Orality and Literacy
in Hellenic Greece

Southern Illinois University Press

CARBONDALE AND EDWARDSVILLE

ORALITY
AND
LITERACY

In
Hellenic Greece

TONY M. LENTZ

Designed by Duane E. Perkins
Production supervised by Natalia Nadraga

92 91 90 89   4 3 2 1

Library of Congress Cataloging-in-Publication Data

Lentz, Tony M.
Orality and literacy in Hellenic Greece / by Tony M. Lentz
p. cm.
Bibliography: p.
Includes index.
ISBN 0-8093-1359-6
1. Greek language. 2. Language and culture—Greece.
3. Oral tradition—Greece. 4. Oral communication—Greece.
5. Written communication—Greece. 6. Literacy—Greece. 7.
Writing—Greece. 8. Greece—Social life and customs. I. Title.

PA227.L46 1989   88-14152
001.54'0938—dc19   CIP

Contents

Contents

Acknowledgments

As a boy I read Thomas Wolfe's *Look Homeward, Angel* one long afternoon in my grandmother's living room, fascinated by references to the classical education of the early 1900s. In graduate school Professor Richard Leo Enos rekindled my interest when he told his classical rhetoric class that the ancient Greeks never read silently. As a Ph.D. candidate in oral interpretation, I was excited by the thought that a world so completely oral had generated the glory of ancient Greece. This book is the result of my pursuit of a clearer picture of ancient oral and written culture through dozens of primary sources, over years of research, and with the help of many friends. The names I must acknowledge range from those who made me a person to those who made me a scholar, and they culminate with the one who provided the support that made the research possible.

Tracing the roots of the research to "first principles," I owe much to my family for the examples they set: persistence and hard work from my father, the late Fred Woodrow Lentz; intellectual curiosity and love of art from my mother, Mary Bridges Lentz; self-confidence and a sense of humor from my late grandfather, John Marion Bridges, Sr.; and from Grandmother Eugenia Bridges, the faith that has supported our family through all life's daily tribulations.

In scholarly endeavors I owe great debts to my teachers and colleagues. To Professor Paul Brandes I owe an awareness of myself as a thinking individual and an appreciation of the rigor that true scholarship demands. To Professor Bert Bradley I owe my understanding of history as a living series of persons and my determination to revive a few of these individuals for myself. To Professors L. LaMont Okey and Richard Haas I owe the extension of this living view of history to the great oral performers in speech communication. To Professor Richard Leo Enos I owe the inspiration and example provided by his energy and commitment to scholarship in the history of rhetoric. The debt I owe this scholar is beyond price and beyond words. *Ho agathos ho anthropos* [hail, good man].

Professor Gerald M. Phillips has been a steadfast friend to his junior colleague, providing encouragement, information, and an occasional libation to the gods. To his experience as an author and editor, and to the stimulation of his incisive intelligence, I owe no less than the successful completion of this written work.

Ultimately, however, I owe the completion of this work to my wife, Alicia Bergey Lentz, who labored as a nurse in a major medical institution so I could enjoy for a time the unencumbered life of a scholar. Many have taken her generous gift of herself for granted; this, at least, is not one of those times.

Finally, I owe to papyrologist Herbert C. Youtie an appreciation of my small niche in the tradition of scholarship. I shall always remember standing with him in the University of Michigan Library, looking out over stately trees and buildings surrounded by youthful— and sometimes scholarly—endeavor. I was acutely aware of his benign indifference to rank and prestige as he helped this anonymous graduate student find references to the cost of papyrus in ancient times. "Yes, I have done some good work in my time," he said, gesturing to the students outside, "but I know there will always be some young person who will do better work one day." He had a quietly sublime vision of his place in the line of scholars reaching back to ancient times, each individual serving history and human-kind in the silent and unglorious pursuit of scholarship. To those scholars of the past and future, and to that vision of their sacrifice, I dedicate this book.

Orality and Literacy
in Hellenic Greece

1

Introduction

Mimi Sheraton described in her *New York Times* column how preconceptions colored her experience with a particular dish.[1] Waiters at an oriental restaurant served the meal on a large number of small plates, and guests helped themselves to small portions of many dishes. Sheraton noticed one small plate with a delicate item crumpled upon it, something apparently dipped in a dark sauce. When she tasted it, the flavor was a severe disappointment. "This tastes like paper with soy sauce on it," she told her husband. "It is," he replied. "You're eating my napkin." Sheraton expected that anything on one of the small plates was food, and she acted accordingly.

Human beings approach the world with certain expectations that inevitably color their view of the world. They expect the soda machine to return a soft drink for correct change. When the machine is out of order, they respond by pounding and cursing, as though the machine had deliberately decided to irritate them. They expect the car to start in the morning as part of the normal order of things, and blood pressure and tempers rise if that normal order becomes, unexpectedly, abnormal.

Scholars are also human beings, and the completion of the syllogism is that they face the world with expectations based on concrete experience that color the way they interpret historical evidence. Scholars, in short, eat their metaphorical share of paper napkins dipped in soy sauce. The only way to avoid being blinded by what we expect to see is to pay close attention to the evidence, all the while reminding ourselves that what we think we see may be a self-induced illusion. While that statement has the familiar ring of a well-worn Socratic quotation, in practice it is often difficult to

1

remember. The history of scholarly views on the oral and written traditions in Greece is no exception.

The culture of Hellenic Greece flourished at the same time that a symbiotic relationship developed between oral and written modes of thought and communication. The oral tradition of memory and performance interacted with the written tradition of verbatim preservation and abstract thought, so that each reinforced the strengths of the other. This symbiosis was integral to the remarkable accomplishments of all aspects of Greek culture, from education to law, and from philosophy to literature. Greek society exemplified a revision of Harold Innis' hypothesis that culture flourished when differing media are in competition for dominance.[2] The lives of the Greeks proved, rather, that culture flourished when differing media interacted symbiotically, so that each supplemented the strengths of the other. Before the second half of this century, however, scholarly preconceptions made this organic perspective on the Hellenic world virtually inconceivable.

The Western academic measurement of success by literacy and printed research colored the expectations of classical scholars as they considered writing in ancient culture. Writing was so important to their world that they assumed it was the key to the growth of ancient culture. The assumption extended to theories regarding the composition of great ancient literature such as the works of Homer. Milman Parry, however, sought to examine the evidence and the assumptions through the eyes of the ancients. Significantly, he began his seminal *L'Epithète traditionnelle dans Homère* by quoting Ernest Renan.

> *How to know the physiognomy and the originality of primitive literatures, if one does not penetrate the moral and private life of the nation, if one does not place oneself at the same spot with the human beings whom it incorporates, in order to see and feel as they do, if one does not consider their lives, or rather, if one does not live an instant with them.*[3]

Parry strongly challenged literate preconceptions by demonstrating the possibility of purely oral composition of literature. He believed, based on new evidence, that the oral tradition had a power and influence that modern print orientations had kept us from appreciating.

Introduction

In this work, I examine the ancients' use of oral memory, oral performance, writing for preservation, and writing for publication. The consideration focuses on the Hellenic Greeks' perspective as recorded in their descriptions of writing, oral performance, and memorization. The examination draws a broad and dynamic picture of the symbiotic relationship between orality and literacy in the ancient world.

ORAL MEMORY AND PRACTICAL SKILLS

In his comprehensive yet concise *Orality and Literacy*, Walter J. Ong defined the oral and written traditions descriptively with a valuable survey of recent research.[4] The difference between the two traditions focused on the individual's perspective on the world. The oral culture functioned on the basis of practical experience, memory, and performance skills. People raised in oral cultures perceived the world in terms of immediate and concrete experience, specific situations they faced daily. They interpreted new events or statements in terms of the specific contexts and objects around them, the settings, people, and tools that made up their daily existence.

People developed sophisticated skills in craftsmanship, and those skills were passed on from one person to another in apprenticeships or face-to-face instruction. Many of the great works of ancient architecture, art, and literature were developed in this way, without the assistance of writing. They preserved words or events in oral memory and passed them down through oral performance. They retained useful words and events much longer, while less important words or events faded from memory through lack of repetition or recall. They developed and cultivated oral performance skills, speaking and singing to each other for both pleasure and practical gain. They were not, however, easily able to abstract themselves from their own existence to imagine the point of view of another. Yet they developed complex cultures and works of art, and their skills in practical craftsmanship, oral performance, and memory remained the foundation of Greek culture.

WRITTEN RECORDING AND AWARENESS OF ABSTRACTION

Literacy became influential due to its power as a support for, or alternative to, memory. Writing preserved words or events ver-

3

batim and indefinitely. Gradually, however, the written tradition became much more than a recording device. Writing constantly reinforced the awareness of symbolic, abstract relationships. Writing was the symbol for the spoken word, which was, in turn, the symbol for thought. People grew aware of categories as they reread and puzzled over relationships between written words, words writing removed from the intonation and situations that make them vocally concrete and contextually specific. Humans developed awareness of abstract relationships between categories as they reread and revised versions of texts. The daily use of the linear sentence, subject–verb–object, encouraged them to focus on cause-and-effect relationships between things. This reinforcement led, eventually, to Aristotle's concern with categories and the relationships between them. The daily use of these abstractions cultivated the ability of people to project themselves imaginatively into situations beyond their experience with the concrete world around them. Gradually the world opened to hypotheses and the projection of long-range consequences for everyday decisions.

Ong cited one experiment that succintly described a basic difference between oral and literate cultures.[5] Researchers asked a person from an oral culture to look at drawings of a hammer, saw, log, and ax, and then to select one that was "different." The individual was unable to perceive a difference. He envisioned a concrete situation, where someone was working on the wood with the tools. As a result, the items all fit in the same category for him. He was unable, in short, to reach the abstract level of categories such as "tool" and "materials." Piaget described a similar stage in the development of children. Up to a certain age, a child was unable to draw a small model of mountains from the perspective of a doll placed on the model. The child was unable, in other words, to abstract itself, to imagine itself looking at the world from a perspective other than its own. At a particular age, however, the child developed the ability to project itself into other points of view. Writing reinforced a similar change in ancient culture. The individual grew in awareness of abstractions; first, by becoming aware of an abstracted self able to act upon the world around it; second, by becoming aware of abstract conceptions like law, truth, and justice as reasons for that action. Such abstractions gradually began to compete with self-interest and the narrow concrete perspective of the individual and his or her tribe.

For the first time, according to Bruno Snell, people became aware of themselves as individual decision-makers responsible for the consequences of their choices. In the great works of Greek tragedy, for the first time, the individual began "to look at himself as the maker of his own decisions."[6] In contrast, earlier people had looked toward the gods as the source of all change. The oral mentality preceding this shift was, simply, unaware of itself through its inability to look at itself from without. As one peasant responded to a researcher, when asked to describe himself: "What can I say about my own heart? How can I talk about my character? Ask others; they can tell you about me. I myself can't say anything."[7] Thus writing helped humankind develop self-consciousness, the awareness of the individual as one who made decisions, acted upon them, and took responsibility for the consequences.

Thus writing was vital to the first attempts of humankind to free itself from the preconceptions of tradition and to examine its "self" world critically. Yet Parry's work showed us that the great early works of Greek literature, particularly the works of Homer, were not solely the result of writing's beneficent influence on culture. These great works, he demonstrated, showed the characteristics of oral memory and performance. His work revolutionized our understanding of the place of writing in the ancient world and increased our respect for the power of the ancients' memory and creativity. Through the work of Albert B. Lord, Berkley Peabody and, in particular, Eric A. Havelock, Parry's new expectations began an extension of our awareness of the powerful influence of oral culture in ancient times.[8] The traditions of memory and oral performance are now accepted as vital parts of life in ancient Greece.

As we grow in awareness of the pervasive influence of the oral culture, however, we grow in appreciation of the importance of writing. Havelock's *Preface to Plato* is another milestone. The book details the place of writing as the source of Plato's understanding of abstractions, and as a direct influence on the origin of philosophy. We see the development of abstractions as reasons for action in daily life which reach far beyond concrete details of the Greeks' daily existence. Havelock stresses the importance of literacy to the development of Greek philosophy through this awareness of abstraction. He moves the date for the literate age back to about 450 B.C. and argues in recent works for a "dynamic tension" between the concrete world view of orality and the abstract thought of literacy, with the balance swinging in favor of writing after Plato.[9] So from a time when scholars cannot conceive of the composition of ancient poetry apart from writing, even as early as 650 B.C., we come to accept a much later date for the advent of literacy. Havelock demonstrates that the oral tradition remains a powerful force up to the time of Plato.

THE DOMINANCE OF THE ORAL TRADITION

This work proposes a continuation of the trend to move up the date of this "balance point." I examine the place of writing, reading, and recitation in various contexts in ancient culture, as the ancients themselves describe it. The overall pattern of the evidence indicates a society that is still largely oral and that is just beginning to become "literate" in the sense that we employ the term. I argue that the "dynamic tension" Havelock describes continued well past Plato and that the balance between orality and literacy only begins to swing in favor of writing following the work of Isocrates (c. 390 B.C.). Writing, while vital to Greek culture, is in many ways secondary to the memory and performance skills of the oral tradition. The symbiosis of the strengths of oral and literate traditions in Hellenic Greece offers a detailed illustration of the importance of both oral and written communication skills to a particular culture. The evidence reveals a pattern of interaction in each area of the culture, an interaction in which the strengths of the new written culture complemented the strong memory and performance skills of the oral tradition. There is, in short, a synthesis of orality and literacy that employs the strengths of both to the benefit of culture.

Memory functioned as a dominant or equal partner in all aspects of the culture. Instruction in the schools remained largely oral, with students learning great works by heart. Most students studied grammar for only a short time, many merely learning to recognize the letters that represented the sounds of the alphabet. The singers and reciters of literature remained a vital part of the culture, and amateur performers recited to one another for purposes of both persuasion and entertainment. The Greeks thus carried their cultural identity complete within their memory, and educated individuals could talk about shared literature and maxims with confidence and ease. Composition took place orally, and authors recited works to scribes who put them in writing to preserve them. The character of individuals vouched for the accuracy of written depositions in court, and the introduction of written evidence did not shorten the time allowed for oral presentations. The Greeks still preferred to hear the witnesses' own testimony and to judge those individuals by the concrete details of their vocal and bodily action.

The powerful memories trained in these situations were important in maintaining the lengthy philosophical discussions of the day. Furthermore, accurate memories and concrete examples remained vital to the epistemologies that were the culmination of the awareness of abstraction. Plato, Isocrates, and Aristotle all recognized the power of the spoken word. Finally, writing never completely broke away from the sound of the human voice. The Greeks never read written words without speaking them aloud. Silent reading was possible, but the Greeks never considered it necessary or desirable to separate compositions completely from their spoken form. Writing was the sign for the spoken word, not its replacement.

CHAPTER SUMMARIES

The overall view of Greek culture, writing, and oral performance in this research argues for an extension of Harold Innis' idea that competition between media contributes to the flowering of culture. I propose instead that competition between media that emphasizes the strengths of each contributes to the growth of culture.

Each chapter following outlines the ways in which writing and the oral tradition interacted in a given aspect of ancient Greek culture. In chapter two, we consider Plato, the only Greek philosopher to relate writing to an epistemology, as he reveals himself to be indebted to *both* oral and written traditions. Plato certainly displays the consciousness of abstraction that Havelock develops so thoroughly in *Preface to Plato;* on the other hand, he remains indebted to both memory and concrete examples in his epistemology. He nevertheless attacks *both* the oral tradition and writing, showing himself to be in the midst of the "dynamic tension" between the media that Havelock identifies.

Chapter three proposes that the rhapsode is a symbol of the continuing importance of oral performance and memory to Greek culture. While the view of the rhapsodes left to us through Plato's *Ion* is apt to convince us of their irrelevance to society, the Greeks indicate that the rhapsodes are successful members of society well

7

beyond the Hellenic era. The laurel and myrtle symbols of their inspiration are common elements of Greek social interaction. Like the philosophers, rhapsodes owe much to writing, for they recite from written copies of Homer and other poets. Their continuing existence, however, illustrates that the oral performance tradition extends its influence well beyond the time of Plato.

In chapter four, the "elementary" educational system of ancient Greece moves slowly toward literacy, but only in an extremely narrow sense of the term. Education involves only limited work in writing, and learning one's letters, or *grammata,* is largely a matter of learning to identify the written symbols for the sounds of the language. The education of the day reaches only a few rather well-to-do individuals, and as a result most individuals in society are not really literate in the sense that we would use the term.

Chapter five details the interaction of orality and literacy in Athenian courts, demonstrating that the Greeks determine the credibility of the written word by the credibility of the sources who were responsible for that word. Writing does, indeed, become more important and is vital to the origins of the laws and the functioning of the law courts. The Greeks still measure the meaning of laws, legal agreements, and written evidence in the courts, however, against the wisdom and trustworthiness of the individuals who are responsible for the protection and enforcement of written documents.

Chapter six illustrates the ways in which Greek philosophy gradually begins to give writing a place as a source of evidence alongside the memory and recitation of the oral tradition. Through the depictions of recitation, reading, and writing in Greek philosophical discourse, we observe the gradual change in the use of writing. From oral composition, preservation by memory, and oral publication, people move to a stage of oral composition, preservation by writing, and publication by recitation. In a final stage, the Greeks display oral composition, preservation in writing, and publication by oral reading. The improbability of lengthy oral recitations shows itself to be a product of contemporary views of verbatim memory, and not necessarily relevant to the ancient conception of memory. The ancients are more concerned with accurate reproduction of arguments than with the verbatim recall modern literates associate with recitation.

8

Introduction

The secondary education of the Sophists is the focus of chapter seven, with the interaction of the logographers, Sophists, and writing providing an example of the tension between oral and written traditions. The first logographers are the historians who preserve important words and events in the culture. Gradually the word's meaning shifts, as the uses of writing evolve into the second stage outlined in chapter six. The word "logographer" then refers to people who write speeches for others to perform from memory. The Greeks attack this practice as a form of misrepresentation, just as they later attack the Sophists on the same ground. The Sophists err in the use of writing, not for the preservation of important words or ideas, but for the preservation and creation of literary devices and sophistic trickery. Isocrates becomes a unique figure in this view, for he moves into the final stage of the use of writing in discourse.

Isocrates emerges, in chapter eight, as the first true writer in the modern sense of the word. He composes from memory, preserves his ideas in writing, and publishes them in oral readings. He is, in short, the first person about whom we can say that he employs writing only for publication by reading aloud. Others employ writing to preserve important words or ideas, or to prepare works that they recite orally themselves. Isocrates becomes the first to conceive of himself exclusively as a writer. Furthermore, Isocrates begins to develop a style characteristic of the written tradition.

The speech of Alcidamas attacking Isocrates for his use of writing nevertheless displays recognition of the growing importance of the new medium. Chapter nine considers Alcidamas as an advocate for the old oral tradition of extemporaneous speaking without the use of writing. Alcidamas finds it necessary to use writing, however, to attack Isocrates for associating with the written word. The composition outlines the oral tradition's case against the new medium, but has the tone of a last attempt to retain a dominance over writing which is clearly lost forever.

Chapter ten considers the descriptions of writing and its use both within and about poetry and drama. Both poetry and drama have paradoxical relationships with writing, for the Greeks increasingly employ writing to preserve compositions in both forms. Yet both forms rely primarily upon performance skill and memory for their "publication." Finally, two extant examples of silent reading in dramatic works provide powerful evidence of the continuing influence of the oral culture. For silent reading is apparently possible, and the question remains as to why it was not more common. In the the light of the previous chapters, the answer is clearly that by ancient tradition and contemporary choice the Greeks, simply, think of literature as oral.

Chapter eleven considers the work of Aristotle exemplary of the continuing dynamic between writing and the oral tradition. Just as the works of Plato demonstrate the interaction between oral and literate traditions, so Aristotle displays surprising connections to the oral tradition of the past. Aristotle, as the originator of the tradition of scientific research in the West, seems largely removed from the oral tradition. Yet even in the works of this most literate of Greeks, we find evidence of connections to the traditions of memory and oral modes of thought. Aristotle's works appear in a form that implicitly accepts Plato's epistemological attack on writing. His early works are composed in the dialogue form employed by Plato, and his later works appear to be lecture notes, or reminders "of that which we already know." Furthermore, his research method blends both abstract first principles, contemporary wisdom, and careful observation in a way that suggests the synthesis of oral and written modes of thought.

The final chapter summarizes the picture that arises from the evidence. The pattern that emerges shows the integration of the strengths of both oral and written traditions in Greek culture. In all aspects of the culture, characteristics of both oral and written traditions are integral to the flourishing of the society. This overview requires a revision of Harold Innis' conception that competition between media contribute to the flowering of culture, to require that such competition reinforce the strengths of each medium.[10] The symbiosis of oral and written traditions in Hellenic Greece offers a detailed illustration of the importance of these skills to society. Orality and literacy contribute to the growth of culture because each reinforces the strengths of the other in their interaction. The result, should the Muses bless our examination of the evidence, will be a clearer understanding of the challenges that face communication in any culture, including our own.

2

The Third Place from Truth: Plato's Paradoxical Attack on Writing

The works of Eric A. Havelock created considerable controversy among scholars in classics and media. His influential *Preface to Plato* stirred up both admiration and dismay among those who felt more comfortable with the traditional view of the relationship between writing and ancient Greek culture. As Havelock himself noted in his recent *Literate Revolution in Greece and Its Cultural Consequences,* early in his research he was "increasingly aware that I was likely to threaten the status of some sacred cows in my profession."[1]

Havelock's work was, in a sense, the culmination of a revolution in the modern conception of composition, recitation, and writing in ancient Greece begun by Milman Parry in the first half of this century. Havelock's *Preface to Plato* demonstrated convincingly the power and importance of the oral tradition in pre-Platonic Greece, delighting those who had become convinced that early Greek literature and civilization were largely oral.[2] One reviewer compared *Preface to Plato* to Werner Jaeger's *Paideia,* and Walter J. Ong, another well-known writer on the oral tradition, said that the "work is so seminal that he [Havelock] could not possibly touch on all the chains of thought it initiates."[3] "Havelock's thesis is a sweeping one and, on the whole, utterly convincing, tying in with the findings of an increasing number of recent psychological, historical, philosophical, and cultural studies."[4]

Other reviewers in classical journals, however, noted several important difficulties in the work. Several were apparently among those who believe writing to have been a vital part of Greek culture and composition long before the time of Plato, and they criticized Havelock's "assumption" that the culture preceding Plato was dominantly oral.[5] Havelock recently clarified his position, noting that it is simplistic to think of oral and written traditions as "mutually exclusive."

> *Those who suppose that I offer a narrowly oralist version of Greek literature extravagantly extended to the death of Euripides lend themselves to an error of oversimplification. If the main stress in these articles falls on the oralist element, this is because a novel thesis requires a restricted emphasis to be put across. But in a larger perspective, the complete genius of the literature and philosophy here placed under inspection is understandable as neither oralist nor as a flaccid compromise between the oral and the literate but as the product of a dynamic tension between them. After Plato, the balance tilted irrevocably in favor of the latter, a tilt in which Plato plays a decisive role, even though his own discourse retains some of the hallmarks of previous oralism.[6]*

The significance of Havelock's scholarly accomplishment, then, was ultimately the creation of a new dynamic perspective upon the culture of ancient Greece, a perspective marked by the critical reexamination of our assumptions about Greek literature, rhetoric, and philosophy.

There are several ways in which Plato's works exemplify this "dynamic tension" between the oral and the literate. I will focus on several apparent contradictions in the relationship between Plato and the new technology of writing and will contrast several points regarding Plato and writing developed by Havelock in *Preface to Plato* with Plato's own view of writing as expressed in the *Phaedrus*. The axis of these apparent contradictions is found in a central assumption of Havelock's view of Plato's *Republic* and its relationship to writing.

THE EPISTEMOLOGICAL PARADOX

In the *Preface to Plato*, Havelock takes the position that Plato was a spokesman for a new scientific and abstract view of knowledge that grew out of a new awareness of the self, a self that traces its origins to the Presocratics. The first half of the book explicates the power of the oral traditions of memory and self-identification with others through poetry. "How," Havelock asks rhetorically in chapter eleven, "did the Greeks ever wake up?" In other words, "given the immemorial grip of the oral method of preserving group tradition," how could a self-consciousness ever have come into being?[7] "The fundamental answer must lie in the changing technology of communication. Refreshment of memory through written signs enabled a reader to dispense with most of that emotional identification by which alone the acoustic record was sure of recall."[8] Or, as Havelock says in the Foreword to *Preface to Plato*, "the crux of the matter lies in the transition from the oral to the written and from the concrete to the abstract."[9] Earlier poets and authors presage the coming importance and impact of the technology of writing, but Plato's view of abstract thought was a balance point in the tension between oral and written traditions. Thus, writing, Plato, and philosophical abstraction intertwine in Havelock's view, with Plato serving as a pivotal point in the transition from a predominantly oral culture to a predominantly written one.

The essential paradox in associating Plato and writing is that Plato criticizes the written word in the *Phaedrus* for the same faults attributed to the poets in the *Republic*. Procope S. Costas notes this point in his review of *Preface to Plato*.[10] A number of paradoxes around the theme are evident. First, it is clear that Havelock associates writing with abstract thought, yet in the *Phaedrus* Plato attacks writing itself for being removed from the mind of "one who knows." The ideal "forms," the ultimate abstractions, exist outside the mind, and yet writing is also attacked for being outside the mind of "one who knows." Second, Havelock associates memory with the oral tradition that Plato attacks in the *Republic,* but memory is vital to the epistemology of the *Phaedrus,* which is the basis for the attack upon writing. A third paradox is that Plato strenuously objects to the self-identification of the individual with the "charming" words of the poet, and yet the dialectic that is the approved path toward truth is a method of carefully examining the opinions of another. He identifies poetic voices outside the self with the oral tradition, but the dialectic that is vital to the pursuit of truth in the *Phaedrus* appears to be an oral method of attempting to "identify" the perceptions of truth in the mind of another. In addition, while Plato clearly expects his attack upon poetry to be unpopular, there is evidence that his attack upon writing on the same epistemological grounds is an accurate reflection of popular sentiment. Finally, the poets appear to have been singled out in the *Republic* for special attention because of their relationship with the oral tradition, but the rhetoricians and Sophists associated with the written tradition are criticized in the *Phaedrus* upon the same epistemological grounds as the poets and rhapsodes.

At first glance, Socrates' criticism of writing seems due primarily to his (or perhaps Plato's) Spartan sympathy for the oral traditions of the aristocratic past, as Plato depicts them in the *Laws* (658D). This perfunctory judgment, however, is unsatisfactory when the objections to writing are placed within the context of Plato's epistemology. Plato's thought directly relates the credibility of the written word to the living intelligence of the author or maker; that is, he measures the written word according to the worth of the knowledge in the mind of its maker. He labels writing a poor substitute for the spoken word of "one who knows." Plato seeks knowledge in the individual's mind, not in the external abstractions of the written word.

This Platonic conception of thought, speech, and written language leads to a criticism of written language on epistemological grounds. Plato pictured the ultimate truth of reality in the *Phaedrus* as a region above the heavens (247A–248E).[11] The well-trained charioteer of a flying chariot is compared to an immortal god, a driver whose training in handling the horses of the soul allows him to view the heavenly plane of absolute justice, temperance, and knowledge while driving upward through the heavens. "For the colorless, formless, and intangible truly existing essence, about which the family of all true knowledge resides in this place [topos], is perceived only by the one who sees, the pilot of the soul" (247C–D).[12] As people attempt to imitate the chariot-driving of the gods, however, the horses distract the attention of their souls, which often lose sight of reality (248A). The souls that through great discipline of mind and toil manage to rise above their limitations in order to see one or more truths, on the other hand, are allowed to stay in the heavenly plane through "the next period of days" (248C). The others, weighted down by evil nature and forgetfulness, fall to the earth (248C).

Those who achieved the longest glimpses of truth enter the souls of philosophers, lovers of beauty, or those who are musical and loving (248D). We should note here that Plato's use of the term for "musical" can refer to all the arts over which the Muses presided, arts of composing poetry, singing song, and presenting choral competitions that are associated with the "old education" tied to the oral past. [13] The second rank goes to a lawful king or warlike leader; the third to a politician, one knowing business, or one knowledgeable about wealth; the fourth to a gymnast or someone knowledgeable about curing the body; the fifth to a prophet or priest; the sixth to a poet or some other imitator; the seventh to a craftsman or farmer; the eighth to a Sophist or demagogue; and the ninth to a tyrant. The "katharsis" or purification of the soul, in this view, might lead to advancement in the hierarchy of knowledge (248E). [14]

The pursuit of truth and ultimate knowledge, in this Platonic conception, rests on the ability of the mind, as the "pilot of the soul," to direct the soul away from earthly distractions. The absence of this "pilot" in writing, as we shall see, leads to Platonic criticism of writing as removed from the rational, and thus from the truth. [15] One of the basic accusations against writing was that the written word could not reply to questions, and therefore could not explain the intended meaning of its words. Papyrus, in short, did not possess the knowledge of the living mind or "pilot."

The charge did not apply only to written words, however. The poets who represented the oral tradition faced the same accusation. Either they were not present with the "pilot of their soul" to explain their ideas when others quoted their words, or they had no knowledge of the things they described. Socrates, for example, dismissed Homer in a discussion of false and true men in the *Hippias Minor*, (365C–D, literally translated) "since it is impossible to ask whatever he was thinking about these things." Note that he quoted Homer from memory and not from a written text. The key point was that the creative intelligence of the maker was not present, and the particular meaning at issue could not be clarified by asking questions. In the *Republic*, Plato wrote that the imitations of the poets are "about the third place from truth" (602B–C). The accusation is also made in the *Protagoras* regarding poetry quoted in discussions. Socrates says that the poet cannot be questioned regarding what the words actually meant (347E–348A). [16] Some say the poet meant one thing, and some say he meant another, and the resulting discussion is generally pointless.

The paradox is that the Socratic distaste for the written word originates in the same view of knowledge in the individual mind as the source of our perception of truth. Written words, Socrates says in the *Phaedrus,* are of value only "to remind him who knows about the things that have been written." No one but the author, in Socrates' conception, knows the truth of the thought behind the letter.

> *For somewhere writing has this marvelous power, Phaedrus; in reality it is very much like the art of painting. For from these works each creature stands like living beings, but if anyone asks them a question, they solemnly remain perfectly still. And these things are also true of written words; for you might think they spoke as one having intelligence, but if you question them wishing to know about the things having been said, they always declare only one and the same thing. And whenever it is written once and for all, a word is tossed about by all, alike by those approve it, and by those who have no relation to it, and it does not know when it is necessary to speak and when it is not. And being mistreated and unjustly reviled it always needs its father to rescue it, for it has not the power to defend or help itself. (275D–E)*

We should note the irony here: truth is clearly an abstraction, based in the ideal plane of the *Phaedrus,* but our perception of truth in this world must come through the knowledge in the mind of the individual.[17] Writing, which makes internal abstraction possible, is too remote from internal abstraction to be trusted.

The same viewpoint is raised in the *Protagoras* when Socrates says that many of the speakers of the day "are just like papyrus rolls, being able neither to answer your questions nor to ask questions themselves" (309A). This is clearly a reference to the speakers of the day who spoke either from rote memory or from memorized versions of a logographer's written work (see chapter seven). The point, again, is that these speakers repeat a string of either spoken or written words, either of which were removed from knowledge in the mind of someone who knows. Thus, while the abstract forms of the *Republic* may have their origins in Plato's acquaintance with the written alphabet, he takes the position that both writing and speaking are separate from knowledge of those forms as it exists in the mind of "one who knows." The important point for our consideration here, however, is that Plato's epistemology is the basis for the attacks upon both the poets in the *Republic* and writing in the *Phaedrus.*

16

There is a further paradox in Plato's hierarchy in this conception of language and reality. For while he implicitly associates forms with the consciousness of abstraction due to writing, he views writing as farther removed from knowledge of these truths than the spoken word. As Socrates concludes in the discussion of language in the *Cratylus:* "Accordingly, in what manner it is necessary to learn or to discover realities, perhaps this is too great a question to have been known by you or me; but one must be content even to be agreed on this, that not from names, but that things are both learned and sought much better from themselves, rather than from names" (439B). Names or spoken words, then, are clearly one place removed from the realities of life as we experience them in our minds. The "Stranger" who is the protagonist in the *Sophist* of Plato describes thought and speech in these terms: "Accordingly, then, thought and speech are the same; except that the inner one, being a dialogue without sound of the soul with itself, this same thing we call thought?" His partner in the dialogue admits that this is certainly true (263E). Thus Plato closely relates thought and speech, making speech an external version of the internal realities of individual experience with external ultimate truth.

Therefore writing is "twice removed" or "the third place from truth," as Plato attacks the poets in the *Republic* for "mimesis at second remove" (597A–E, 602C).[18] As Havelock notes in the *Preface to Plato:* "Roughly the first two-thirds of the attack is levelled at the character of the poetised statement. The problem here is epistemological."[19] In the Platonic conception, Socratic dialogue is the appropriate method for the pursuit of truth. The seventh of the *Letters* attributed to Plato states that

> *by toil and pain, being engrossed in these things, each compared to the other—names and definitions, things having been seen and perceived—in gracious refutations testing them and without jealousy using questionings and answerings, the light of intelligence shines on each thing and on the mind, exerting to the fullest the best possible of man's capabilities. (344B)*

The author, while possibly not Plato, continues with a statement in apparent agreement with the criticism of writing examined above. No serious person considers his best compositions to be in writing; these are rather to be "stored up somewhere in the fairest part of himself," in his mind (344C–D). If indeed a man does put his serious works into writing, then mortal men have "destroyed his senses completely" (344D).

The truths of the world, then, exist for Plato in the reality of human experience, in the "fairest region" of man's thought. This conception cuts across the boundaries of speaking, poetry, and writing of all kinds, as we have seen above. The ultimate charge against the written word is that it exists two places apart from the reality of human thought and experience. The evidence cited above demonstrates that Plato viewed the spoken word as the sign of the soul and the written word as the sign of the spoken word. The written word Plato conceives in the *Phaedrus* is thus a more remote expression of the best compositions or "makings" that a man as to offer from the realities of his experience (276A).

The speeches or poems or writings of man, then, are the results of his activity, of his existence, or "imitations," as Plato would have said. These are not, however, identical with the reality of the individual "maker's" experience. The Platonic condemnation of the written word, seen in this context, is not merely the opinion of a conservative Athenian with ties to the aristocratic oral traditions of the past. Plato bases his objection to popular acceptance of the written word upon his theoretical conception of language and creativity, a conception with apparent ties to written abstraction. The written word, when someone other than the author reads it, is lacking the soul of the writer, of the "one who knows." Writing is also "the third place from truth," from the glimpses of ultimate knowledge that the author might have in his experience. For this reason memory is considered vital to man's intelligence, for men must remember these brief glimpses of truth that are the basis of their pursuit of wisdom, if these glimpses are not to be lost forever.

THE PARADOXICAL DEFENSE OF MEMORY

Havelock identifies memory as the "preserved communication" of preliterate Greece, its linguistic statement of the political and private mores of the society. "In a preliterate society, how is this statement preserved? The answer inescapably is: in the living memories of successive living people who are young and then old and then die."[20] Thus memory, paradoxically, is a vital characteristic of the oral tradition against which Plato's intellectual armory is arrayed, and yet memory remains a vital component of his epis-

18

temology. Indeed, a second basis for Plato's attack upon the written word, beyond its being "the third place from the truth," is his certainty that it will damage the memories of men. This particular statement seems a little out of touch with the thrust of history to the modern reader, as it possibly did to some in Plato's day. Historians surely view writing as a means of preserving their learning, as Herodotus notes in his introduction, "So that their knowledge may not be destroyed as time weakens the memories of men" (1.1.1–2). In the famous passage in the *Phaedrus,* however, Socrates takes the opposite position, defending the memory that is vital to dialectic against the written technology that will lead to its deterioration.

Plato presents Socrates telling the story of Theuth, the Egyptian god, who invents letters (274C–275E). The ruling god, Thamus, viewing this marvelous invention that would, Theuth said, strengthen the wisdom and memory of man, replies that indeed it would do precisely the opposite.

> *For this thing will cause forgetfulness in the spirits of those learning it through neglect of their memories, seeing that because of trust in writing by unnatural signs outside themselves they are not using the memories within themselves; therefore you have not discovered a medicine for memory but for reminding. And you furnish your students with the appearance of wisdom, not truth; for having heard much without instruction they will appear to be sagacious, nevertheless being ignorant upon most topics and difficult to understand, being wise in conceit as opposed to wisdom. (275A–B)*

Phaedrus replies that Socrates makes up stories easily about any country he likes, implying that the Theuth story was convenient fiction. Socrates replies, however, that it makes little difference who the speaker is if he speaks the truth (275B–C). The philosopher may indeed make up the story, but clearly it represents his view of writing, at least as Plato presents him in the dialogue. The argument seems straightforward enough, but takes on new significance if placed in the context of Plato's thought about memory.

Plato conceives of the memory as a vital part of man's conceptual capacity, uniting with the senses in the work of forming opinions about the world around man. As Socrates says in the *Philebus,* "Memory meets with the senses in this, and each thing that occurs between them appears to me at that time almost to write words in our souls" (39A). Plato writes again of memory in the same context when Socrates says in the *Theaetetus* that the image of two friends in his mind is like two wax imprints of signet rings. He "seals" the image into the mind for comparison to incoming perceptions through the senses (193B–C). The soul includes, then, a metaphorical "wax block" that records the imprint of the perceptions. As Socrates describes it:

> *Then grant me for the sake of argument that in our souls there is one wax tablet on which impressions are made, and in some the wax tablet is larger, and in some smaller, and in some the wax is cleaner, in some dirtier, and in some harder, in some softer, and in some of the appropriate quality. . . . Accordingly let us say it is a gift of Mnemosyne, the mother of the Muses, and into this, that whatever we ourselves had wished to remember—something being seen or heard or thought—that holding this wax out to the perceptions and thoughts, we stamp them, just as seal-ring impressions are made. And whatever is imprinted, we remember and know so long as the image is in the wax; and whatever is wiped out or is such that it cannot be imprinted, it is forgotten and is not known. (191C–E)*

Again we find a reference to the Muses, the goddesses of the musical culture of the oral past, and to Mnemosyne their mother, the goddess of memory. Note the multiplicity of ironies here. Socrates thanks the goddess of memory for the preservation of perceptions, although he attacks the poets of the oral tradition for whom she and the other Muses are the patrons. He employs the memory of the oral tradition to preserve concrete perceptions of the world necessary for the verification of abstract thought associated with the written tradition. Socrates makes it plain in the ensuing sequence that the functioning of the memory is vital to his conception of thought. The rigorous pursuit of knowledge is the careful examination of things he seals in the memory in comparison with the perceptions of the immediate world (192A–194C). Thus the proper functioning of the memory is vital to the growth of wisdom among men. As Socrates concludes:

> *On the one hand, whenever the wax in the soul of a man is deep and wide and smooth and appropriately kneaded, the images through the senses, being pressed into the "heart of the soul"—as Homer says in intimating its similarity to wax—whenever these things happen the impressions are unspoiled and of adequate depth and they hold for*

a long time. Men of such quality are the first to learn, and afterwards remember, so accordingly they do not interchange the impressions of their perceptions, but hold true opinions. For being clear and uncluttered these men quickly assign their perceptions to their places, which are then called realities, and such men, then, are called wise. (194C–D)

The opposite, he continues, is true of men with impurities in their memories, the equivalent of improperly formed wax. "Thus all these men hold such false opinions. For whenever they see or hear or think, they are not able quickly to apportion things, are slow, and assigning them wrongly most of the time they see badly and hear wrongly and think in error, and such men are thus called deceived about realities and unlearned" (195A). We note in passing that it is ironic that Socrates describes the memory in terms of the practice of writing—making impressions on wax like a Greek schoolboy might have done. This is another paradoxical illustration of Havelock's assertion that Plato's conception of abstraction may have its roots in the written tradition of the Hellenic future. In spite of this ironic twist to the argument, the fact remains that Plato associates strength of memory with wisdom. The importance of memory, however, goes beyond the organization and evaluation of impressions from the senses.

The view of heaven in the *Phaedrus* cites "forgetfulness" (*lēthē*) as one of the "weights" drawing the soul away from the ultimate truths (248D). Too much reliance on the external means of recording by writing, Plato might say, results in the improper care of the internal "wax" of the memory that is necessary for a man to be wise, or even to seek wisdom. The philosopher relies on memory to maintain contact with the vision of those heavenly realities that his soul glimpses before falling to an earthly life (249C).[21] The most important function of the memory, in short, is the maintenance of the memories of ultimate truths that lift the soul upward toward perfection.

This Platonic link between concrete and abstract through memory foreshadows Aristotle's more rigorous focus on the relation between abstract and concrete, as we see in chapter eleven. The Aristotelian conception of the dynamic tension between abstraction and concrete perception forges the link between abstract and concrete that becomes the link between hypothesis and data. Thus memory remains vital to a central ingredient of the mixture that provides the core of scientific method and the possibility of cultural change based on research.

The Socratic condemnation of writing as destructive to memory, in summary, does not rest solely on a conception of appropriate pedagogy, or on an old man's concern for laziness among the youth of Athens. He attacks writing in defense of his understanding of the functioning of the mind in the pursuit of knowledge. The quality of the "wax," again, declines with disuse. Socrates does not disapprove of writing solely because he does not employ it in his personal pedagogy or because he is in sympathy with the oral traditions of the aristocratic past (*Laws,* 658D). As he sees it, the downgrading of memory, through the use of writing and the encouragement of mental laziness, leads to less accurate, less "true" knowledge of the world. Men with bad memories, in Plato's view, are "deceived about realities and unlearned," and their pursuit of knowledge becomes the pursuit of the appearance of knowledge.[22]

The memory associated with the oral tradition, in sum, is a vital part of Plato's epistemology. He defends it as an essential component of the pathway to abstract truth, applying a tool of the oral tradition to remember perceptions of this truth—an abstract truth that grew out of the written tradition.

THE PARADOX OF DIALECTIC IDENTIFICATION

A third paradox evident in Plato's epistemological attack on poetry and writing is the position of dialectic as our only measure of the truths individuals perceive with the help of memory. Havelock sees dialectic as the tool of the new abstract thought implicitly related to writing, and yet Plato's description of that process clearly involves two people in *spoken* discussion. This discussion implicitly involves a form of "identification" with the perceptions of another through spoken language, but it is clearly very different from the "rhapsodizing" of the poets. The abstract writing that influences the Platonic conception of knowledge, however, is not evident as a part of this single Platonic pathway to truth. Dialectic is spoken, one mind to another in the form of language closest to thought.

Havelock sees self-identification with others as Plato's deadly enemy.

> *But if we remember the centuries of old habit, which had fused subject with object in sympathetic self-identification as a condition of keeping the oral tradition alive, we can realize how this inherited state of mind was for Plato the enemy, and how he would wish to frame his own doctrine in language which met it head on, and confronted it, and destroyed it.*[23]

The major weapon in opposition to self-identification is fifth-century dialectic, "a weapon for arousing the consciousness from its dream language and stimulating it to think abstractly."[24]

Dialectic as Plato describes it, however, is a matter of close and careful attention to another's views in *spoken* language. One dictionary definition of "identification" is "to make oneself one with another person by putting oneself in his place." This sounds very much like the description of dialectic Socrates gives in the *Protagoras* as he derides discussions in which men quote poets who cannot be questioned.

> *But this sort of conversation is avoided gladly by those who converse with each other directly, each man in his own words testing the other by taking and giving. Such men, it seems to me, you and I should rather be eager to imitate, putting the poets aside to make our discourse to each other through ourselves, and making trial of the truth and of ourselves. (347E–348A)*

The key phrase is "to make our discourse to each other through ourselves, and making trial of the truth and of ourselves." Note the parallel between "the truth" and "ourselves." The truth regarding the issue is to be found within the making of the individual's existence, not within external sources that cannot be seized and tested. The same writing that is the source of this view of abstract knowledge in the mind, in short, is also an external source that cannot be questioned.

Training in dialectic is the highest form of study for the young guardians in the *Republic*, but training in *grammata*, or letters, is of only minor importance. Dialectic, we learn, leads to the limits of the "intelligible" truth (532A–B), is set above all other studies (534E), and should involve five years' training (539E). In the *Laws*, however, only three years of training is to be provided for the study of "letters," and neither the students nor the parents may change the length of the term of instruction (809E–810A). Students learn sufficient *grammata* to be able to read and write, but great speed and beauty in writing is not to be encouraged (810A–B).

Thus the writing that is the apparent origin of Plato's understanding of abstract thought and knowledge, ironically, is not necessary for the pursuit of that knowledge. Plato does not, in fact, even mention it in the *Republic* as one of important studies that the guardians of the ideal city should pursue (521C–541B). The pursuit of truth, from our assumptions up to first principles and then back down to conclusions about the world around us, takes place in spoken language (509D–514B). The search proceeds without the help of the further abstraction of written language. The written word, it seems, leads the attention of the soul back to external sense images, to visible earthly distractions from the intelligible thought that provides the stepping stones to truth.

Those who would call themselves philosophers, Socrates says at the close of the *Phaedrus, must* name themselves by the knowledge in their minds that makes "the things having been written" trivial (277E).

> *If he collects these writings having knowledge of the truth, and is able to support them in vigorous discussion, and to demonstrate in himself the power to show that the things having been written are trivial, he must not call himself by name from things he possesses such as these writings, but from the knowledge of the truth that he has taken seriously. (278B–D).*

The pursuit of this knowledge through dialectic, then, relies upon the spoken word, and not writing. Those who would move one place closer to the perception of truth in the mind of a person who knows must do so by a careful attention to the words spoken.

The difference between self-identification with a poet's discourse and the pursuit of another's perception through dialectic resides in a similar conception of abstraction. The poet presents an imitation of an external object, and worse, often he presents an imitation of an object (or series of events) with which he has no personal experience. The audience member listening to the poet (or rhapsode) willingly accepts the poet's version of things, but an accepting partner in dialectics, as Socrates says in the *Republic,* is not in the least helpful (450D). The partner in dialectic must help his companion in discussion as he seeks to move up the ladder of abstraction, testing the speaker's perceptions lest he miss the truth (450D). This, to Socrates, is serious business, so serious that he believes homicide—and the blood curse it entails—to be less an evil than misleading others regarding the truth (451B).

This strength of feeling makes the paradox regarding dialectic even more powerful in its impact on modern scholars. For it is clear that Plato's dialectic is preserved for us in written form, the very written form that he feels is "the third place from truth." This paradox leads scholars to go so far as to allege, through an astonishing leap of faith, that Plato could not really mean to attack writing.[25] The essential idea behind this position is that the written words of the *Phaedrus* are permissible imitations because they call attention to themselves through Socrates' criticism of writing. Imitation that does not intend to deceive is thus excusable, it is argued, for it serves as "a reminder to him who knows," the only use for writing to which Socrates will admit in the *Phaedrus* (275C–D). Scholars move to this conclusion and beyond to the postulation of a Platonic "art of writing," driven by the power of this paradox. The resulting syllogism runs thus: Plato attacks writing; but Plato writes; therefore, Plato must be kidding. He intends this "playful" tone, the argument continues, to show us the *Phaedrus* as a classic example of Platonic/Socratic irony, with Plato using the character of Socrates to attack writing, while demonstrating the brilliance of the new technology in his own writing of the dialogue.

The difficulty with such desperate attempts to resolve the paradox rests upon two objections, one that we do not know and one that we do. First, in Socratic style, we must remind ourselves that we do not, literally, know that Plato is a writer, at least not in the modern sense of the word. Socrates states in the *Phaedrus* that writing to record in the archaic tradition of listing and preserving is the only real value of writing (275C–D).[26] Perhaps we should reconsider whether Plato writes in the modern sense of composition, or in the archaic tradition of preservation of important spoken words representing the important ideas of the culture. Here we see the oral tradition's preservation by memory overtaken by the new technology of writing as it preserves the laws and records of the city at the Royal Stoa and later at the Mētrōon, or sanctuary of the Mother of the Gods.[27] It is certainly true, as generations of scholars agree, that Plato is one of the great stylists of the classical period.

The question we must ask is whether that style is an outgrowth of the written tradition, of the oral tradition, or of a dynamic exchange between the two. We must remember the only apparently ironic statement by R. C. Jebb that "the distinquishing characteristic of the best Greek literature is its constant and intimate relation with living speech."[28] Perhaps, to a great degree, Plato's works are an attempt to preserve in writing the great spoken words and ideas of Socrates as Plato held them in his memory. They could thus serve as a "reminder of that which he already knows," a function consistent with the Socratic attack upon writing. As we shall see in chapter six, this possible preservation is supported by the ancient conception of memory as a means of preserving arguments, and not necessarily verbatim accounts.

We move toward this reexamination of our assumptions under the force of the second objection, that which we do know. It is, as Havelock says of Plato's attack on poetry, that the problem "cannot be solved by pretending that it doesn't exist, that is, by pretending that Plato cannot mean what he says."[29] Plato bases his attack on writing upon epistemological grounds, as we have seen. Further, he applies this epistemological foundation to attacks aimed consistently at poets, rhetoricians, logographers, and rhapsodes. To say that Plato is "playful" in his attack on writing, or further, to say that he actually presents an ironic example of philosophic writing, is to say that Plato's attacks upon the poets, the rhetoricians, the logographers, Sophists, and rhapsodes are all in jest. As Shorey notes in his introduction to the *Republic,* Plato considers all literature a form of jest *except* dialectic.[30]

To claim, in all seriousness, that the dialogue format of the *Phae-drus* illustrates a "playful" imitation of the dialectic pursuit of truth, complete with Socratic tongue in cheek,[31] is to call the the entire epistemological foundation of Plato's works a playful exercise in legerdemain. Such hermeneutic sleight-of-hand more closely resembles the sophistic exercises of the *Euthydemus* (302A) than the earnest pursuit of truth in the *Republic* by a Socrates who would later die for his belief in absolute truth (517A).[32] A theory of knowledge so unpopular as to lead to this result would not be a matter for lighthearted treatment. This unpopularity, indeed, leads us to another paradoxical dimension of Plato's attack upon writing.

Plato's Attack on Writing

THE PARADOX OF POPULARITY

Havelock's portrait of Plato's attack upon the poets and Socrates' tone of voice in carrying on the discussion both lead us to surmise that he expected the popular reaction to his attack to be hostile. As Havelock writes, "He thus exhorts us to fight the good fight against the powers of darkness."[33] There are indeed, indications that the rhapsodes and poets were highly popular, as we shall see in chapter three. The paradox of this popularity is that Plato's attack upon the written word, on the other hand, was also a reflection of popular feeling about the new technology.

First, we find that Aristotle and others apparently accept Plato's understanding of the written word as removed from knowledge. Of particular importance in our study is the special relationship between the maker and his work of art as Aristotle conceives it. In the *Nicomachean Ethics* he describes the mutually beneficial relationship between a benefactor or patron and the artist the philanthropist supports.

> *Indeed it seems to be in this fashion with the patrons; for the person receiving their wealth is their work of art, and indeed he loves this work more than the work loves its maker. And the reason for this is that all existence is the object of desire and love, and we exist by activity (both in living and doing). The person making a work by any means exists through activity; thus he cherishes his work, for the same reason that he cherishes existence. This is the order of nature: for the work a thing does reveals its strength and ability through action. (9.7.2–4)[34]*

The last sentence bears more literal translation: "And this is nature: for what a thing is with respect to strength [ability], this the work [of the thing] reveals with respect to action."

Aristotle makes two points of importance to our examination of Plato's condemnation of written language. First, we note that the power, the strength, and the ability (dynamis) are part of the living, breathing maker or artist. We exist in activity, in living and in doing, and the artist exists actively because he makes something. Second, note that the thing being made, the work of art, is the demonstration or revelation of that energy, the result of that action. It is not, however, active on its own. The work does not exist (by living and doing). It is, however, a means of revealing the dimen-

27

sions of the existence humans cherish because it is the result of that existence. The thing made is of value because it reveals existence to those who are living and doing.

Aristotle writes in the *Metaphysics* that "whenever one thing makes and another thing is made, there is between them a making" (1022B). The constant in the Greek conception of man and his making with reference to writing and poetry is that they are separate from the life force of the maker when written down or recited from memory by another. The key seems to be the concept of an active making, the direct contact with the living experience of the author. The *Regimen* in the Hippocratic corpus speaks of writing as an art similar to that of the statue makers, who "imitate the body with the exception of the soul" (1.22–23). They do not make intelligent things, the author continues, and writing is a similar art. "The art of grammar is such as this: the putting together of figures, signs of the human voice, an ability to remember the past, to indicate what must be done." The writing, however, does not have the soul or judgment of the author to give it life. Aristotle notes the distinction in the *Politics* when he says that it seems to be a bad thing to doctor oneself by a "do-it-yourself" book on illness rather than to call in the expertise of the physician. That is, of course, unless you think the physician has a reason to kill you—then you should doctor yourself "by the books" (1278A–B). Aristotle does place writing among lists of "arts" such as medicine in his other works.[35] It is clear from the example above, however, that he understands the significance of Plato's objections to writing, and agrees with them. We must also recall the common description of the *Rhetoric* as "lecture notes" in style, and wonder if we see a reflection of writing as a "reminder of that which one already knows" consistent with Socrates' attack on writing. Chapter eleven addresses this issue more thoroughly.

There are many other clear indications of popular mistrust of writing. There is the reluctance of early orators to have their speeches written down, as we see in chapter seven. There is Xenophon's attack in the *Cynegeticus* upon the Sophists and the "many worthless things" about which they had written (13.1–2). There is the epithetic use of the writing associated with "speech-writing" in attacks by Aeschines (1.94; 3.173) and Demosthenes (19.250; 58.19). Written evidence in the law courts gains acceptance only gradually, and then only when credible witnesses provide support, as we shall see in chapter five. There are indications, in short, that other Greeks of the Hellenic period agree with the Platonic criticism of writing as two removes from the intelligence of the author. Furthermore, the unpopular attack upon the poets that originated in the consciousness of abstraction compares ironically to the apparent popularity of Plato's opinion of the written word that gives that abstraction birth in the ancient Greek consciousness. The final contradiction, however, is that Plato applies the same underlying epistemology to both attacks. In fact, Plato applies the same epistemological standard evenhandedly to all others, whether he associates them with writing or merely "removes them from truth."

THE PARADOX OF CONSISTENCY

We might expect Plato to single out the poets for special attention in his crusade for abstract thought, for as Havelock writes, they are the representatives of "the Homeric state of mind [that] was a general state of mind."[36] Surely his attack on the poets interweaves in the length and breadth of the *Republic,* which is, as Shorey writes, "the central and most comprehensive work of his maturity."[37] Surely it is as vigorous as any of Plato's criticisms of his society when Havelock speaks of poetic statement as "*the* enemy."[38] The rhetoricians and Sophists we associate with writing, however, face Platonic attacks upon the same epistemological grounds as writing. That is, epistemology paradoxically provides the basis for the attack upon both the poets of the oral tradition and the writing technology of the new written tradition. This standard is consistently applied as the basis for criticism of rhetoric, Sophists, and rhapsodes alike.

Writing was the tool that could lead, as we saw above, to an appearance of reality and wisdom, and to the destruction of memory. The rhetoricians, Sophists, and rhapsodes were those who employed writing, speaking, and recitation to create consciously this illusion of reason and wisdom. Whether it be in the written speeches of the logographers, the written discourse of an Isocrates, or recitation from memory by a rhapsode, any work separate from the rigor of dialectic thought in the mind of an individual was not a pathway to truth. Socrates says in the *Phaedrus* that he belongs to

*the many who believe that in the discourses having been written about
each topic there is necessarily much that is childish, and no discourse
yet written, either with or without meter, was worthy of much serious
attention, nor recitation such as those of the rhapsodes that are delivered
for the sake of persuasion without questioning or instruction, but [the
discourses] are a reminder for those who know [the truth].(277E–
278A)*

That man was closest to the truth, Socrates continued,

*who believes that clarity and perfection and worthiness of serious
attention exist only in things taught and words spoken earnestly for
learning, and, in fact, written in the soul about justice and beauty
and goodness. Such discourses of his own must be accounted to be
legitimate sons—first the discourse within himself, if it exists there
after being discovered, and secondly if any offspring or siblings have
similarly grown correctly in the souls of others. The man who believes
this and who bids farewell to all other discourses, this is the sort of
man whom you and I would pray that you and I might become,
Phaedrus! (278A–B)*

The person who would be a true rhetorician, either in speaking or
writing, had to meet several rigid criteria. Plato based these criteria
on the rigorous pursuit of truth through dialectic in both preparation
and in presentation (277B–278C).[39]

The man who simply composes in writing at his leisure without
knowledge or the living wisdom of internal reality is not a true
rhetorician but merely a poet, or speechwriter, or writer of laws
(278E). Note that the qualifications for truth in speaking are very
similar to those for truth in writing. In the case of writing, however,
the lack of intelligence with which to defend itself prevents the
written word from ever meeting the test.

Plato attacks the Sophists for their reliance upon the appearance
of knowledge in both writing and in rote memory. As we shall see
in chapter seven, the Sophists and writing are both are unable to
defend themselves with the word of truth, the mind of one who
knows. The man who knows a thing, in other words, is able to
explain his knowledge, and defend his position. The measure of
reality is not the appearance of the man or his works, but the
undiluted strength of the living intelligence. The truth is fired in
the furnace of intellectual combat, and the Sophists, insecure about

their tricks, avoid head-to-head combat in uncontrolled situations. Others attack the Sophists for their reliance upon memorized tricks and memorized speeches, many apparently taken from the first *technai* that writing preserves. As Aristotle notes in the *Sophistical Refutations,* the techniques of learning by rote and memorizing speeches may result in rapid teaching, but the instruction provides little of permanent value to the student's thought (171B).

The rhapsode suffers under similar harsh criticism. Socrates spends much of the *Ion* convincing the rhapsode of that name that he does not speak Homer with knowledge of the things the poet says (537A–541E). The rhapsode, in short, was once removed from the spoken word of the poet, just as the written word was once removed from the spoken word. The poets, Socrates says, are literally "out of their minds," inspired by the gods, and function as interpreters/messengers of the gods. The rhapsodes, he continues, are the interpreters/messengers of the poets and must rely on similar inspiration (533D–535B). The poets and rhapsodes, in other words, substitute the inspiration of the gods for the connection with the internal reality of the living maker that Plato requires of the true rhetorician and the true author. The rhapsodes' laurel staff is a symbol of this inspiration, as we shall see in chapter three. Socrates concludes the *Ion* by offering the rhapsode a choice.

> *Now if on the one hand being an artist, as I was just saying, you deceive me by promising to display knowledge of Homer, you are unjust; on the other, if you are not an artist, but knowing nothing from out of Homer you speak many and beautiful things about the poet being possessed by divine providence, just as I said about you, you are not unjust.(542A)*

The key phrase for our consideration here is "knowing nothing from out of Homer." This takes on new significance in light of the examination of the Platonic objections to writing above. The rhapsode, a self-proclaimed expert on Homer, knows nothing directly "from out of Homer." Through divine intervention the rhapsode becomes an interpreter/messenger for the interpreter/messenger of the gods, and in reciting he is possessed by the same divine spirit that possessed the poet. Thus the reciting of poetry, along with the reading of the written word, is an irrational endeavor, by Platonic definition, because it is not in contact with the living spirit of the maker. The rhapsode does not become a true artist like the rhetorician or the writer, by knowing his subject completely and being able to defend it in person with the living knowledge of his soul; indeed, the rhapsode does not become an artist at all in the Platonic sense of art or craft. The rhapsode is *to theion,* sent by or from the gods, divine, replacing the living spirit of the maker with the living inspiration of the gods.

This is not to say conclusively that Plato saw no place for rhetoric and rhapsodes in society, even though poets and other imitative artists, craftsmen and farmers, Sophists and demagogues, were all near the bottom of Socrates' hierarchy of the knowledgeable in the *Phaedrus* (248D–E). Plato, as E. R. Dodds wrote, maintained a healthy respect for the inspiration of the gods.[40] He also placed those of a "musical" nature on the same rung of the hierarchy with philosophers and lovers of beauty. Plato clearly revised the definition of the *mousikē* associated with the oral past by his attack on the poets. He has not, however, completely abandoned this connection with the old education of the oral past. It remains part of the training for the guardians of the *Republic,* a source of harmony in the strains between reason, appetite, and high spirit in their characters (441E). Plato was clearly emphatic, however, in his assertion that both rhetoric and the rhapsodes were considerably beneath dialectic in the hierarchy of methods leading toward the ultimate truth.

All of which reinforces Havelock's conclusion regarding the important problem of Plato's banishment of the poets. Poetry does indeed "cripple the mind," for the poet has no knowledge of the things he describes.[41] Homeric battles are the representations of an inspired poet who never sees the battles; he never knows Achilles or Hector. Poetry is thus one of the temptations that man must resist in his pursuit of knowledge, one of the earthly distractions (though divinely inspired) that draws men away from the remembrance of the plain of ultimate truth Plato describes in both the *Republic* (608B) and the *Phaedrus* (248E). Havelock, then, is clearly correct in his analysis of Plato's attack upon poetry as removed from abstract knowledge, and the epistemological basis for that attack is consistently applied throughout Plato's works. The suggestion that writing is related to this knowledge, however, clearly deserves further study in the light of Plato's paradoxical objections to writing. As we shall see in the chapters that follow, the paradoxical connections between writing and the oral tradition in Plato's thought are symbolic of the interaction of the two media in all aspects of Greek culture.

SUMMARY

We see now that Plato's work personifies the tension between the written and the oral traditions in ancient Greece in several dimensions of apparent contradiction. These suggest that the oral tradition retains considerable influence upon Plato, the individual who is demonstrated by Havelock to have been pivotal in the struggle between the two traditions. Furthermore, they illustrate the power the conflict generates in his thought.

The paradox of Plato's attack upon writing, however, is not an excuse for the dismissal of the substance of that attack, nor a justification for dismissal of his attack upon poetry as insightfully explicated by Havelock. Instead it presents a dynamic picture of Plato as a thinker on the edge of the change in human thought and society brought about by the new technology of writing. His thought shows the influence of a consciousness of abstraction that was not aroused in our own written culture until I. A. Richards' *The Meaning of Meaning* and S. I. Hayakawa's *Language in Thought and Action*.[42] These seminal works brought our consciousness of the differences between written words, spoken names, and things to the level experienced by Plato, as the oral tradition struggled to maintain its power against the new wave of *grammata*. Plato's theory of knowledge retains links to the oral past through the importance of memory and spoken language in the individual struggle to pursue this same abstract consciousness.

There seems to be little reason for sophistic struggles to resolve the paradox; indeed to make the attempt lessens both the abstract brilliance and the individual power of Plato's accomplishment. A conservative with many reasons to sympathize with the discipline and tight structure of the more Spartan Greek past, Plato blends the best of both the oral past and the written future in a call to reason that has stirred the imaginations of truth-seekers for thousands of years. We must not attempt to lessen that achievement by applying nineteenth- and twentieth-century assumptions about writing technology to an ancient culture where men still recited their cultural tradition as it had been passed down for hundreds of years.

Plato's paradoxical attack upon writing, in essence, provides a remarkable paradigm for the employment of the strengths of both the written and the spoken word. The powerful memories of the day are evident in the recitations that provide the dramatic frame of eight of the Platonic dialogues, and in the implicit recitation of the *Republic* itself. The participants in the *Republic* are engaged in a lengthy and complicated endeavor, and yet their memories keep the discussion consistent throughout the elaborate structure of abstract events. The intricate tracings of abstract relationships between abstract ideas, in addition, display the consciousness of abstraction that is the power of the written word. They avoid the weakness of the written tradition as a method of preserving sophistic gimmicks or appearances in pretty words that distract us from the pursuit of truth. The written form of these dialectic struggles toward virtue is not a "playful hint" that Plato means to say something that he does not. These writings are a preservation of thought in the only format consistent with his epistemology—the dialogue—and possibly in the only form consistent with his attack on writing, as written reminders of the spoken word representing the perceptions of truth in the mind of one who knows. They remain for us to examine in the form he intended to pass on to future generations, a preservation of the spoken words that remain humankind's only approach to truth.

3

The Rhapsodes Revisited: Greek Society and the Messengers of the Muse

Perhaps the earliest depiction of a singer "making" poetry is in the brilliantly colored fresco at the Palace of Nestor at Pylos. The performer sits upon a stone with a lyre in his hand as a colorfully depicted dove flies away from him.[1] The bird is almost as large as the singer, and by sheer size calls to mind the more than one hundred references in Homer to "winged words."[2] The connection of the dove to the song is clouded, of course, by the long history of the dove as a religious symbol in the eastern Mediterranean.[3] Certainly there is no hard evidence that the bird is a representation of words and music, but with a small flight of fancy we can picture the singers of the *Odyssey,* Demodocus (8.44–45) and Phemios (1.154), seated in the hall of a Mycenaean noble. Surrounded by brilliant colors and famous warriors, the power of the song matches the size and brightness of the singer and his lyre.

The idealized Homeric view of the ancient bards and epic poets was only a memory by the time of Plato. The heirs to the tradition of recitation in Hellenic Greece were the rhapsodes (*rhapsodoi*), the "song-stitchers" or "rod-chanters" who recited works of literature verbatim as a profession.[4] These heirs to the tradition of the Homeric bards (*aoidoi*) have been examined and rehabilitated somewhat by scholars in recent years, but the most powerful image of the rhapsode is still that of the affable bumbler Ion in the Platonic dialogue of the same name.[5] As we have seen in the previous chapter, how-

35

ever, Plato owed more than a few debts to the oral tradition in his own view of the world.

In the following, I will argue that the rhapsode stands as a personification of the continuing interaction between orality and literacy in the fifth and fourth centuries B.C. The argument follows several lines. First, as we noted in the previous chapter, Plato bases his criticism of the rhapsode as lacking in *technē,* or scientific knowledge, upon epistemological grounds. He applies the same commonsense criticism to other individuals and areas of study. Further, there are indications that he considers the rhapsodes an accepted part of society, despite his dismissal from the Republic of the poets they preserved. The second main argument is that while the rhapsodes are heirs of the oral tradition, they owe their existence to writing. The verbatim memory we associate with the rhapsodes, in other words, does not become possible or desirable until "standard" written texts of literature appear. Third, while the rhapsodes appear as specialists after writing, they clearly represented a tradition of oral performance that was commonplace in the time of Plato. Finally, the rhapsodes remain a significant part of Greek culture for a long time, indicating a strength in the oral tradition that continues well beyond the Hellenic period.

THE RHAPSODES' RELIANCE ON WRITING

Plato aims the Socratic criticism of Ion on epistemological grounds consistently at rhetoricians, Sophists, and others in Plato's work, as we saw in the previous chapter. The rhapsode in the *Ion* does not know anything "out of Homer" (542A); he is removed from the poet, just as the written version is. The rhapsode is not, however, singled out for criticism while others remain unscathed. Indeed, many of those on the receiving end of Socrates' biting wit would rejoice to have even the backhanded compliment regarding Ion's "divine inspiration," that he "speaks many and beautiful things about Homer while possessed by divine providence" (542A). Few of Socrates' partners in dialogue receive such kindness at his hands.

The rhapsode, in short, is another case of paradox regarding the Platonic attitude toward the advent of writing. Plato attacks the rhapsode for a lack of knowledge, the same grounds upon which he attacks writing. Yet he shows respect for the work of the rhapsode, just as he owes a debt to the consciousness of abstraction that writing makes possible. Further, the rhapsode is a representative of the old oral tradition in Plato's mind, and yet the position of the rhapsode as a performer distinct from the older bards or *aoidoi* would not have come into existence without writing.

The difference, of course, is that by the fourth century the rhapsodes are verbatim reciters who memorize from a written document and perform works without changes. Scholars are apparently in agreement that the change took place around 450 B.C.

> *The rhapsodes of the fourth century were mere reciters, but those of the sixth and early fifth were to some extent composers as well as reciters; some may have been pure composers. Therefore the rhapsodes of the sixth and early fifth centuries included a substantial number of men trained in the complex technique of oral composition.*[6]

The ironies, we find, begin to multiply. The rhapsode is famous for preserving the tradition of Homeric verse as writing preserved it, and for popularizing that tradition through oral performance. Writing shapes that performance, however, as the ability of written copies to preserve works verbatim eliminated oral composition techniques.

Further, the highly emotional and implicitly flashy renditions of Homer to which Plato alluded in the *Ion* (535B–C) resulted from changes wrought by the written tradition. For example, style became more important to the rhetoric of the Roman era when substance was limited by the emperor's likes and dislikes. By the same token, when the rules prohibited creativity in oral composition, and the rhapsode was judged partially by his ability to remain true to the written text, the style of his oral delivery became all the more important.

So writing reduced the creative aspects of poor Ion's profession to matters of delivery, and then Plato criticized him because he cannot discuss those performance skills scientifically. Ion would have found sympathetic company among both the elocutionists and contemporary scholars in speech communication. As Mino concluded after a survey of research on delivery in speech communication, "there seems to be ambivalence and controversy concerning what effective communication skills are and how the components of effective communication should be defined and taught to our students."[7] The vocal and physical variables in such oral performances, in short, were so complex that three thousand years later we were still in the process of exploring them, and often in terms not much more sophisticated (literally) than Ion's.

THE RHAPSODE AND THE DIVINE

While Plato belittles Ion's lack of knowledge of his craft, however, the rhapsode maintains an attitude of blithe equanimity. While Truman Capote's theory about good actors being stupid may apply, an alternative explanation is suggested by the rhapsode's popularity with the rest of his society. Clear evidence links his work to the other oral performances that abounded in fifth and fourth century Greece.

Aside from the rather lavish dress of the rhapsode, scholars most often associate this wandering reciter with his trademark, a bay laurel staff. A parallel is found in the association of myrtle wands with the recitations that are an important part of Greek social life. These informal performances provide information that throws a new light on Socrates' comment in the *Ion* that the rhapsodes are divinely inspired (534A–535B).

Hellenic Greeks highly valued in their social life the ability to recite poetry or other literature from memory, and in some cases that value was measured in life and death terms. Plutarch reported in the *Life of Nicias* that after the catastrophic Athenian defeat at Syracuse, many men avoided dying as slaves in the quarries because they recited Euripides (29.2–3). The residents of Sicily were extremely fond of Euripides' works, and they were willing to pay for access to his work.

> *It is said that many of those reaching home safely greeted Euripides warmly, and recounted detailed stories, some saying that they were released from slavery for repeating as much as they could remember of his poetry, and some that they received food and drink in exchange for singing some of his choral songs while wandering about after the battle.*

On another occasion, the Sicilians actually refused, as Plutarch records the story (29.3), to admit a ship of the Caunians to the harbor at Syracuse until the people on board reported that they did, indeed, know songs by Euripides. The ship, it should be noted, was being pursued by pirates at the time.

These two stories certainly may be exaggerated, but they probably do not overstate the case for the ancient Greeks' affection for singing and reciting at social occasions, a tradition known to have been popular since the time of Homer. Plutarch reports a telling comparison in his *Life of Cimon* (9.1–2). He criticizes the great hero Themistocles, who was instrumental in the defeat of the Persian fleet at Salamis, because he had not learned to sing or play the lyre. At the same time, he praised Cimon because he sang well as the wine was passed. The ability to recite or sing was apparently a mark of intelligence as well as education.

The evidence demonstrates that such recitals were quite common at dinners. Aristophanes and Xenophon both record instances of singing as after-dinner entertainment, and Plato indicates in the *Symposium* (214A–B) that Greeks expect speech, recital, and song with the wine after dinner. "So are we neither to say nor sing anything over the cup," Eryximachus asks Alcibiades, "but simply to drink like thirsty people?" Xenophon's *Symposium* (3.1; 7.1) also records singing after a repast, both from a professional entertainer and from the group as a whole led by Socrates. Aristophanes records references to singing after dinner in *The Clouds* (1364–65) and *The Wasps* (1222), the two plays describing a game the Greeks play that is similar to the "capping" contests in Elizabethan courts. They play the game with lyric poetry, and one genre of poetry, the *skolion*, takes its name from this contest of wits and drinking stamina. The scholiast on *The Wasps* (1222) writes that the guests passed a wand (*skēptron*) of laurel or myrtle around, the first singer passing the wand to indicate who must pick up the song where it was left off.[8]

Holding the laurel wand while singing links these social performances to the passage of the *Theogony* (29–34) in which Hesiod describes the inspiration of the Muses and their selection of him as a singer.

> *So said the daughters of great Zeus, ready of speech; and they plucked a sweet-smelling laurel staff and gave it to me, their admirer, and breathed into me the human voice of divine inspiration, in order that I might celebrate the things that shall be and the things that were before. And they commanded me to sing of the race of blessed ones who live forever, and of themselves to sing forever first and last.*

The staff of Hesiod and the later rhapsodes symbolizes the power through which the Muses inspired the singer, and the symbol lasted for generations.

The *skēptron* (staff) of which Hesiod speaks also means "scepter." The scepter is a symbol of kingly power in the *Illiad* that Agamemnon passes to those who ask to speak, implying with its presence that the king gives them permission to speak.[9] The Greeks associate the same bay-laurel (*daphnē*) with temples of Apollo, the god of prophecy who spoke to men through divine inspiration.[10] The laurel or myrtle wand thus appears as a symbol of divine inspiration to the singer from the earliest recorded time. The concept of divine inspiration thus remains a symbolic part of Greek recitation through the staff or myrtle wand, whether it is in the hand of a rhapsode at a festival or the hand of a private individual at a symposium.

Ancient sources provide differing versions of the origin and nature of the *skolion,* the song sung over the wine.[11] The number of sources referring to such a game, however, makes it clear that the Greeks sing poetry in a test of memory, one person picking up the song where another leaves off.[12] The commentaries also make it clear that the Greeks consider individuals who refuse the wand and decline to sing "unmusical" (*amousos*). The word implies not just a lack of musical skill but also a lack of cultural refinement and taste.[13] The literal translation would be "without the Muses," or without the performance ability their presence ensures. Social recitation of poetry from memory is thus more than just a form of entertainment; it is the mark of education and culture. In addition, these recitations maintain a direct symbolic link to the "divine inspiration" of the gods through the passage of the laurel or myrtle wand.

The wand's link to "divine inspiration" provided a symbolic, if not real, replacement for the living intelligence of the poet or "maker" who composed the poetry. The original maker appealed to divine sources to aid in his composition of poetry; the reciter held a symbolic link to the gods as he reproduced the making. This symbolism was an obvious parallel to the staff traditionally carried by the rhapsodes and provided evidence that Socrates' description of the rhapsodes in Plato's *Ion* (534A–535B) as interpreters or messengers of the gods was not in the least ironic.

Perhaps, in other words, the Platonic refusal to accept the rhapsode's work as an "art" or *technē* is not quite as harsh as it first appears. The religious symbolism of the staff or wand and its relationship to divine inspiration is a common and accepted part of

40

Greek culture; Socrates' praise of the rhapsode Ion (542A) as one inspired by the gods may not be faint praise at all. Thus Ion's gushing self-confidence may be based on more than his blithe enjoyment of the sound of his own words.

THE RHAPSODE'S SUCCESS

Ancient sources reported that the rhapsodes of Hellenic Greece had become both specialized and successful. Scholars differentiatied them from their predecessors, as we have seen, by the fact that they did not usually compose their own works and by the fact that they recited verbatim. Neither did they play the lyre or harp.[14] As Plato noted in the *Ion* (530D), the rhapsodes had become so specialized that some, perhaps all, performed the works of only one poet. Ion told Socrates that he recited only Homer and that discussions of other poets had no interest for him at all (532B–C).

The rhapsode earned classification in a category separate from contemporaries who recited poetry, such as actors. While in the *Ion* (532D) Socrates spoke of rhapsodes, actors, and the men whose poems they recited in the same breath, in the *Republic* (395A) Plato wrote of the rhapsode's art as being so complex that the same man could not have been a good actor and a good rhapsode at the same time. This specialization also differentiated the rhapsode from the Homeridae, a society, clan, or "tribe" devoted to the preservation and study of Homer. Strabo (14.1.35) reported that they centered on the island of Chios and claimed to be descendants of Homer. Plato referred to them in his general reference to "those clever at knowing Homer" in the *Cratylus* (407A–B) and in his quotation of their work in the *Phaedrus* (252B). Again, the group mentioned by Plato claimed to be the descendants of Homer.[15] The characteristic verbatim recitation thus separated the rhapsodes from the earlier bards, from contemporary poets and musicians, and from the Homeridae, indicating that the rhapsode had a unique function and a recognized position in Greek society.

The rhapsodes, in addition, were quite successful in the pursuit of their profession, despite the oft-quoted remarks about their stupidity. This rather pleasant empty-headed quality was an identifying trademark of the rhapsode Ion, at least as he was portrayed by Plato.

agreeing with Socrates in the *Memoribilia* (4.2.10) that rhapsodes are very stupid, and in his *Symposium* (3.4.6), the company concluded that, indeed, the rhapsodes were the most stupid of all "tribes" of men.

The apparent financial and social success of the rhapsodes, however, argues against this unqualified view of their mentality. First, the rhapsodes remain a feature of Greek culture for hundreds of years, as the existence of odeions in many Greek cities would suggest. Enos writes that the rhapsodes remain an important part of Greek culture for "at least nine centuries."[16] He argues on the basis of epigraphical evidence that rhapsodic competitions continued well into the Roman Empire.

Further, society valued the talents of the rhapsodes. Plato noted in the *Ion* (530B) that this rhapsode was well dressed and financially successful. The rhapsodes would not have been either if they were not skilled in the eyes of many of their contemporaries. In fact, this was a significant part of Plato's case in the *Ion;* the dialogue sought to demonstrate the lack of conscious craft or art beneath the adept facade of the rhapsode.

The success of Ion was also a sign of the level of sophistication that the rhapsodic competitions had reached, approaching the standing of the theatre, at least in terms of individual monetary support and status. In the *Laws* (843E), Plato spoke of the regulation of the rhapsodes and their escorts, those who followed in service of the rhapsode. The fact was that rhapsodes were either wealthy enough to afford a retinue of servants or popular enough to attract a group of followers who accompanied them without pay.

Such success led to official recognition of rhapsodic competitions in the official calendar. In the *Laws* (834E–835A), Plato took rhapsodic competitions for granted in ordering the festivals and contests of the religious calendar, along with the choral competitions of the theatre and the athletic games. Plato stated, in addition, that rhapsodic competition was one of the components of the "music" (*mousikē*) that was such a vital part of the Greek concept of education. In the same passage of the *Laws* (834D–E), he noted that the discussion had outlined the regulations for contests and learning in gymnastics, both with respect to contests and daily teaching. The laws, he continued, had been proposed for most of music as well, with the exception of the work of the rhapsodes and their escorts. Immediately afterward, the discussion turned to the choral competitions that were a part of yearly religious life and theatre.

So despite Plato's apparent contempt for the rhapsode's intelligence, he clearly thinks of rhapsodic competitions as a part of the "musical" education of society, a continuing education of the citizenry in the traditions of the Greek oral past. In short, despite his reservations about the rhapsode's personal knowledge of his art as Plato portrays it in the *Ion,* the philosopher does recognize the place of the rhapsode in society.

It is odd, however, that Plato does not specifically ban the rhapsodes from his ideal city in the *Republic* (376E–389A), or discuss them when setting the tight restrictions to be imposed upon the poets. He bans the poets, as he criticizes the rhapsodes, on the epistemological grounds that they have no knowledge of many of the things they teach through description. Rhapsodes would be one source of the Homeric epics that he would severely edit or completely ban. We must wonder if it is his intention to ban written versions of the poets solely, or if he would allow rhapsodes to perform only certain versions of the poets.

Perhaps, however, even Plato would not risk speaking ill in writing of those chosen by the gods as the special messengers of divine inspiration. If there is a hollow ring to the Socratic praise of Ion's profession, it may originate in a hyperbolic attempt to placate those upset by his earlier criticism of the rhapsode. Perhaps even the theoretical banning of the special messengers of the gods approaches a heresy uncomfortably reminiscent of the charges against Socrates. But Plato attacks the oral tradition with few signs of temerity, as we see in chapter two. Could it be that we have evidence of yet another Platonic paradox? Does Plato himself have mixed feelings about the banning of the recitations of the rhapsodes?

I argue on the basis of the evidence that Plato feels a conflict in this case between his abstractly aware intellect and his "musical" heart. Even though he includes the poetry of Homer in the ban on "imitative" poetry, Homer's work is clearly respected above all other poetry in the *Republic* (386A–387B, 595B–C). As Paul Shorey writes, Plato's concern about poetry is an expression of his sensitivity to its power.

> *He himself wrote verse in youth. His imagery, the invention of his myths and the poetic quality of his prose rank him with the world's*

43

He himself wrote verse in youth. His imagery, the invention of his myths and the poetic quality of his prose rank him with the world's major poets. He quotes poetry with exquisite and fond aptness throughout his writings. And there are no more wistful words than his reluctant dismissal of the supreme poet, the author and source of all these beauties of epic and tragedy, the Ionian father of the rest—Homer.[17]

So the dismissal of Homer comes reluctantly. But Plato does ban the poets, however politely he packages the blow. Why do we not read a simple statement banning rhapsodes and rhapsodic competitions as well?

Whether self-preservation motivates the omission, or it comes as a Freudian slip, we find the rhapsodes in place in the *Laws* (834E) as an expected part of society. They are not mentioned in the ideal *Republic*. One may reason from that premise that Plato would not forget to ban the rhapsodes from his ideal society without motivation. The simplest answer is that he assumes the rhapsodes to be the source of any recitations of Homer that might be discussed. In other words, that poetry was heard and not read goes without saying. Other evidence, outlined in chapter ten, supports this proposition. The rhapsodes and their oral performances are such an integral part of society, as the *Laws* suggest, that banning the poets is equivalent to banning the rhapsodes. Yet even so we find another point of paradox in Plato's position on the turning point between the old oral tradition and the new written tradition. Despite Plato's conception of the rhapsode as unintelligent, despite his protrayal of Ion as one who practices his art without knowledge, he nevertheless suggests respect for the function of the rhapsode in contemporary Greek society.

SUMMARY

In summary, the rhapsode emerged as a figure whose value to society grew out of the interaction between oral and written culture. The rhapsode owed his existence to writing, and he performed those written words orally. His creativity was limited to divinely inspired powers of delivery because he reproduced the written text verbatim, yet on the basis of writing's awareness of abstraction he faced attack for lack of awareness of those delivery skills. Without the written text, he would have become another type of performer, but the use of it limited his potential for creativity. Nevertheless, the rhapsode was the publicizer of the great epic tradition, an apologist for literature who used the power of the oral performance tradition to acquaint the illiterate with the greatest poetry of his day. Despite his apparent lack of intellect in the literate, philosophical sense, the rhapsode stood as a model for the oral performance of literature. He succeeded in the midst of a changing society as an apologist and publicist for literature, employing the skills of the oral performer as a means of engaging imaginations with the best in written literature.

The final portrait of the rhapsode removes some of the sting of Plato's portrayal of Ion as an interpreter-messenger of the gods, a man who has no rational explanation of his work. This rehabilitated picture of the rhapsode reveals that Ion, like Plato himself, is a product of the continuing interaction between writing and the oral tradition. Unlike Plato, Ion relies primarily upon the oral performance tradition for his success in life. He does not preserve his words for all time in writing, for his craftsmanship forms art from the evanescent breath of life. But the extension of his profession into the Roman era shows that at least one facet of the interaction between orality and literacy continued through Greek civilization and beyond.

4

Orality and Literacy
in Basic Education

A story from an old Athenian manuscript symbolizes the tension between orality and literacy in Greek attitudes toward education.[1] "The Sailor and his Son," tells of a sailor who wants his son educated in grammar. After some time in school the son reports that he knows grammar and wants to continue with the study of rhetoric. His father consents, and the son shortly becomes an accomplished rhetorician. One day at the dinner table the father admits that he does not really understand the value of rhetoric. "About the art of grammar I have heard that it is the foundation of all the arts, and that one who understands it [grammar] is able to write and speak without stumbling; but I have never known what rhetoric is capable of doing." The son quickly agrees with the father on the value of grammar, but says that rhetoric is even more powerful. Rhetoric, he says, can demonstrate everything and make even false things seem true. The father quickly parries this assertion, challenging the son to make the two eggs on the table into three. The son says it would be easy and asks his father to begin counting the eggs. When he gets to two, the son stops him and asks him if one and two do not add up to three. Yes, the father agrees, it does, but replies that he is going to eat one egg and his wife the other and that the son could eat the egg he "made" with his rhetoric.

Grammar, in the father's view, was clearly useful in teaching the recognition, proper combination, and recording of letters that represented the sounds of the language. He displayed the continuing attitude toward writing that it was useful for preservation of words, a handy tool. He has come further, recognizing the value of order and correctness in speaking the language, showing that literacy has begun to impose the alphabet's order and discipline upon his conception of language. Any literary arts beyond these necessities of life, however, both he and others regarded with considerable suspicion, as we shall see in chapter seven.

Yet even in the education of the Hellenic Greeks in basic written grammar we find evidence of the continuing tension between orality and literacy. First, education in Hellenic Greece begins with strong ties to the oral traditions of the past, and to the social tradition of education as leadership training for young aristocrats. Second, the educational practice of the Hellenic period at all levels demonstrates continuing ties to both the oral tradition and to the tradition of aristocratic leadership. Memory and recitation play a large role in the education of the day, demonstrating the continuing vitality of the oral tradition. Children of aristocrats and the wealthy, those who could afford to pay, predominate. Students study "grammar" for a brief period, and many have the feeling that the student should learn only such "letters" as are useful. The Greeks relate their very conception of grammar to the archaic conception of writing as a means of preservation. Grammar is for them a method of identifying spoken letters in order to record them accurately in writing. Finally, even the new sophistic and philosophical schools retain important ties to the oral traditions of the past.

Education, in short, was training for the aristocratic youth who eventually were to guide society in its governmental functioning. They learned to recognize the written letters for each sound of the language and the way those sounds—and thus letters—interacted. This was apparently the limit of that which was considered "useful" education in writing. The oral tradition of memory persisted as students memorized and recited from dictation in classroom exercises. In this society, writing was a means of recording and preserving the spoken word of the aristocrat or leader in society. Memory was vital to the proper functioning of the leader's mind, and recitation was a means of strengthening that memory. The more advanced forms of education by the Sophists and the later philosophic schools moved away from that tradition, as we shall see in chapter seven and beyond. Nevertheless, their instruction was primarily oral, and they transferred some of the archaic feeling for musical education as a virtue in itself to the appreciation of philosophical abstractions and argumentation. Basic education in writing, however, was apparently a useful tool for recording and preserving words and lists in the archaic tradition. Literacy as we know it was not a conception, much less a goal, in elementary education.

EDUCATION IN TRANSITION

Like the sailor's son, those who undertake the study of Greek education must be careful to count their evidence carefully. Harold Frederick Cherniss writes in *The Riddle of the Early Academy* that modern scholars often impose the modern usage of "academy" on their conception of that ancient Greek institution. German scholars, he writes, describe it as a kind of German university, French scholars describe it as a kind of French university, and an Englishman writes that it "resembled a modern college . . . with its Masters, Fellows, and Scholars."[2]

In reality, Hellenic education was not a stable institution, a well-defined part of society like the modern university. As George Kennedy wrote in an article in *Western Journal of Speech Communication,* Greek education during this period was part of an intellectual revolution.

> *The revolution involved a transition from a predominantly oral culture to a culture in which writing played a major role, from a culture passed on and preserved by word of mouth to a culture written down, from an educational system based on imitative action to an educational system based on original action as guided by written rules.*[3]

This revolution paralleled the changing meaning of the term *engkyklios paideia,* the equivalent of the Latin *artes liberales* or liberal arts education.

L. M. De Rijk claimed that from the early fifth century B.C. *engkyklios paideia* referred to all aspects of choric (or choreutic) education, including rhythm, harmony, word, and gymnastics, all "training to make a man 'harmonious.'"[4] By around 450 B.C., however, the term differentiated between the sister arts of music and gymnastics, with "the arts of the Muses" (*mousikē*) referring specifically to literary culture. Music itself was further divided into several *technai:* grammar, stylistics, and poetics. This took place at approximately the same time that speeches were first being written down.[5]

Further evidence for a revolutionary change in the relationship between writing and education appeared in Frederick A. G. Beck's collection of school scenes as depicted on vases and in other media.[6] Only a few vases or sculptures that can be dated prior to 460 B.C. pictured writing or writing materials; most are dated in the mid to late fifth century. Both verbal and visual evidence, in sum, indicated a shift toward writing in education.

By the fourth century B.C., basic instruction in writing began with a period of primary instruction under the *grammatistēs* at the very beginning of the student's career.[7] Plato wrote in the *Euthydemus* that the *grammatistēs* would be expected to write and read letters better than any other individual, as that was his area of specialty (279E). The *grammatikos* supervised a secondary period of education. He taught a wide range of subjects, including interpretation and exposition of a wide range of poets, and other subjects.[8] With the sophistic or philosophical schools as the third level, this basic framework of educational practice remained in place until the end of pagan education in the sixth century A.D.[9]

These changes clearly depicted an evolving conception of education as the culture became more complex and writing became more common. Yet writing in Greek education had not instantly become, to paraphrase Cherniss, similar to writing in an American educational institution. In fact, the change indicated the beginning of the interaction of orality and literacy in education, because prior to 450 B.C. writing and literacy apparently had little or no place in formal Greek education.

THE OLD EDUCATION

Even before grammar and writing, the students of ancient Greece were no more appreciative of school than modern students, as this brief poem from the *Anacreontea* shows.

> *Why teach me laws*
> *and constrain me with words?*
> *And indeed such words*
> *utterly without use?*
>
> *Rather teach me to drink*
> *the tender draught of Bacchus.*
> *Rather teach me to play*
> *with golden Aphrodite.*[10]

The poem, while probably not a genuine work of Anacreon, did represent in spirit the feelings of a student compelled to memorize when he would rather have been playing. The student's resentment against the constraints forced upon him by education may be one of few constants in the changing history of Hellenic education. The poem also illustrated, as other sources attested, that memory and oral performance dominated what Henri Irénée Marrou termed the "old education."

Marrou compiled a picture of education at the beginning of the period, calling it the "old education" after a passage in Aristophanes.[11] The early fifth-century B.C. Athenians apparently considered even basic education as a sort of cultural training for the upper classes.

> *Such was the old Athenian education—artistic rather than literary, athletic rather than intellectual: in the account in the* Clouds, *Aristophanes gives only eight verses out of more than sixty to the teaching of music; he says nothing about the teaching of letters. The remaining verses are concerned with physical education, and especially its moral aspects. This is a point to be emphasized: the education was in no sense technical; it was still designed for the leisured life of the aristocracy.*[12]

Marrou noted that grammar was the "third brand of learning" after gymnastics and music but did not date its appearance.[13] Evidence for formal schooling in "grammar," he wrote, consisted only of sources indicating that Greeks could read.

Ancient authors support Marrou's conception of an "old education."[14] Quintilian writes that letters and music were once united, with music more esteemed than letters.[15] Quintilian also quotes Sophron as saying that the same teachers were employed to teach both and cites several other authors of plays who show their characters to be trained in music. In the same section, he cites Cicero's comment that Themistocles, the engineer of the Greek victory at Salamis, is considered to have an "imperfect education" because he cannot play the lyre.[16]

More recent authors generally agree that prior to the end of the fifth century Greek education is largely a matter of choral movement, music, and recitation, but that by the beginning of the fourth century a dramatic change occurs. Freeman writes that Solon is said to have made letters compulsory in the sixth century, and that a secondary stage of education in "grammar" begins in the end of the fifth century.[17] He also notes that while letters are compulsory at Athens, music and gymnastics are almost universal in the Greek world.[18] Beck agrees with the general dating of the origins of schools and with the conception of the old aristocratic education as one that is "not in letters and literature."[19]

Walden dates the change to the same era and states forcefully the goal of the "old education." "The chief aim of the Athenian education appears in the point of view from which the poets were studied: they were looked upon primarily, not as literary artists, but as moral preceptors, and were required, not so much to form the tastes as to develop the characters of the pupils."[20] The students memorize the words of the poets to embed permanently the maxims of the oral culture in their characters. In the same way the Spartan oral law proposes to change each citizen by becoming part of his character, as we shall see in chapter five. So the origins of education reach back to an oral tradition of memory, recitation, and oral performance as training for the youth of the aristocracy.

WRITING CHANGES EDUCATION

The growing complexity of economics in Athenian society demanded greater knowledge of letters, and the growth of schools seems to parallel this rising demand.[21] The educational heritage of the period and its tradition of oral instruction, however, strongly influenced the teaching of letters. Frederick A. G. Beck wrote that the meeting of the aristocratic tradition and the study of letters had a "twofold effect": changing aristocratic culture, but at the same time moulding the instruction in letters so that teachers offered them "not as a technique, but as a discipline."[22] Thus, throughout this revolution in all levels of Greek education, the oral culture and traditions of the past remained powerful influences.

By the mid fifth century B.C., the vocabulary of education began to include specific terminology that demonstrated increasing sophistication in the use and study of letters.[23] The above-mentioned differentiation between the positions of the technically oriented *grammatistēs* and the secondary *grammatikos* was evidence of this change. The Greeks eventually recognized the *grammatikos* as a part of the tradition of *mousikē*, and by the fourth century paid him a little more than the average laborer, something over a drachma a day.[24] Schools taught reading and writing along with literature, demonstrating writing's acceptance as part of the normal curriculum of the day.[25] Music and gymnastics remained the two major parts of the Greek concept of education, but there were complaints that many were neglecting gymnastics.[26] These changes were all characteristic of the "new" attitudes toward education. Clarence A. Forbes noted that Athenian interest in physical education peaked after the great victories over the Persians in the sixth century and the first half of the fifth, then faded with the growing affluence of the city and the influx of the sophistic movement.[27] Yet while education changed, many of the changes were more in style than in substance.

GRAMMAR SCHOOLS

The pedagogy, conception of grammar, and discipline of the "new" grammar school all reveal ties to the "old education" of the past. The evidence shows that reading aloud and recitation are essential parts of the daily routine and yet offers no clear instances of reading silently in school. The basic teaching of grammar subordinates writing to the knowledge of the sounds of the language, revealing a conception of writing as a means of preserving the spoken word in the best Archaic tradition. The discipline of the grammar school seems suited to the aristocratic aim of developing hardened leadership for the state.

First, the Greeks apparently read written texts aloud in grammar school. The single reference that described reading in the grammar schools occurred in the *Symposium* of Xenophon (4.27) when Charmides teased Socrates about his prurient interest in reading. "I have seen you myself, he said, by Apollo, when the two of you searched for something in the same papyrus roll at the school, having head to head and your naked shoulder against the naked shoulder of Critobulus." Unfortunately, Charmides did not detail the context of this event. The reading may have taken place near the school instead of within it, and the word for "search" (*masteuō*) did not necessarily relate to reading. Xenophon, in fact, appeared to be playing with the word's secondary definition of "crave" or "desire," as though Socrates "craved" the young boy's company more than the understanding of the letters.

It is clear, however, that the two are sharing a book. This is apparently the norm. We know from Plutarch's *Life of Alcibiades* (7.1) that grammar teachers do not all own complete libraries of Homer, for Alcibiades reportedly beats one poor teacher who tells the young man that he has *no* papyrus rolls of Homer.[28] This suggests that reading aloud and recitation might play a large part in the learning of letters, for Herodotus (6.27) says the students in any one grammar school were probably numerous. If papyrus is scarce and expensive, as we have reason to believe, to the tune of a full day's pay for a grammarian per papyrus roll, then the most obvious way to share a papyrus roll is to read aloud or recite from the papyrus.[29] Socrates says in the *Apology* (26D–E) that one can sometimes purchase a papyrus roll of Anaxagoras in the orchestra for a drachma, but the price of clean papyrus in antiquity is that much or more.[30] This suggests that the roll of Anaxagoras is a secondhand copy. As Marrou notes, one drachma is the equivalent of a full day's wages for a laborer and nearly so for a teacher of grammar in the fourth century.[31] The cost of written works apparently does not encourage the establishment of libraries for grammarians and thus encourages the practice of reading aloud or memorizing from the written page for recitation.[32]

Furthermore, the teaching of grammar, in fact, subordinates writing skill to the knowledge of the sounds of letters, for Greeks view writing as a way of preserving spoken words. There is an intriguing reference in Plato's *Charmides* (159C) to writing and reading in the grammar school.

SOCRATES: *Which is most honored in the grammar school, to write the same letters rapidly or cautiously?*

CHARMIDES: *Rapidly.*

SOCRATES: *And what of reading? Rapidly or slowly.*

CHARMIDES: *Rapidly.*

SOCRATES: *And further not only to play the lyre rapidly but also to wrestle nimbly is much more highly honored than to do so cautiously or slowly?*

CHARMIDES: *Yes.*

Socrates proceeds toward proving an unrelated point about temperance, but his use of the word "cautiously" (*hēsychos*) is of interest.

The word also means quiet, at rest, at leisure, or still. The reference does not clearly support the conclusion that instructors encourage students to write quickly rather than quietly. The passage does suggest, however, that classroom writing may have been rapid and thus, perhaps, sloppy and difficult to read. The goal is not, in short, attractive writing but the preservation of the words.

The famous passage in the *Protagoras* of Plato (325D–326D), in addition, indicates that boys learned the alphabet and some grammar before they received written works to read. More importantly, however, the section portrays writing as a means of recording for memorization. The parents, Plato states, tell the teachers to expend more concern upon correct behavior in the aristocratic tradition than upon letters and harp playing.

> *The teachers take charge of these things, and when the children know the letters and are about to understand the things having been written, just as formerly they understood the spoken language, the teachers place before the students upon the benches the poetry of the good poets and compel them to memorize—poetry in which there are many admonitions, many descriptions and praises and encomia of good men in the past—in order that the boys through admiration may imitate them and yearn to be like them.*

Writing appears as a means to memorization, memorization that would continue the tradition of making leaders through the power of poetic maxims and examples.

Much later evidence from Dionysius of Halicarnassus in his work on *Demosthenes* (52) suggests that students partake of a thorough grounding in the grammar of the spoken language before they begin writing and reading themselves. "For when we learn grammar in detail, we first memorize in order the names of the elements of sound, which we call letters [*grammata*]. Then we memorize the shape and meaning of them. When we know these things, then we memorize the syllables and the modifications of their forms."[33]

Thus the student learns to identify the sounds of the language first, and *then* learns the means of writing them down through making written symbols for them. Afterward the student studies the parts of speech, long and short syllables, high- and low-pitch accents, gender, case, number, moods, and myriads of other things. After all these steps, he finally begins to read and write, slowly, step by step, syllable by syllable. Plato implies in the *Charmides*

Basic Education

(161D) that teaching the children to write their names may have
been a part of the process. Dionysius' description clearly outlines
more intensive instruction in grammar than Plato's, but one point
remains constant: the student learns to identify the parts of the
spoken language first, and then he learns to write them down.

Grammarians clearly became aware of the parts of speech, and
so on, through the use of writing. Then they taught students orally
to identify the abstract relationships between words *before* they
learned writing. This suggests an organic interrelationship between
writing and the spoken language, a point that will be developed
later in this chapter.

In addition, the pedagogical practice of the day retained strong
ties to the aristocratic traditions of discipline for the future leadership
of the city-state. The learning process, in other words, was not
very pleasant for the students, as the discipline in grammar school
was evidently quite strict. Students went to school at daylight,
according to Plato (*Laws* 7D) and Thucydides (7.29.5). The face
that greeted them was not, apparently, a friendly one. Xenophon
described the tough general Clearchus in the *Anabasis* (2.6.12) as
"hard and fierce," then stated that as a result the soldiers felt toward
him as boys felt toward their schoolmaster. Plato noted in the
Protagoras (325D) that parents straightened their children with blows
as they might a twisted piece of wood, and this description appeared
just before he reported how the parents instructed the teacher in
the care of their children. The tools of the teaching trade also fitted
the model of strict discipline in grammar school. A small poem in
the *The Greek Anthology* (6.294) listed the tools of the schoolmaster
of the third to first century B.C.: walking staff, leather strap, a cane
he kept beside him to strike children's heads, a lithe sweetly singing
whip, single-soled shoes, and a covering for his bald head. All of
these were in evidence in depictions of grammar-school work on
Hellenic pottery of various types.[34] Interestingly, the poet did not
mention papyrus, pen, or wax tablet among these "symbols of the
teaching of children." Discipline, on the other hand, was a large
part of classroom life.

The direct evidence regarding reading and grammar school pedagogy, in summary, shows that reading aloud did take place and
provides no certain examples of reading silently. Writing allows
the preservation of poetic works for memorization and clearly influences the understanding of the abstract relationships between

55

parts of speech. Yet the basic teaching of grammar subordinates writing to a knowledge of the sounds of the language, placing writing in the position of a means of recording the spoken word. The strict discipline of the grammar school is in keeping with the traditions of the aristocratic past.

Further evidence provides examples of ties between the grammar schools of the Hellenic period and the "old education" of the aristocratic past. Basic education relies heavily on memory and recitation, limits attendance to those who can pay, offers strictly restricted instruction in writing, and defines grammar in terms of the sounds of the spoken language.

MEMORY AND RECITATION

While the awareness of the parts of spoken language was a vital part of the conception of grammar, the oral tradition of memory training retained its central role in Greek education. In addition to, or perhaps, in the process of teaching students their "alpha, beta, gamma's," the grammarian apparently recited to the children and required them to memorize what he said. Plato's *Euthydemus* (276C) framed a clear description of this in such a casual way as to make this cycle of recitation, memorization, and recitation seem a common practice. Dionysodorus has the following exchange with the young boy Cleinias. "But what happened, Cleinias, whenever the grammarian recited to you, which of the boys learned the things being recited, the wise or the foolish? The wise, Cleinias said. Then the wise learn, but not the foolish." Contemporary authors accept the fact that, as Clarke wrote, "memorization continued to be the practice throughout antiquity."[35]

Indeed, once the primary instruction in writing was complete, recitation and study of the poets became a major concern. As Kenneth J. Freeman wrote, "Even letters, when the elementary stage was past, meant reciting, reading or learning by heart the literature of the boy's own language."[36] Plato mentioned in the *Laws* (810E) the great numbers of poets composing in all types of meters, some serious and some comic, and then said that some people believed in stuffing children full of poetry. "The countless majority of people say that it is necessary, for the proper upbringing of the young, to bring them up in these poets and to stuff them, and having heard and learned much poetry and great learning in the readings, memorizing whole poets by heart." Furthermore, Plato continued in the same passage, many people compiled summaries and collected specific passages, saying that for any child to obtain a complete education, that young person must have memorized all the passages in their collections.

This use of writing to collect maxims and bits of wisdom for memorization matches the first *technai* collected by the Sophists, as we will see in chapter seven. The passage may well be a lightly veiled criticism of sophistic education, which as we will see Aristotle later reflects. Aristotle also specifically mentions in the *Metaphysics* (1050A) teachers who think they achieve their end when they display their students "in action," suggesting a kind of public recitation or "recital" as a part of the normal school routine. This evidence makes it certain that memorization and recitation are established, if not expected, portions of the pedagogy of the grammar school.

Furthermore, we find another link between writing and the oral tradition of memory and recitation. Clearly these collections that Plato mentions are in writing. Just as the rhapsodes rely upon written copies of the great works of Greek literature for their existence, so grammar-school practice in the oral recitation of literature (probably composed orally) relies upon written copies of the poems for their preservation. And, presumably, the critiques of the instructors concern themselves more and more with the accuracy of the verbatim repetition of the work and less and less with the life of the poem's spoken meaning.

There are several much later references to the work of the grammarian in *The Greek Anthology* that imply that the *Iliad* of Homer was the first thing taught to the children, certainly at least the first lines.[37] The *Anthology* attributes to Lucian (11.401) an epigram about a physician who sends his son to learn from the grammarian. The boy learns three lines from the first three verses; "Sing the wrath," "Imposed a thousand woes," and "Many strong souls he sped to Hades." Then the father quits sending him to school, telling the teacher: "Thanks to you, my friend," he says, "but the boy can learn these things from me. For truly I send many souls to Hades before their time, and for this I have no need of a grammarian."

Another epigram in the *Anthology* that scholars attribute to a fifth-century author notes that "the beginning of grammar is a curse in five lines," referring to the first five lines of the *Iliad* (9.173). Stephanus the grammarian is the apparent author of a little work in the same collection (9.385) that may be representative of the other kinds of poetry the students were required to memorize. The piece is an acrostic poem, each line beginning with a letter of the alphabet, from alpha to omega, each a brief summary of the contents of a book of the *Iliad*. These works provide additional, if extremely late, evidence to support the position that memorization and recitation were important parts of the students' training in grammar school.

ACCESS TO BASIC EDUCATION LIMITED

The ancients limited education, even in reading and writing, to the more aristocratic and wealthy elements of society. Plato wrote in the *Protagoras* that students received the basic education in letters, music, and gymnastics in rough proportion to the wealth of the families who paid their fees. "This is what people do, who are most able; and the most able are the wealthiest. Their sons begin school at the earliest age, and are freed from it at the latest" (326C). Aristotle noted in the *Politics* (1313A–B) that some states limited education to protect tyrannies, because education breeds pride and confidence. Much later Plutarch observed in *On the Sign of Socrates* (593A–B) that training in written language was quite unknown to the common herd of men.

Other sources concurred. According to Diodorus Siculus (12.12.4–12.14.2), the legendary (and perhaps mythical) Charondas of Thurii wrote the first laws that provided for public payment for education of the citizens. Thus all the sons of citizens learned to read and write, because otherwise society denied men without wealth the opportunity for noble endeavor. The cost of basic education was apparently too much for many citizens. Plutarch reported in his *Life of Demosthenes* (4.2–3) that guardians of the great orator deprived him of a proper education when they did not pay his teachers. Demosthenes himself gave a stirring example of the prejudice that grew up among educated citizens against those who were less fortunate in this attack on Aeschines' childhood: "Through your childhood you were raised as one among the many in need, at the same time remaining beside your father at the grammar school, grinding the ink and sponging the benches and sweeping out the student's room, stationed as a slave, not as a boy having freedom" (18.258–59).[38] Xenophon, in his Hellenized and fictionalized account of

Persian history, the *Cyropaedia* or *Education of Cyrus* (8.3.37), recorded one character's telling of his father's scrimping and saving
to give him an education.

Advanced education was even more expensive. Socrates, in Plato's *Cratylus* (384B–C), recorded that Prodicus had a price range
from fifty drachmas to one drachma for lectures, with the fifty-
drachma lecture guaranteed to deliver knowledge about certain
things. If the drachma represented a day's wages for a workman,
going to secondary school could have been quite expensive.[39] As
Wilcox concluded, "That only the rich could afford higher education
at Athens needs little proof."[40]

Many references show that basic education was a proper thing
for the gentleman of quality, but that this proper education had
strong ties to the "old education." No one, for example, enjoyed
being called a Sophist, a clear association with the "new education."
As Socrates told Hippocrates in the *Protagoras* (312A–B) regarding
the education of the grammar-teacher, the lyre-master, and the
gymnastics instructor: "for you did not learn of these things from
the instructors for art (*technē*), as one going to practice a trade, but
for education (*paideia*), as becomes a private citizen and a free man."
Just previous to this passage, Hippocrates admitted that he would
be ashamed to be called a Sophist (312A). Even the Sophist Protagoras, later in the dialogue, said that he considered knowledge of
poetry and skill in its interpretation to be the largest part of a man's
education (338E–339A). These examples illustrate a preference for
the "old education" with its stress on teaching young gentlemen
the finer things regarding poetry and music.

An imitator of Plato supports this interpretation in the *Theages*
when Socrates asks Theages a question regarding his education.
"How so? Has your father not been teaching you and educating
you just as the others here have been educated, the sons of good
and noble fathers, in such as letters and playing the harp and wrestling and the other contests?" (122E). Plato also mentioned the
trilogy of letters, harping, and wrestling in the *Alcibiades* as part of
the young man's education (106E), and as the ward of Pericles he
probably received the best of training. Education was, it seems, the
birthright of the sons of noble fathers and wealthy families, and it
was shameful to deny them that right, as in the case of Demosthenes.
On the other hand, we cannot be certain how those outside aristocratic or wealthy families fared educationally.

Little information is available regarding the actual population of Athens. Estimates of the number of people in Attica show that the wealthier class of citizens enrolled as cavalry or hoplites ranged from roughly 5 to 8 percent of the total population, including noncitizens.[41] Armor and horses certainly cost more than grammar school, so this is clearly an uncertain estimate of the number of people who could afford education. Even if every one of those citizens learned to read and write, however, and many of the wealthy noncitizens as well, it seems reasonable to say that many citizens of Athens did not learn to read and write.

Kennedy wrote that literacy in Athens must have been similar to that of cities in the United States and Western Europe at the turn of the century.[42] Census data showed that only 10.7 percent of the population of the United States was illiterate at that time.[43] The explanatory notes, however, indicated that respondents took no specific test of writing or reading. Census takers asked respondents only if they could read and write, and if they said they could write, they were called literate. Furthermore, officals had to warn census takers *not* to classify someone as literate just because the individual could write his or her own name! Some analysts made the assumption that the illiterate population was composed of those with no schooling at all, but later census work showed this assumption to be unfounded. So our definition of "literacy" is open for interpretation.

One recent study, for example, shows that ninety-five out of one hundred young American adults can read at the fourth-grade level, but four out of five cannot use a bus schedule correctly to select arrivals and departures.[44] The figures Kennedy suggests become more believable if we define literacy as merely the ability to identify the written signs for the sounds of the spoken language, or what Havelock terms "craft literacy." In other words, we must recognize that many we might label minimally literate remain unable to think in the abstract, logical way we associate with literacy. They are, in fact, semiliterate, and function in ways more oral than literate in orientation.[45] So even if we accept this limited general comparison to contemporary literacy, we must remember that many in that category were literate only in the narrowest sense of the term. We must also remember that the time spent in the study of writing in Hellenic education is much more limited than that of any modern grammar school.

BASIC EDUCATION LIMITED IN TIME OF STUDY

Education in reading and writing at the primary level was limited both in the length of time spent in the study of grammar and in the scope of the overall instruction. Xenophon wrote in the *Lacedaemonian Republic* (2.1) that many Greek states placed students under the care of a type of chaperon or moral tutor (*pedagogos*) and sent them to school as soon as they were able to understand the things said to them. The actual length of time spent in school by the student, on the other hand, he left uncertain. Later in the same work, Xenophon reported that some cities released the student from his "pedagogue" and from the schoolmaster when he left childhood and reached puberty (3.1).

The actual time spent in the school depended on both the parents' desire for education and their ability to pay.[46] Plato wrote in the *Laws* (809E) that the three years from ten to thirteen were a reasonable time for the study of letters, and that neither the students nor the parents would be allowed to extend or shorten the three-year period in the system he would establish. Some years later, Aristotle claimed in the *Politics* (1336B) that children should begin attending lessons at the age of seven with the elementary education completed at puberty or around the age of fourteen. There was probably much variation in the actual length of study by students in writing and reading depending on parental finances, perhaps within the limits roughly established by the theoretical schools of Plato and Aristotle.

The apparent difference between Aristotle and Plato regarding the length of time to be spent in learning letters is intriguing, suggesting greater acceptance of letters with the passage of time. Plato's mention of a limitation that neither parents nor students could alter indicates a severely limited conception of the time required to become "literate." Plato states in the *Laws* (810A–B), for example, that students must learn sufficient *grammata,* or letters to be able to read and write, but instructors would not encourage great speed or beauty in writing. Not only do students study writing and reading for just a few years, but ancient sources clearly display a negative attitude toward writing and reading that reflects the influence of the "old education" and its links with the largely oral past. There is also significance in the fact that most references, like the one by Plato above, do not pair "writing and reading" as we do in our modern idiom. Most sources speak of teaching or learning "letters." This implies a conception of the written symbol as a means of transcribing the spoken language that the student already knows. The student, in other words, does not need a great deal of instruction to be able to identify the symbols for the sounds of the language that he speaks.

Socrates hinted at this attitude in the *Protagoras* of Plato (312A–B) cited above. Hippocrates and Socrates agreed that the young man did not study grammar, the lyre, and gymnastics with a technical view toward practicing a trade "but for education, as becomes a private citizen and freeman." The clearest evidence of the "old education's" attitude toward writing was in Sparta, where young men received considerable training in athletics and gymnastics, but little in reading and writing. Xenophon, for example, described this training in detail in the *Lacedaemonian Republic* (2.3) but did not mention writing. Plutarch wrote in the *Life of Lycurgus* that Spartan youths of his subject's day learned only such *grammata* as were useful, while all the rest of their training focused on making good soldiers (16.6). He repeated the statement in the *Moralia* (237A) and noted further that Spartans banned all other forms of education beside reading and writing from the country. The ban apparently included teachers and their lectures and writings. Isocrates backed up these statements in the *Panathenaicus* (209) saying that the Spartans had dropped so far below Athenian culture and philosophy that they did not even try to learn *grammata*. This also suggested greater acceptance of writing by Isocrates than by others, a point to be considered further in chapter eight.

The Spartan attitude toward reading and writing paralleled much in Socrates' attitude toward education, at least as portrayed by Xenophon and Plato. Xenophon wrote in the *Memorabilia* (4.1.1–5) that Socrates stressed the importance of education to all. In many areas of study, however, he thought there was a limit to the instruction needed. As a result, he urged his companions to study geometry, astronomy, and arithmetic only to the extent that was useful for everyday life (4.7.2–10). Socrates saw little "useful" in the written word, as Plato recorded in the *Phaedrus* (275B). Socrates said that the written word was of no use except to remind the person who had made the writing. Perhaps Plato's limitation of the study of reading and writing to three years was rooted in Socratic and aristocratic attitudes tied to the "old education's" oral tradition.

This was consistent with Plato's attraction to Spartan discipline and aristocratic culture. Aristotle's more extensive period for study of the basics of grammar reflected a later acceptance of and attention to the study of reading and writing and announced the beginnings of a more clearly written tradition in education.

Such speculation finds support in the fact that by the time Aristotle examines education in the *Politics,* probably some years after Plato's death, Aristotle apparently feels the need to defend the place of music in a young man's education (1337B–1342B). At the same time, on the other hand, he accepts reading and writing offhand as a normal part of one's basic education, as a useful study with practical application in business, managing a house, and learning (1337B–1338A). Then he proceeds into a lengthy examination of the role and importance of music, ultimately concluding that Socrates was wrong to criticize music as something that merely charms or intoxicates (1342B). This passage shows that, while the Greeks limited education in writing and reading, writing was nevertheless gaining acceptance as a part of the basic curriculum.

GRAMMAR AND SOUND

Another tie between education at the basic level in Hellenic Greece and the "old education" of the past exists in the definition of the art of grammar (*grammatikē technē*) in terms of the sound of the language. Several definitions of this "art pertaining to letters" in classical literature define the word in terms of the spoken language. Aristotle states in the *Metaphysics* (1003B), for example: "And of each class of things there is both one perception and one science, just as grammar—being one science—studies all articulate sounds." The reference clearly states that the perception of articulate sound is the "one perception" of grammar, with no reference to writing. Plato presents a similar definition in the *Philebus* (17B) when Socrates says, "but knowing that of which the number and quality of sounds consists, this it is that makes each of us grammarians." Plutarch's much later definition summarizes this concept of grammar in *On Music* (1131D) as, "an art useful for the production of sounds and storing up sounds by letters for their recollections." The Greeks conceive grammar itself, in short, in terms of the spoken language, even though the name of "the art pertaining to letters" refers directly to writing.

Aristotle offers a definition of grammar with an even more interesting twist in the *Topics* (142B). The following passage occurs
in a discussion of the commonplaces of definition. "Furthermore
you should determine if the word being defined by reference to
many things has not accounted for all of them, for example, if
grammar is the knowledge of writing the things being dictated; for
it also requires knowledge of reading." The construction is parallel
in a way that could lead to a translation of the last phrase in this
manner: "for it also requires knowledge of reading [the things dictated and written]." This illustrates a conception of writing based
not upon a concern with the written word but upon the original
spoken word that the written word records. Our conception of
writing and reading argues against this, and there is no conclusive
evidence in the passage itself. The very suggestion that grammar
is defined in terms of "writing the things being dictated," on the
other hand, leads us to a Greek conception of grammar much different from our own.

Several clues to the actual techniques considered a part of the
knowledge of grammar illustrate this conception. Plato mentions
in the *Cratylus* the correct assignment of letters to names as part of
the art or *technē* of grammar (431E–432A). In the *Politicus* of Plato
(285C–D), the author says that teachers often ask students what
particular letters compose a given word. Children apparently make
mistakes as they begin, first learning the letters of short syllables
because they have difficulty with the longer syllables, even when
the longer syllables contain the same letters (277E–278C). In the
Euthydemus (279E), the participants agree that writing and reading
letters are two matters in which the primary grammarians are most
successful, because these are their specialties. Part of the art of
grammar, Plato says in the *Sophist* (253A–B), also concerns the
knowledge of which individual letters could combine with different
letters to form syllables and words, a knowledge that was not readily
apparent to the uneducated. Aristotle suggests in the *Categories*
(8.10B) that this knowledge of identifying and combining letters is
possessed in varying degrees, just as some people are more healthy
than others, and some more just than others. Some people know
more about grammar than others, in other words. In the *Theaetetus*
of Plato (207D), Socrates describes someone as being without
knowledge when he tries to write but puts down the wrong letters
for certain syllables. The common thread throughout these varied

examples is a relationship between letters and the syllables that represent the basic units of sound in speech.

There is obviously not an exclusive concern with spoken language in the Greek conception of grammar in the Hellenic period. The students learn to write, and considerable time is spent with stylus and wax tablet in hand. At the same time, it is clear that the word "grammar" does have strong ties to the sound of language, to the identification of letters as they are heard in various combinations, and to the identification of the written letters that represent the sounds. The training in grammar that many students receive in Greece during this period, then, focuses on the use of the new system of letters that is growing more useful in business affairs and learning. Grammar, as taught in the schools of Athens, and probably elsewhere as well, is the kind of knowledge Plutarch describes in *On Music* (1131D), "an art useful for the production of sounds and storing up sounds by letters for their recollection."

The irony, of course, is that the classification of the spoken language represented by the categories and definitions of grammar finds its origins in writing. As we note in chapter six, the Sophists begin their intellectual labors with the examination of definitions and categories, early in the period when writing begins to encourage awareness of words as abstractions. As Walden writes, "The science of language, the study of the forms and meanings of words, inflexions and the rules for correct speech, originated with the sophists; Protagoras, Prodicus, and Hippias all had linguistic interests."[47] So the study of the organization of the sounds of language originates with writing and the awareness of abstraction. Then teachers pass on that knowledge orally in tandem with the writing skills that ensured the preservation of the spoken sounds thus identified. So the very conception of grammar as practiced in Greece is the product of the interrelationship of orality and literacy.

THE SOPHISTS

The Sophists established the first type of secondary school in a fashion complementary to the elementary practice of the day. The school of the Sophist was not, however, a formal institution; it might have met in a home, or in various other locations around the city.[48] These relatively informal classes began the tradition of advanced education in Western civilization.[49] On the other hand, the old education system strongly influenced even the new schools of the Sophists. First, as Werner Jaeger wrote in his *Paideia*, sophistic education remained in the aristocratic tradition.

> *From its first appearance, therefore, the aim of the educational movement led by the sophists was not to educate the people, but to educate the leaders of the people. At the bottom, it was only the old problem of the aristocracy in a new form. It is true that nowhere else had even the simplest citizen so many opportunities of acquiring the foundations of elementary education as he had in Athens—even without a state-directed educational system. But the sophists always addressed themselves to a select audience, and to it alone.[50]*

Second, the Sophists were the "heirs of the educational tradition of the *poets*," [Jaeger's italics] and they sometimes openly competed with poetry in their prose.[51] They did change the poetic heritage, adapting it to methodical instruction and a new rational view of ethics and politics.[52] And the public mind clearly associated the Sophists with writing, as examined in chapter seven. In fact, writing made the early study of rhetoric possible, as people were able to preserve their words in writing for later study, and to make lists of new stylistic techniques and organization plans for future use. Yet the beginnings of the "new education" of the Sophists in Athens grew out of and complemented the older aristocratic and largely oral tradition.

THE PHILOSOPHICAL SCHOOLS

Major figures such as Isocrates, Plato, and Aristotle established permanent institutions of higher learning around 390 B.C. or earlier.[53] These institutions developed from the more informal sophistic schools, differing in the basic fact that they were permanently established in a given location. Ironically, they were often in the same locations where the Sophists first gathered students from the three gymnasiums—the Lyceum, the Academy, the Cynosarges—and other public places.[54] John Patrick Lynch argued in *Aristotle's School* that drawing an extremely clear distinction between sophistic schools and the more permanent philosophical schools was "to foster a rather extreme form of the Platonic viewpoint."[55] He pointed out many essential similarities between the sophistic schools and the schools of the philosophers. Both arose from the lack of advanced education in Athens; both received support from individual fees or contributions, not from the state; both lacked "a defined graduated curriculum" similar to the one outlined in Plato's *Republic;* and all other schools were of the same general type, searching for the same students. The students stayed in school as long as they wished or could afford.[56]

Perhaps the most valuable distinction between sophistic and philosophical schools lies not in the characteristics of the schools themselves, but in their degree of self-awareness. Jaeger notes that the final defeat of Athens in 404 B.C. brings a new sense of awareness and a desperate intensity of life as the Greeks develop "*a conscious ideal of education and culture*" [Jaeger's italics].

> It was simply because the Greeks were fully alive to every problem, every difficulty confronting them in the general intellectual and moral collapse of the brilliant fifth century, that they were able to understand the meaning of their own education and culture so clearly as to become the teachers of all succeeding nations. Greece is the school of the western world.[57]

In a sense, Greek education becomes aware of its "self" just as writing, Snell believes, makes the ancients "self" conscious.[58] Perhaps the establishment of this "conscious ideal" delineates most clearly the nature of the differences between sophistic and philosophical schools in Hellenic education. The Sophists teach techniques that served a purpose beyond the instruction in the concrete world of the courts and the assembly, as shall be seen in chapter seven. The philosophers, on the other hand, perceive education as a virtue in itself or, as Plato might say, as the pursuit of virtue.

The philosophers developed a concept of education through abstraction taken from writing, and yet their attitudes toward writing retained the mistrust of the oral past. The old education, as we have seen, considered music good for the personal character.[59] In precisely the same way, the philosophers valued education in the abstract definitions, logic, and argument developed through the influence of writing. Such knowledge they felt was good for the personal character, as we saw in chapter two. Yet the aristocratic tradition looked down on technical education as beneath the dignity of a gentleman, and saw writing as a kind of technical education.[60] Letters thus remained remained a tool for the preservation of the oral poets in primary education, and schooling in grammar was limited.

Abstractions growing out of the awareness of words fostered by writing, however, were the *sine qua non* of philosophy.

One significant difference between the philosophical and sophistic schools was in the critical distinction between word and thought. Sophists, as we will see in chapter seven, viewed the manipulation of words in writing for persuasion as an end in itself and thus defied the aristocratic disinterest in technical education. The philosophers knew the uses of writing but remembered the Platonic admonition that thought existed in the mind of the individual who had knowledge, not in the written words that represented thought.

The nature of educational practice, in any case, was quite different from that which we might have expected. Clearly the great schools of Athens did not mirror our modern conception of a school classroom with the teacher imparting knowledge to the students. Instead, scholarship was a group effort, with the leader—say Aristotle or Plato or Isocrates—as *primus inter pares* [first among equals].[61] Many scholars at a given school, for example, were contemporaries of the *scholarch* or leading scholar, and many, such as Aristotle, left one important school to establish another of their own.[62] The new philosophical schools, in short, developed out of the same trends as the sophistic movement, with some ties and many similarities to the older more informal institutions. And the instruction apparently continued in the conversational give and take termed dialectic, or literally, "through talk."

Thus, while the new schools advanced the study and uses of grammar, they retained elements of the old aristocratic view of education. H. Curtis Wright believed that the appearance of the sophistic schools was in "solid alignment with the coming literate period" and implied that the philosophical schools continued this progression.[63] The evidence supported that basic position, as will be seen in later chapters. Wright made two vitally important observations, however: first, that Plato aimed his well-known distrust of the written word at the Sophists' "exaggerated respect for the written word"; and second, that this distrust reflected an antipathy to the written word that the Greeks never completely forgot.[64] In other words, even the most advanced educational institutions of the Hellenic period retained powerful links to the oral traditions of the past and maintained a suspicion of the relatively recent practice of writing upon which they grew to rely.

This paradoxical relationship suggests consequences that seem puzzling to today's thoroughly literate academic. We can only speculate, for example, as to the number of scholarly works that history loses before the students in the great schools begin to collect the works of their masters in writing.[65] We can, however, examine in detail the evidence of interaction between writing and the oral tradition in other areas of Greek culture.

SUMMARY

Greek education during the Hellenic period was in a period of change and growth. The "old education" the Greeks based upon aristocratic ideals interacted with the growing written tradition through the rise of the Sophists and the advancement of the philosophical schools. The oral tradition retained great influence in the schools where people were taught to read and write and in the attitude of society toward education in reading and writing. Teachers did not all have large libraries of papyrus rolls, and the numbers of students in a given class probably necessitated the frequent use of reading, memory, and recitation. The ancients expected teachers to have access to written literature, however, and to master the use of letters to represent sounds. Students evidently learned the sounds of the language, the letters that symbolized them, and some basic rules about syllables before they began to read and write.

The very teaching of grammar, in other words, demonstrates the tension between oral and written culture. Students do learn to write, but *first* they learn the system of sounds the writings will represent. The system of sound they are taught, in turn, owes its existence to the awareness of abstractions fostered by writing.

Further connections with the "old education" were evident. As students learned writing, they also learned the oral skills of memory and recitation. Children memorized many poems and passages of other works. The old educational values established a limit to the knowledge of letters that Greeks expected of a freeman and a citizen. The brief length of study in grammar, probably between three and seven years, reflected this limitation. The Greeks found grammar a useful knowledge that should not be studied to excess. Many children probably did not learn to read and write. Education was expensive, and the individual's ability to pay had much to do with the quality and quantity of a student's education in grammar.

In sum, writing and the oral tradition interacted to the benefit of Greek education. Students learned much good literature preserved in writing that might otherwise have been lost to memory. They also gained awareness of spoken sounds as an abstract system. The rules of grammar provided the foundation for the rules of logic and reasoning that students might have met in study with a Sophist or philosopher. At the same time, students learned to use their memories, placing the wisest and most beautiful expressions of their language at their command. Furthermore, they learned to perform these expressions orally, providing performance experience in a culture where speaking was a path to power and influence. Grammar school, despite its name, was a place where the oral and written traditions merged their strengths to the benefit of Greek culture. Finally, even the sophistic and philosophical schools retained strong ties to the oral tradition of the Greek past and showed evidence that writing and the oral tradition each reinforced the strengths of the other. So while writing was the vehicle moving Greek education toward change, the driving force remained the power of the spoken word.

5

⊰⊱

A Question of Credibility:
Spoken versus Written
Inartistic Proof in Athenian Courts

Scholars in oral interpretation have long made reference to indications that citizens of the ancient world always read aloud. As Bahn and Bahn wrote, "To Greeks the spoken word was a living thing and infinitely to be preferred to the dead symbols of a written language."[1] Authors have often quoted the well-known passage in which St. Augustine described his surprise at seeing his teacher Ambrose reading silently. They have considered it an indication that most, if not all, ancient reading was reading aloud.[2] Scholars in classics have generally agreed with this position regarding reading aloud, primarily due to the lack of evidence of silent reading, a matter considered in more detail in chapter ten.[3]

There has been less certainty regarding the influence of the written word upon the ancient Greek conception of literature and rhetoric. Some scholars believed that writing was in use as an aid to poets as early as Pindar.[4] The most widely accepted perspective upon the growing use of writing and its impact upon the Greek mind has been that argued by Eric A. Havelock, as noted in chapter two. In *Preface to Plato* and later works, Havelock proposed that the growing use of writing reinforced the consciousness of abstraction evident in the *Republic*.[5] He argued for a "dynamic tension" between written and oral cultures in which the balance shifted toward writing after the time of Plato.

There are two interesting highlights to this conception of the power of the written word in Hellenic Greece as it is used in the law courts. The first is the context of Plato's own paradoxical criticism of writing through Socrates in the *Phaedrus* (247A–248E), criticism he firmly grounds in his epistemology (as discussed in chapter two). Plato attacks writing because knowledge exists in the mind of one who has glimpses of the truth in his search for virtue.[6] He then examines these glimpses in the purifying fire of dialectic combat to determine their validity.[7] Writing is suspect upon two grounds; first because it is the sign for the spoken word, which is itself a sign for thought; the written word is thus two removes from knowledge.[8] The second ground for criticism of writing is that it weakens the memory, a vital link in the search for knowledge; man must remember the glimpses of truth he sees, and weak memories lead to less accurate perception of the truth.[9] This perspective appears to link Plato with the oral tradition, which Havelock recognizes as a highly sophisticated cultural tradition.[10]

The second highlight of the relationship between the written and the spoken word lies in ancient references to writing and its use in Hellenic law courts. These references indicate that the Greeks accept the use of writing reluctantly and that the establishment of credibility for this new technology is a long, gradual process. This chapter addresses the second aspect of this interaction as regards the use of written inartistic proof (and the reading aloud of same) in the law courts of Athens. I argue that the use of written evidence in the law courts of Athens is a popular reflection of the attitude toward writing Plato expresses in the *Phaedrus*. The ancients measured the trustworthiness of the written word in direct proportion to the perceived trustworthiness of the person whose spoken word (and thought) the words represented, and to the trustworthiness of the persons responsible for the writing's safekeeping. This position is supported by two lines of argument: first, the Greeks introduce written pleadings and evidence late in the fifth century B.C. with apparent reluctance; second, the Greeks do not trust written inartistic proof as completely as the spoken word of a credible witness. Written forms of inartistic proof are, indeed, vital to the functioning of Athenian society as described by ancient authors, as the growing references to them in the courts attest. The ancients, however, are reluctant to change from the oral traditions of the past, as we see in the gradual introduction of written pleadings, and are reluctant to admit extensive preparation for speaking.

A man's spoken word was his bond, and jurors clearly preferred the spoken word of a trusted individual to the written representation of a witness' testimony. The measure of the credibility of documents and written testimony was the character of the individual who vouched for the accuracy and meaning of the written words. Thus the ability of writing to preserve great detail accurately was employed so as to augment the memory and oral performance strengths of both speaker and juror. Speakers were able to place large amounts of information at the service of the jury without losing their speaking time. Speakers and jurors with trained memories could call upon a great store of common wisdom in both literature and maxims. The same memories made possible the handling of lengthy presentations of evidence in both oral and written form. Writing increased in use but remained dependent upon the testimony of respected witnesses to vouch for its authenticity.

WRITING INTRODUCED GRADUALLY

Litigation, at least in the democracies of Hellenic Greece, was a very popular pastime. In the Athenian government, one of the most effective means of opposing a given politician was to tie him up in lengthy court proceedings. Such a charge by Aeschines against a friend of Demosthenes produced *On the Crown*.[11] In fact, Demosthenes said that going to court was so popular one politician was well known primarily because he had never been indicted (18.251).

Written documents and the reading of these documents aloud played a large role in the proceedings of court trials in Athens and presumably in other Greek city-states as well. The gradual increase in the use of written materials in Athenian courts, however, showed that the society was reluctant to accept writing in the courts.

Calhoun demonstrates clearly in his work on the use of written materials in Athenian courts that the introduction of written pleadings and evidence is a gradual process. The beginnings of Athenian justice predate the introduction of writing into general society, he notes, and even "after the introduction of written law there was still a time during which the procedure was entirely oral." Following this period there is a length of time "during which public actions were entered in writing, but private actions were not."[12] By 425 B.C., Athenians write their complaints in both public and private actions, apparently by speaking the statement to a clerk or other functionary. The final phase of the transition, Calhoun believes, begins about 378–377 B.C. when the individual initiating an action writes both pleadings and evidence down.

This gradual transition in the status of writing in the courts showed that the new technology was not immediately accepted in Hellenic society. There was reason to believe, as Calhoun wrote, that necessity brought about at least part of the change. The final shift to writing of pleadings and evidence by the participants and not by clerks took place in a time of severe stress upon Athenian society.[13] The city suspended the normal rules of jury selection, for example, to ensure that there would be enough jurors. Preparations for war with Sparta in 378–377 B.C. apparently made this necessary. Under those circumstances clerks may have been as hard to find as jurors, due to the organization of men and materials for war. The citizenry may also have just been becoming literate enough to do their own writing.[14] The central point was that the change came about at a time of great stress, and that stress may have caused it.

SPEAKER'S TIME NOT SHORTENED

Another indication of a reluctance to introduce written material was the fact that the speaker's time was not reduced by the reading of such evidence, for the water clock was stopped. Demosthenes, for example, told his listeners in one speech that he would read depositions regarding the character of his opponents because the water clock did not allow him enough time to recount the events leading up to the trial.[15] There were many examples of speakers urging the clerk to read a document and to be careful to stop the water clock during the reading. Research for this chapter uncovered over one hundred instances of documents being read in court, including lists of names, leases, affidavits of witnesses, letters, decrees of the Assembly, oaths, inventories, records of other proceedings, and, of course, the laws.[16] The practice of reading evidence aloud in court trials was clearly well established, and was an aid to speakers because the reading did not subtract from their time.

This showed a reluctance to introduce written material as a substitute for the spoken word of a witness, for two reasons. First, the Greeks introduced writing in order to avoid reducing the time the jurors had to examine the words and demeanor of the speakers.

Writing was probably admitted to court with this specific provision in order to appease conservative Athenians who preferred to see and hear a living witness. Second, a great number of such readings postdated the transition to written pleading, suggesting that the change to written evidence was made reluctantly.[17] During a period of wartime stress upon the society, it was impossible to ensure that witnesses be present at a trial. They might have sailed or marched off to battle, and they might have been killed. The courts may have introduced written materials by necessity under such circumstances and then have accepted writing as speakers discovered that they could supplement their speaking time.

ARTISTIC PROOF SPOKEN

Circumstantial evidence regarding written artistic proof also supports this conception of the transition. For while the Greeks clearly accept reading evidence in the court, they certainly question the reading of speeches. The *Rhetoric to Alexander* (1444A–B), devotes a section to the responses against charges that one had prepared a speech in advance.

> But if they reproach us because we speak discourses [words] having been written or [because] we practice speaking or because we plead someone's cause for payment, one must respond to such things by attacking with sarcasm, and say about the writing that the law does not forbid one saying things having been written by oneself nor one's opponent [saying things] without writing; for the law does not permit certain actions, but it allows one to speak in whatever manner one may wish.

The charge applies to reciting a speech the rhetor prepares beforehand, as the author suggests in the phrase "saying things having been written." It is unlikely that a written manuscript is ever present in a speaker's hand.

Indeed, even careful preparation involving writing left a speaker open to criticism. Demosthenes told the audience in one trial (58.41) that they must uphold the laws, whether they were presented in studied language or in everyday speech. He himself met the charge of too much preparation in one speech by reading all his memoranda to the audience. He then openly admitting that he had carefully thought out and prepared his remarks (21.130, 191). That may have been the closest that an orator of the canon ever came to manuscript speaking. Plutarch showed in two instances that Demosthenes' opponents perceived such reliance on careful preparation as a weakness, as they criticized him for spending too much time developing his speeches. Apparently Demosthenes developed retorts for such charges. Plutarch's *Life of Demosthenes* (8.3–4; 11.5–6) recorded the story of one Pytheas, for example, who told Demosthenes that his arguments smelled like lamp oil. Demosthenes replied that clearly his lamp and Pytheas' were put to different uses. Pytheas apparently had a lively reputation as one who used lamp oil to find Athenian night spots.

Any speaker who read from manuscript would have revealed openly that he had prepared in advance and was unable to defend himself spontaneously. The Greeks considered the living word of a speaker more genuine, more trustworthy, than written representations. Preparation thus implied misrepresentation, for a man who spoke only the truth could have relied upon his memory of what had happened. This conception led to the claim of "everyday speech," a common rhetorical device of the day that was similar to the modern "unaccustomed as I am to public speaking." Socrates, for example, made much of the fact that his opponents in Plato's *Apology* (17A–C) were orators while he was not, and he made the charge in a statement replete with elaborate and ironic rhetorical figures. The claim to being an average citizen, not an orator, was doubtless grounded in the Athenian legal requirement that litigants speak for themselves, a provision of the law that again reflected a preference for the presence of the spoken work of the individual over the preparations of a written substitute.[18]

The change to the use of written materials as inartistic proof in Athenian courts, in summary, was a gradual process, with timing that showed a reluctance to abandon the presence of the individual witness. The Greeks used the written word more and more often but not without some opposition to the new technology. Furthermore, there was good reason to mistrust all the forms of writing found in the courts.

WRITTEN EVIDENCE SUSPECT

The legal situation promoted use of written evidence as Athenian procedure grew more complex.[19] Eventually, Demosthenes said, clerks read aloud all the documents related to a given trial in the presence of the parties concerned, including indictments, affidavits, lists, and records (54.26). Further, he reported, each side made copies of these and then sealed up the documents and gave them to an official for safekeeping until the trial (16.21; 53.24).[20] In Xenophon's *Symposium* (5.3), Socrates said that in general these preliminary hearings provided an opportunity for the defendant and the accuser to question each other as well.

The procedure was standard in hearings for all major trials. The participants sealed up written charges, testimony, affidavits, and any other written documents in a container and gave it to the four judges who supervised the trials of the defendants' tribe. That was unless, of course, the Arbitrator who supervised the hearing could have brought the matter to a close. Aristotle outlined the steps in detail in the *Athenian Constitution* for civil cases involving more than ten drachma (53.2). The sum amounted to ten days' wages for a day laborer, so logically the Greeks would expect similar procedures in trials involving more serious matters.

Once the container was sealed, the rules permitted the introduction of no new evidence at the jury trial if either side appealed. Plato wrote in the *Theaetetus* (172D–E) that the law provided for the sworn statements to be the basis for the trial, and the speakers watched their opponents to make sure they did not deviate from their original statements.[21] In one instance Demosthenes attacked a piece of evidence as fake because it did not come from the container (45.17). However, the Greeks maintained a healthy suspicion of all types of written evidence, despite their apparent reliance upon writing, and this meticulous procedure for its use.

The ancients often called the written word into question because it did not have the authority of an honest man's character to support its credibility. In fact, Athenians had good reason to mistrust all of the major forms of written inartistic proof, including the laws, depositions of witnesses, registers and enrollments, wills, and contracts.

LAWS

The laws were the most important documentation in the courts, and in the Hellenic period the Greeks wrote them down as a matter of course. Solon composed the first written laws in Athens. The city had them written on white wooden tablets that revolved, and the citizens called the tablets "axles."[22] Plato later associated the *Laws* with writing saying that all other writings should be compared to the laws (858E). By the time of the *Rhetoric to Alexander* (1422A), the author defined law in terms of writing.

The growing identification of writing with the law, however, still competed with a recognition of and respect for the unwritten laws defined by custom. These established moral standards through a common oral culture. This unwritten law, in effect, substituted the commonsense and standards of behavior in the individual Greek's knowledge of the world for the narrow application of what we might call today "the letter of the law." The status of the unwritten law showed that the ultimate judge of judicial truth was the knowledge of fairness in the minds of the citizens. The Greeks exhibited great concern over possible misrepresentation of the law to subvert this unwritten law of fairness.

The Greeks observed the importance of the written laws by expecting citizens to know them and by punishing those who broke them. Ignorance, Aristotle said in the *Nicomachean Ethics,* was no excuse, because men might know the laws without difficulty (3.5.8). Hellenic citizens appreciated the value of the written law as an equalizer between the wealthy and the weak, according to Euripides' *The Suppliants* (433–34). As Aristotle quoted Solon in the *Athenian Constitution* (12.4): "And laws established equally for evil men and good,/ Strict justice suited to each case,/ I drafted." The citizen, in short, benefited from the knowledge of the law and suffered punishment if he violated the law through ignorance.

At first that knowledge was relatively simple to acquire. Solon wrote the laws quickly and published them for all to see, but by the time of Isocrates' *Panathenaicus* (12.144) the laws upon papyrus were "without number."[23] The city made two additions to the Royal Stoa in the Agora to accommodate more stylae with laws inscribed upon them.[24] Aeschines later charged that things had become so complicated that many invalid laws remained written alongside the valid (3.39). Aristophanes parodied the situation in *The Birds* when a statute-seller offered to sell written copies of laws made to order for given situations (1035–55). This was a root cause for much of the uneasiness with which the ancients approached writing. With such a great number of laws, writing might have given the appearance of authenticity to something that had been forged.

78

Eventually laws were so numerous that the city stored them on papyrus in the Mētrōon at the Agora, and a great deal of care was taken to maintain accurate copies of current statutes. Lycurgus noted in *Against Leocrates* (66–67) that if anyone had entered the archives in the Mētrōon and had erased a law he would be sentenced to death. Aeschines cited the value of preserving the public acts in writing (3.75), because they did not alter themselves to suit the political tides.[25] The Greeks, however, did not regard the laws as sacrosanct. They revised them periodically.[26] Such revisions could be made only through regular procedures; one of the most serious accusations made against an individual was that he had altered the law.[27] Anyone who even suggested an illegal motion could be subject to penalty, Aeschines said (3.192), "if only one syllable [of the law] is contradicted." This concern for accuracy in the written law was more than sensible. The Athenians had experiences with the written law that made such precautions necessary.

The story told by by Lysias in *Against Nicomachus* (30.1–29) offered the strongest explanation for the reluctance of Greeks to trust written documents. Nicomachus was an underclerk the city appointed to rewrite the laws during the rule of the hated oligarchy called "The Thirty." Nicomachus held the laws hostage for six years, refused to give the archons the copy of the laws in his possession, and assumed improper authority over the whole legal code of the city. The Thirty created legal chaos in Athens by effectively erasing the written legal tradition of the city. The story exposed the weakness of that tradition, for Nichomachus rewrote the laws to suit the enemies of Athenian democracy. The rewritten laws required more frequent and more expensive sacrifices than the ancient laws of the city at a time when Athens was hard-pressed for funds. Lysias even accused Nicomachus of displaying a new law on the day of a trial that resulted in the death of a man accused by two members of The Thirty. The oligarchs employed the growing respect for the written tradition of the law, in other words, to provide a semblance of respectability for a plot to eliminate a political rival. Writing, in effect, misrepresented the knowledge of fairness in the "unwritten law of humanity." One could scarcely have imagined a more striking illustration of the reasons for strict precautions to protect the written laws in the Agora.

Nevertheless, the written laws of Athens, and presumably of other city-states, developed a credibility that was lacking in other written documentation. This credibility grew precisely because all citizens had access to the essential tenets of the law, at least originally. The law was thus part of the collective consciousness of the citizens. The primary value of the written law was that it was familiar to all citizens and thus remained unchanged, as Aeschines notes (2.68). As a result, no tyrant or demagogue could "rewrite" the law by spoken whim. The essential point was that the law remained alive in the minds of the citizens. Writing did not make a law legitimate but symbolized the sanction the people gave the law. The democracy originally employed writing to make the law accessible to all. The Athenians clearly saw that tyrants could also use writing to give injustices the trappings of legality. As Aristotle noted in the *Nicomachean Ethics* (10.9.14), whether a law was written down or not had no apparent impact upon its functioning in society.

In fact there were two types of unwritten law that played an important role in Hellenic life. The unwritten law of fairness was the center of much attention in Greek life. The funeral oration of Pericles, for example, urged the Athenians to obey the unwritten laws that all men recognized as valid.[28] Several ancient sources mention these unwritten laws of ethics and morality.[29] Aristotle described them in the *Rhetoric* (1374A) as the unwritten principles of equity that allowed people to decide justice on a case-by-case basis when the written law was too general. "For that which is fair seems to be just, and fairness is justice that goes beyond the written law." There was, in short, a recognized unwritten law both accessible and highly credible to the average citizen, the "common law of all men" to which Demosthenes appealed (23.61) This unwritten law resided in the living intelligence of the community as a whole.

The Spartan legal system provided a second example of unwritten law. Lycurgus the lawgiver composed an entire set of laws that were to be memorized by the citizens of Sparta. Plutarch wrote that one of the laws, or *rhētras*, actually forbade writing the laws.[30] The young were taught to recite the laws as a part of their education.

> For he believed that if the most authoritative and greatest things for the prosperity and virtue of the city were established as principles in the customs and training of the citizens, they would remain untouched and constant, having a deliberate and binding course of action stronger than force, and put in motion by a system of education created in the

> *children, a design of the lawgiver being turned out complete within*
> *each one of them.*

Isocrates defended the same principle (4.78; 7.41) in discussing the old democracy in Athens, saying that the old ones understood that with "good and honorable men" many written laws were unnecessary. The written law, again, was only a reflection of the community's unwritten principles of equity.

Aristotle supported this position in the *Nicomachean Ethics*, praising the Spartan law as the only one, to his knowledge, that promoted the virtue of its citizens (10.9.13). Then he noted (10.9.14) that laws do not necessarily have to be in writing to develop virtue among the citizens of the state.

> *For it is clear that public affairs should take place according to law,*
> *and that these affairs are made equitable through good laws; and*
> *whether they are written or unwritten, would not seem to make any*
> *difference, nor if through these laws one person or many are to be*
> *educated, just as it makes no difference in music or gymnastics or any*
> *other field.*

The person who wished to direct others into virtue, he continued, must have a broad knowledge of the general principles of his art or science (10.9.16–17). The molding of character was thus a task for the man with knowledge of the general principles of the law that he could apply justly to individual situations (10.9.17). The question, in other words, was not whether the law was in writing, but whether it functioned in the living mind of one with comprehensive knowledge of the law and legal principles. The law of Sparta, in this context, was the only one to promote the virtue of its citizens, because it was the only law that was part of the consciousness of all the citizens.

Note the obvious parallel to the Platonic accusation that writing cannot get up from the page to defend itself. The essential point is the clear distinction between writing and the law, the law being the general principle of justice alive in the mind of man and applied to individual circumstances. Knowledge of justice, as Plato might say, resides in the minds of those who understand the basic unwritten laws of humanity. Aristotle extends that definition to include the application of those general principles in the real world.

We consider this difference between Plato and Aristotle in more detail in chapter eleven. For now, we note that writing still refers back to knowledge in the mind of the individual for its credibility. The principle also applies in the taking of written depositions by witnesses.

The same concern for the security of written copies of the law extended to the written depositions that became a vital part of Athenian legal procedure. Isaeus wrote in one case (9.17) that he had convicted people of "writing what was not true." False written evidence, then, formed clear grounds for prosecution. Furthermore, the Greeks evaluated written evidence by its relationship to a credible witness. Speakers presenting a written deposition from a witness had to prove that the individual had actually written those words. Isaeus, for example, accused his opposition of presenting a false deposition in order to deny its validity (3.18–19). He then showed that the credibility of such documents rested primarily on the character of the witnesses who could testify to their authenticity.

> *And regarding the witnesses themselves being presented in these matters, whoever they might be, these are the witnesses we are compelled to use; but whenever anyone makes a deposition from a witness being ill or about to go abroad, each of us sends for the best of the most capable and best known citizens, and not with one or two, but with as many witnesses as possible are all depositions made, in order that the one making the deposition might not later deny utterly being a witness, and in order that you [jurymen] might better trust the deposition by the testimony of many good and noble men. (3.20–22)*

This passage demonstrated the dependence of such written documents on the word of living witnesses to back up their meaning.

The attitude toward "witnesses" from the past, however, displayed many of the same paradoxes of attitudes toward the law. The written law received great respect, with the reservation that the ultimate judge of equity was the principle of fairness in the mind of men. In the *Rhetoric* (1376A), Aristotle considered the "ancient witnesses" a form of inartistic proof that commanded great respect regarding the justness of a given act: "The ancient ones are the most trustworthy, for they are incorruptible." The ancient ones were "the poets and distinguished individuals of the past whose judgment is widely known" (1375B). As a result, Dorjahn writes, "The primary purpose of quoting poetry in the courts was not to entertain and amuse the jury with a view to gaining acquittal as a recompense. On the contrary, poetry was quoted to decide an issue . . . or to reenforce some point in an argument by elaborating the sentiment."[31] These poets and individuals were part of the common knowledge shared by Athenian jurors, a position shared by the "unwritten law" of the Greeks.

Aristotle stated in the *Rhetoric* (1376B) that the measure of the trustworthiness of a witness was the character of the individual. To paraphrase, the measure of the trustworthiness of a written deposition was the character of the individual who vouched for its validity. The poetry and testimony of the ancients, on the other hand, needed no assistance precisely because it was alive in the minds of the hearers. These inartistic proofs were a popular reflection of Plato's belief that knowledge existed in the mind of one who knows, not in words written upon a page.

REGISTERS AND ENROLLMENTS

The records Greeks cited in the courts descended directly from the earliest use of writing, that of maintaining lists of important items.[32] The various registers and enrollments associated with government and the military were vital to daily life. The most important of these was the roll of citizens, which had a direct bearing on the individual's inheritance rights, voting privileges, tax liabilities, and civil rights.[33] Thus the registers held considerable importance. Citizens closely questioned newly elected archons, who would supervise the courts, for example, regarding their ancestry.[34] The appearance of their names on a list of citizens was crucial evidence in such cases. Lists of men eligible for service in the military were another important form of record-keeping. The commander of each *taksis* (or company) kept lists of the men in armies and used the lists to divide spoils or to give rewards to groups that displayed valor.[35] The cavalry kept similar lists, possibly basing them upon the registry of citizens kept by each *dēmos* or tribe.[36]

The registers and lists of financial transactions common throughout the Greek world were also of great importance.[37] Clerks read aloud to the Assembly many such lists of financial details, inventories of estates being confiscated, and lists of inheritance suits; surely they must have read similar documents aloud to the *Boulē* as well.[38] Such written records of all sorts of financial transactions were essential to the Greek economy. Trial speeches of Demosthenes, Isaeus, and Lysias made references to written records kept by grain commissioners, governmental clerks keeping documents, inventories of inheritances, personal financial agreements being hidden, and deposits with bankers being recorded with names and witnesses.[39] The fact that speakers cited these writings in the midst of court trials demonstrated their integration into the financial society of Athens. As important as registers, enrollments, and other lists were, however, the Greeks frequently questioned their credibility.

For example, Lysias said in *Against Agoratus* (13.72) that some people bribed the individual who proposed the names of those who had so benefited the democracy that they should be added to the citizen's roll. Such attempts led to precautions to ensure the security of the lists. Lycurgus reported in *Against Leocrates* (117–18) that a priestess, presumably less corruptible than other citizens, was required to seal certain registers with her personal seal. These efforts, however, were not always successful. Demosthenes charged in one speech (55.26) that the voting register of one *dēmos* was actually lost. Lysias said the knights' rolls were more credible than the registers (16.6–7), but Aristophanes made them a joke in *The Peace*. The lists, he said, were accurate only as long as the officers were in the field (1179–81). As soon as the troops were safely home, the officers changed the lists unfairly, adding and striking out names in random fashion. Greeks had reason to mistrust financial records as well. Demosthenes notes that laws were passed against erasing names from the state debt register if the amount due had not been paid (58.50–51). Passage of the law was evidence that the citizens feared that the lists had been or could be falsified. Isocrates said in the *Trapeziticus* (17.134) that even documents stamped, sealed, and guarded on the Acropolis had been altered.

All of these examples demonstrate a concern for the accuracy and credibility of the written registers and enrollments that were so vital to Athenian society. They also show that the security and trustworthiness of the documents rest upon the character of those responsible for their safekeeping. The tribal commander, for example, is responsible for the list of his men and presumably knows who should be on the list and who should not. Aristophanes' joke implies that commanders know you as long as they need your weapon in the field, but back in the security of the city they feel free to drop your name from the lists at will. Once home, the more soldiers there are on the list, the more people share in the booty. The principle of personal knowledge and responsibility as a measure of the written word is clearly at work here.

Nowhere was this principle more evident than in the abuses perpetrated by The Thirty, who supervised the oligarchy that ruled Athens after its final and crushing defeat by Sparta. The city originally established The Thirty as a committee to oversee the compilation of a list of three thousand citizens to govern under Spartan supervision.[40] Being enrolled on the list of three thousand eventually became a matter of life and death, as the new laws gave The Thirty the power of life and death over the remainder of the population.[41] The ultimate example of the dependence of written lists upon the character of their caretakers was the condemnation of Theramenes, one of the original three thousand. When he became a threat to them, The Thirty simply struck his name from the list and condemned him to death; the whole procedure was performed in front of the *Boulē*.[42] Left in the hands of unscrupulous men, the written registers and enrollments of government and finance were clearly unreliable.

WILLS AND CONTRACTS

One of the most important written documents for the Athenian citizen was his will, or "the writings having been left," as Demosthenes said (41.6). Isaeus wrote (10.10) that a citizen of Athens could make a legal will any time after his enrollment as a citizen on the registry of his *dēmos*. These documents were of vital importance to those who would inherit a citizen's property, and they often involved large sums of money.[43] Contracts were of great importance as well, Isocrates wrote (17.20), for Greeks signed them regarding all types of agreements. As he said in another composition (18.28), "they have such power that most of the livelihoods of both Greeks and barbarians are made through contracts."[44] The Hippocratic corpus, for example, recorded that physicians required students taking the oath to sign a contract of indenture, and Aeschines even accused someone of being a prostitute *kata grammateion,* or "under written contract."[45] Writing thus developed great influence as a means of preserving transactions of all kinds of business, including the inheritance of property.

Demosthenes illustrated the importance of these documents, often written upon small scraps of papyrus, in his description of the care taken to ensure their validity (54.37). The sums of money involved and the ease with which writing could be forged led to special controls that he described in another speech (45.17). Isaeus, for example, compared the weakness of a written will to public adoption procedures to establish lines of inheritance (7.1–3). The citizen adopted a new son by taking him to the shrines, presenting him to the relatives, and enrolling him on the appropriate registers. This publicly established him as an heir, illustrating once again the importance of knowledge in the mind of those who knew the family. The procedure established witnesses who could vouch for the son's acceptance by the father, as well as written records for which they could vouch.

On the other hand, the citizen could keep his wishes secret in a will and deposit it with responsible individuals. In this case, Isaeus says, a dispute is more likely.

> *For by the former method he establishes his wishes by proceeding in the open, confirming the whole matter, providing for the adopted son according to the laws; but the man who seals his wishes up in a will makes them unclear [uncertain, unknown, secret], because of which many resolve to dispute the provisions, alleging them to be forged.* (7.2)

If the record is in writing alone, in short, it is more likely to come under question. The falsification of contracts and wills, as a result, is often the subject of court proceedings, for the adopted son stands to receive the entire estate.[46] Isaeus even charges in one trial (9.25) that he has witnesses to prove that an individual goes around the city offering to produce a will in favor of anyone who will share the estate in question with him. Of course, this evidence is from speeches in trials where many allegations were made and many were left unsupported; this mitigates the distrust of the written will somewhat. The fact remains, however, that these charges are self-defeating if such written wills are not suspect in the minds of many Greeks. The documents need support from the living word of a credible witness.

Spoken *versus* Written Proof

A similar concern for the validity of contracts led Aristotle, in the *Politics,* to include in his list of indispensable magistrates the superintendant of the market, who supervised contracts and good order (1321B). Aristotle also included the "sacred recorder" who received copies of written private contracts and the decisions of the law courts (1321B). The credibility of these documents, again, rested in the trustworthiness and knowledge of the individual who cared for them. As Aristotle wrote in the *Rhetoric.* "So in reference to the establishment of trust or lack of trust nothing differs from the procedure regarding witnesses; for of whatever sort those may be who signed and guarded [the contract], the credence of the document is the same" (1376B). But reliable guardians were not the only requirement for trustworthy documents; trustworthy witnesses were needed for their creation, as well.

The presence of credible witnesses was necessary, Hyperides wrote, to avoid the equivalent of modern "fine print" that developed when only one individual read the document and there were no witnesses to the other party's interests (3.8). The speaker described the purchase of a slave.

> For when speaking to him I agreed to these proposals, and immediately taking from his lap the writing he began reading what he had written. They were the same proposals as far as I knew; on one hand I was hearing a part of the things being read, but nevertheless I was anxiously waiting to control that for which I had come. He sealed the agreement immediately in the same house, in order that no one thinking well of me would hear the things having been written, and he added beside my name that of Nicon of Cephisia (3.10).

The speaker was anxious because he found the young slave attractive. Unfortunately, the pretty boy also owed a large sum of money; one of the small clauses of the contract noted that the purchaser was liable for "anything that Midas might owe any other person." Once again someone employed the appearance of authenticity in the written word as a means of misrepresentation.

Each of the forms of written evidence in court trials, in summary, gave Athenians reason to treat it with a little suspicion, and each relied upon the presence of a credible witness who had knowledge of the proceedings. The written evidence that the Greeks trusted in court, in other words, was either a part of the knowledge of a trusted individual or part of the public's knowledge of law and fairness. The measure of the knowledge to be gained from the written word in court trials was the knowledge in the mind of one who knew something about the case in question, who had seen the document signed, heard it read, and touched the seal upon the vessel that preserved it. This principle was a popular reflection of Plato's theory of writing in the *Phaedrus* and illustrated that the "common law" and common memories of the oral culture balanced the importance of writing to Greek culture.

SUMMARY

The frequency and importance of the uses of writing in the courts demonstrated that the Greeks used writing more and more often. Writing, however, remained a tool for maintaining records in the Archaic tradition of lists and a means of recording the spoken words of a witness if the man himself could not be present at the trial. Writing was, in short, a tool for the preservation of the spoken word, but it relied upon the spoken word to vouch for its authenticity. Contrary to modern presumptions the ancients mistrusted written documents and carefully controlled them with seals, witnesses, and guards. They related the credibility of such documents directly to the character of the living witness who could testify to the integrity of the writing. They even called the written law into question by appeals to the unwritten law of higher morality. Aristotle clearly considered the written law a mere tool in the hands of intelligent rulers, one that represented the knowledge in the minds of those who knew how to govern. The ancients carried abstract principles of justice in their minds that they applied to particular cases.

Writing thus remained subservient to the spoken word of a living man in Hellenic courts, either as a means of recording the spoken word in the Archaic model of writing, or as a less credible substitute for the word of a respectable authority. The spoken word remained the closest substitute for the knowledge in the minds of men who knew, for the truth of individual experience as it was to be measured in the court. The written word remained the sign of the spoken word. It became credible by establishing a direct relationship with the one whose speech it represented or by finding credible witnesses who would vouch for its authenticity. In short, the most credible form of inartistic proof continued to be the knowledge of events in the mind of an honest man as he spoke to the court. The mind of man was thus the measure of all things in court, and the spoken word remained the primary source.

6

From Recitation to Reading: Memory, Writing, and Composition in Greek Philosophical Prose

One might logically have expected the genre of philosophical discourse in ancient Greece to provide a clear exception to the reliance on the oral tradition of memory that the Greeks closely associated with poetry and drama. As noted in chapter two, Eric A. Havelock proposed a causal relationship between writing and the abstract thought that made philosophy possible in *Preface to Plato*.[1] Even the philosophical discourse the Greeks carefully preserved with the aid of writing, however, retained strong connections to the traditions of memory and recitation of earlier times. Isocrates, for example, stated in the *Panathenaicus* that men have received more knowledge through hearing than through sight, because they heard of greater and nobler deeds than those that they have been able to witness themselves (150). This statement was ironic from the pen of Isocrates, the one author of discourse in Hellenic times who most certainly associated himself with writing, by his own testimony (204–32).

Havelock believed that written signs made abstract philosophical thought possible, despite the concrete, emotional power of the oral tradition.[2] "Nonliterate speech had favored discourse describing action; the postliterate altered the balance in favor of reflection," Havelock wrote. "The syntax of Greek began to adapt to an increasing opportunity to state propositions in place of describing events."[3] Havelock also recognized the significance of memory and oral statement in all facets of Greek society. He argued that 430 B.C. was a time of transition from the "craft literacy" of a fundamentally oral society to one that relied heavily on the written word, and that "after Plato, the balance tilted irrevocably in favor of the latter."[4] He described this transition in terms of a "dynamic tension" between the oral and literate traditions.

This chapter argues that Greek philosophical works from the sixth to fourth centuries B.C. illustrate this tension as oral preparation, preservation, and publication gradually became oral composition, written preservation, and publication by reading aloud from written texts. I defend the position along two lines of argument. First, the ancient canon of memory emphasizes the memory of argument associated with topics, not verbatim memory. Thus, lengthy recitations are not as improbable as our modern preconception makes them seem. Second, the philosophical works of the period give us graphic illustrations of tensive interaction between memory and writing in three stages: oral preparation, preservation, and publication; oral preparation, written preservation, and oral publication; and finally, oral preparation, written preservation, and oral publication by reading of written documents.

MEMORY OF THINGS, NOT WORDS

Charles W. Lockyear, Jr., argued that oral recitations and memory displays in ancient authors from Plato to Seneca were literary devices, forms of obeisance to the oral tradition of the past, and not accurate representations of ancient practice. "Plato, as a writer, had taken the first step away from the wholly oral tradition. But it was a reluctant step, as we can see from the fact that he wishes to preserve the illusion of oral transmission even in writing."[5] The essential arguments were that: 1) written sources were available, and 2) recitation of such lengthy, involved prose was implausible, and therefore must have been a literary fiction.[6]

The writing of prose about 400 B.C., however, is still a relatively recent event in Greek culture. The response to Lockyear's first argument is that written sources are *not* available in great numbers, especially in comparison to the plethora of written works we have that date after 400 B.C. There is no tradition of Attic prose writing style before the time of Antiphon, the first orator to record his speeches in writing, and his extant works apparently date to the late fifth century.[7] The philosophical works of the Presocratic period are only available in fragments, suggesting that they may originate late in the fifth century after a period of oral preservation.[8] Havelock states flatly that "Greek society before 700 B.C. was non–literate," and dates the "literate revolution" in Athens to the beginning of the fourth century.[9] Writing is, at the very least, a relatively new influence on a previously oral culture, and the tradition of memory is the power against which written preservation would be measured.

The response to Lockyear's second position is that our modern preconception of memory makes the recitation of lengthy philosophical discourse appear much more implausible than it is. Ancient theory and practice focus on the memory of things or arguments associated with *topoi,* not on the verbatim memory that we often associate with the term. "Topics," according to Frances A. Yates, "are the 'things' or subject matter of dialectic which came to be known as *topoi* through the places in which they were stored."[10] Yates, tracing the formal study of memory to ancient Greece, finds two memory techniques named in fragments from the *Dissoi Logoi* or *Dialexeis* of about 400 B.C. Her outline of memory technique provides the basis for my argument that memory does not necessarily require the verbatim recitation that modern preconceptions demand.

Yates identifies two types of memory techniques studied by the ancients, memory of "things" and memory of "words." "'Things' are thus the subject matter of the speech; 'words' are the language in which that subject matter is clothed."[11] Things also refers to the objects in memory, such as items placed around a room, which represent arguments the speaker wished to remember. Cicero and the other ancient sources indicate that "memory for things" is sufficient and admit that mastering "memory for words" is difficult.[12] The recitation of a philosophical text, for example, might be evaluated by correct statement of the sequence of arguments, and not by word-for-word reproduction of the entire treatise. This seems logical in the context of a society in which oral literature dominates. In this tradition, words and word forms might vary according to metrical structure, but the order of the events being narrated would remain the same.[13] Thus, the ancient Greek theory may not require memory of words, or verbatim recall, but may necessitate only accurate reproduction of the arguments or events in a particular recitation.

The extensive recitation depicted in Greek prose is, therefore, more probable than our preconceptions suggest and is illustrative of the "tension" between the oral and written traditions. I argue that this tension can be outlined in three paradigms for the use of memory as described by Yates. This chapter examines these three stages through examples of composition, preservation, and publication from the philosophical works of the Hellenic period. These examples picture three stages in the transition from oral to written traditions in which the Greeks: (1) compose, preserve, and publish philosophical works orally; (2) compose orally, preserve in writing, and then publish by recitation from memory; and (3) compose orally, preserve in writing, and then publish by reading aloud from the written text.

ORAL COMPOSITION, PRESERVATION, AND PUBLICATION

We may trace the origins of philosophical thought to the written word, but, as even Havelock recognizes, philosophy begins in a time when memory and oral performance are still the norm. Hussey, in *The Presocratics,* notes that many of the words that survive the Presocratics are in poetic form.

> *Verse was still appropriate, and felt to be appropriate, for any pronouncement intended to be particularly memorable. Written books existed, and many states displayed their laws and decrees publicly in writing; yet the habit of relying on the written word was not widespread or of long standing. An educated man was one who had things by heart, and verse is more easily memorized than prose.*[14]

Ancient sources record that one of the Presocratics, Hippias, is notable for his tremendous memory.[15] Plato quotes Protagoras' statement that the greater part of a man's education is skill in understanding poetry.[16] The context of the origin of philosophy, then, is a primarily oral culture, and the early philosophers composed much of their work in a form suitable for oral preservation.

Furthermore, evidence supports the argument that many of the fragments and *testimonia* we have regarding the Presocratics originate as oral works or stories that men preserve in memory and write down much later. First, Xenophanes, Empedocles, and Parmenides compose their works in the poetic form that we associate with an oral culture.[17] Democritus, as well, leaves us over two hundred maxims or *gnomai* associated with the "wise sayings" that provide many of the commonplaces that early rhetoricians memorize.[18] We must also note, as Wheelwright does, that most of the surviving evidence dates from a much later, more literate era.

> *Except for a few pages in Plato and a larger number in Aristotle, practically all the documentary evidences about the Presocratics, whether fragments or testimonia, are to be found in post-Aristotelian writings— most of them in Greek, a few in Latin. The latter, being culturally and linguistically more remote from the originals, are at best of a secondary and confirmatory value.*[19]

The date of the evidence thus leaves its form open to question.

Works composed in poetic form, then written down much later in a more literate time, may have changed from a poetic form to a prose form in the process. As Hussey wrote about Pythagoras, "Even towards the end of the fifth century, when history begins to be written in earnest, there was probably rather little surviving in the way of reliable information about the facts of his life, his teachings, and the activities of his sect or school in the cities of Great Greece."[20] Much of his history, in fact, derives from teachings called Pythagorean *akousmata*, or "things heard about Pythagoras."[21] Such stories and details preserved in memory were doubtless subject to change over time.

Furthermore, those late scholars intent upon the preservation of Presocratic thought might well have been more interested in the preservation of the argument than in the exact wording or the poetic form. One of the largest collections of material surviving the era, the *Dissoi Logoi,* included both prose and poetic form in a collection of arguments or sayings from the growing sophistic tradition that were not written down until about 400 B.C.[22] Both types of memory were in evidence here—the verbatim memory of poetic statement and the memory of argument as later preserved in writing.

Certainly considerable overlap and intermingling with the growing written culture provide evidence for Havelock's argument that writing made abstract thought possible. The denial of sense perception in Parmenides, one can argue, presages the ultimate abstraction of Plato's ideal.[23] The progression of Zeno's argument demonstrates a growing awareness of words as abstractions, and that awareness is seen in the development about 450–400 B.C. of the concept of a *techné* as a "clearly articulated system of theoretical or practical knowledge."[24] Prodicus extends this awareness of abstraction with his concern for precise definitions of words, pursuing the need to establish clearly the relationships between abstract terms.[25] Without doubt, however, the written word is only beginning to make its influence felt in the Presocratic era.

MEMORY AND RECITATION IN DISCOURSE

Greek philosophical literature offers many examples of memory and oral performance in use as support for serious discussions. These texts illustrate our first paradigm of the use of memory and recitation in philosophical discourse, with literature that the ancients compose orally, memorize, and then recite from memory without reliance upon writing. Plutarch records an anecdote in the *Lives of the Sophists* that describes the use of memory and recitation in Athenian life and shows that such recitations were not only for entertainment (8.1–3). Solon, the great lawgiver of Athens, feigning madness, composes and memorizes one hundred verses of a poem urging the Athenians to war with Megara over the island of Salamis. According to Plutarch, he is successful in provoking a conflict which the Athenians eventually win. The story does not mention writing, demonstrating the influence oral performance has on the outcome of events.[26]

Philosophical literature of the period illustrated the fact that recitation was a frequent part of the intellectual life of Athens. The discussions recorded in writing a reliance upon memory surprising for a period that began the written literary heritage of the Western world. The "dynamic tension" between writing and memory was evident in the fact that the evidence discussed in philosophical works was largely oral. In the *Menexenus* of Plato, for example, Socrates recited a speech that Aspasia, the mistress of Pericles, allegedly composed (236A–249C). The length of the composition, which filled almost the entire dialogue, displayed Socrates' considerable ability for memorization. The display was apparently unremarkable, for Socrates promised to relate many other fine political speeches by Aspasia (249E).

Xenophon's *Memorabilia* recorded another story of Socrates' reciting, in this case a long composition entitled *Heracles and Virtue,* which he attributed to Prodicus (2.1.21–34). Apparently the lecture was the one that Philostratus claims Prodicus recited for money in cities throughout the Greek world—the "fifty-drachma lecture" mentioned by Aristotle.[27] Socrates might have seen a copy of the discourse or he could have borrowed the fifty-drachma fee. Prodicus probably would not have authorized copies of his expensive lecture for circulation, however, and Socrates would probably have lacked the funds to purchase it.

Yates' conception of the memorization of things suggests that Socrates, after hearing the lecture from another or memorizing a version of it, is remembering the *arguments,* not offering a verbatim account. Greeks of the period apparently memorize many poetic works verbatim, as Plato shows in the *Protagoras.* Protagoras asks Socrates if he knows an ode of Simonides; if not, he says, he will recite the work (339B). When Socrates replies that he does, Protagoras continues the discussion. The memory of argument, on the other hand, would be more important in the preservation of a work not in poetic form. In any case, no reference to writing or written copies appears in the course of Socrates' recitation.

Other references provided evidence that many lectures were often delivered from memory on various topics. The ancients knew Protagoras for his voice and for his ability to enchant audiences as Orpheus enchanted trees and stones.[28] Hippias delivered discourses worthy of display.[29] *The Suda* noted under "Herodotus" that the historian recited part of his work in Athens. Even sources in the Hippocratic corpus mentioned physicians who made their reputations through recited lectures and public readings rather than through knowledge of the physician's art.[30] Recitation and memory were clearly an accepted and important part of Greek life. Most of the early lectures probably involved recitation from memory. Indeed, the ancients would have criticized a philosopher who relied too much upon notes for being unable to defend his ideas without the aid of "letters."[31]

Plato provides the most powerful evidence for the importance of memory in Greek philosophical writings. Eight Platonic dialogues involve lengthy recitation from memory as the origin for the entire composition. Furthermore, these examples span the early, middle, and late categories accepted by most scholars.[32] The use of this recitation model throughout Plato's career indicates that oral memory and recitation continue to be an important part of philosophical discussion throughout the Hellenic period. The paradigms for the use of writing in the preservation of philosophical discourse occur in later dialogues, as we shall see.

The early dialogues *Protagoras* and *Euthydemus* establish the pattern for later works, with a recitation as the dramatic context for an entire dialogue. The *Protagoras* begins with Socrates meeting a friend who asks him where he has been, and who accuses him of chasing the beautiful Alcibiades (310A). Socrates then recounts his entire discussion with Protagoras only a short time (in dramatic terms) after it happened (310A–362A). We find the same introductory formula in the *Euthydemus,* when Socrates relates a discussion of the previous day in the Lyceum (271A, 272D–E). The philosopher recounts the entire dialogue without reference to writing as an aid in the presentation (272D–290D).

Of the middle dialogues, the *Phaedo* and the *Symposium* employ a similar setting. Phaedo recounts the story of the last dialogue between Socrates and his friends, one of the most moving and powerful moments in literature (57A–59D). His account carries the authority of an eyewitness. In the *Symposium,* however, we learn that accounts of dialogues from eyewitnesses were learned by others and then repeated by those who were not originally present. Apollodorus reports that he heard a version of the banquet from Aristodemus, for when the *Symposium* occurred Apollodorus was only a child (173A–B). In addition, Apollodorus has talked to Socrates, and was "not careless" in discussing the party with him (173B–C). Apollodorus then recounts the entire story of the *Symposium,* including speeches attributed to people in attendance at the original banquet (177E–178A, 180C). Again, no mention appears of any written support for this recitation.

Strikingly, recitation provided the dramatic context for three of the very latest Platonic dialogues. In the *Parmenides,* recitation was at an even further remove from the original participants. One Cephalus recited the dialogue as Antiphon told it to him. He, in turn, had heard it from Pythodorus, who was present for the original conversation among Zeno, Parmenides, and Socrates (127A–B). Antiphon studied the dialogue well in his youth, and at first was unwilling to repeat it, because it was a great deal of trouble to do so.

The *Timaeus,* which scholars have dated even later, provided perhaps the most striking example of reliance upon memory. Critias first related a story that Solon supposedly composed. Critias had learned the work at age ten from an elder Critias, then ninety (21A–E). The day before the dialogue, Socrates recounted many of the details of the story in another discussion (25D–E). Then, Critias said, he went home thinking over the story, told it to friends as he remembered it, and reviewed it during the evening. On the day of the discourse, Critias was prepared to recount the entire tale of Solon as told to him by the elder Critias (26A–B). First, he said, Timaeus the astronomer was to begin with the origin of the universe (27A). Timaeus' lecture consumed the remainder of the lengthy composition (27C–92C). Another lengthy recitation continued the dramatic situation in the *Critias.* Critias repeated the story he had memorized, including a description of Atlantis as it appeared in Greek myths (108E–121C). None of the characters mentioned the use of written material in the delivery of either long discourse.

Among the Platonic dialogues of doubtful authenticity the *Cleitophon* portrays the character Cleitophon chanting in imitation of Socrates. He speaks like a god in the theatre, as if to mimic Socrates as he appears on the comic stage (407B–E). He recites for Socrates an earlier attack upon Socrates' instruction, and this recitation constitutes the entire work. Plato, in summary, employs recitation from memory as an accepted introduction and conclusion throughout his career, and three of his latest dialogues consist of lengthy recitations.

Even the mighty *Republic* shows the influence of the memory/recitation paradigm, for while Socrates establishes no specific dramatic context, he relates the entire work to an unnamed listener (327A). Interestingly, the work dates to the middle of Plato's career, as though this more abstract setting for an implied recitation is a step toward narrative that develops as the Greeks become more proficient with the new skill of writing. It may also be a precursor to the explicit use of writing in two late dialogues, as we see below.

The fact that Plato found this recitation paradigm so useful—and employed it so often—suggests that memory was a vital part of contemporary philosophical inquiry. It was highly unlikely that Plato built entire dialogues around events that were not only untrue but also atypical. These incidents were not isolated exceptions in Plato, for they occurred in one-fourth of the undoubtedly genuine works, in one of questionable authenticity, and in the *Republic.*

Indeed, Socrates suggested in the *Lysis* that attending to a discourse or intellectual dialogue customarily involved an attempt at memorizing as much as possible of the discussion (211A–B).

If one places these examples of lengthy recitation in the context of tensions between oral and written traditions, they become far more likely than they appear to contemporary minds. Such recitations are even less surprising when we remember that the speakers concern themselves more with the preservation of argument than with repetition of exact wording. Thus, taken in context, Greeks expect memory and recitation as a matter of course in the intellectual life of Hellenic Greece.

WRITING FOR MEMORIZATION

Not only was memory the predominant source of evidence in intellectual discourse, but when the ancients first employed writing in intellectual discourse they used it to aid memory. Havelock's "dynamic tension" was evident in the use of writing to preserve the spoken word and to refresh the still-powerful oral canon of memory. The appearance of this paradigm of oral composition, written preservation, and the use of writing to prepare for oral performance dated to Plato's late dialogues. The well-known example, replete with irony, was in the *Phaedrus* of Plato, before Plato's epistemological attack upon writing (230E–279C). Phaedrus, who has been memorizing a composition by Lysias with the aid of a written copy, met Socrates while walking outside the city wall of Athens (228B–C). Having listened to Lysias repeat the piece many times, Phaedrus proceeded outside the city wall with his written copy to hone his memory (228A–C). The written copy in this case was not an end in itself but a tool for aiding the memory. Phaedrus recorded important words for their preservation, in much the same sense that Mycenaean Greeks employed Linear B to record property in warehouses.[33] This practice was also the only use of writing for which Socrates admitted value (275C–D). Socrates, however, refusing to let Phaedrus test his memory with him as an audience, requested that Phaedrus read the speech (230E). Phaedrus apparently read with great expressiveness, because Socrates said that his appreciation of the reading drew him into a divine madness sent by the gods (234D). Phaedrus reread the beginning of the discourse in the ensuing discussion (262D). In addition, Socrates later asked

Phaedrus to read the beginning: "Speak, in order that I may hear the former [Lysias] himself" (264E).

"[Lysias] himself" may be a reference to the fact that Phaedrus has been learning the speech from Lysias, with all the variety in intonation and expression that the author can provide for Phaedrus' memory. The phrase may also refer to the difference between memory of things and memory of words, for writing makes it possible to preserve the exact wording of Lysias, whereas Phaedrus, in his recitation, would presumably present the arguments without the exact wording stored in the papyrus. We find here the clearest example of writing for the preservation of words to be memorized *and* an example of reading aloud that presages our last paradigm of writing intended primarily for public reading.

Plato tells us elsewhere in the *Phaedrus* that men find knowledge in the mind of the person who knows something (275D–E). Socrates thinks of the written word here as the best substitute for the presence of Lysias himself, but clearly he prefers the word read aloud to the word written. He does not, for example, ask Phaedrus to let him read the passage silently for himself, even though the section in question is brief. Possibly Socrates cannot read, but we have evidence to the contrary in Xenophon's *Symposium* (4.27) and in Plato's *Phaedo* (98B). Socrates wants to hear the words *as Phaedrus heard them from the author,* because the spoken word is closer to the author's mind; *and* he wants to hear the composition verbatim from the written text. Ironically, Socrates criticizes writing because it does not preserve the knowledge in the mind of the author, but he prefers the verbatim record that writing offers to the emendations that might appear in Phaedrus' performance from memory. We can clearly see the conflicting forces that led to the final paradigm in our transition from recitation to reading, that of oral composition, preservation in writing, and publication by reading aloud from a written text.

ORAL COMPOSITION, WRITING, AND READING ALOUD

The late dialogues offer other descriptions of the use of writing, including numerous clear examples that establish that writing philosophical prose for reading aloud to groups is a common event by late in Plato's career. The first may even predate the attack on writing in the *Phaedrus* and may be an introduction or inspiration for that attack.

In the *Parmenides* Plato advances his argument against writing in an ironic dramatic setting (127B). A young Socrates requests the rereading of the first thesis of a work by Zeno and then questions the author about the significance of his statement (127D). Here we have the model for Socrates' criticism of writing in the *Phaedrus;* he cannot force the writing to defend itself, but he can question the author (275D–E). When Socrates teases Zeno regarding the length of the treatise, Zeno attempts to prove that existences are not many. Socrates replies that the "many" of his written words are proof against all the arguments in favor of "one" existence (127E). Here Socrates brings the written word to the test through the author's knowledge in actual practice, an example of the theoretical position he takes in the *Phaedrus*.[34] We also have a highly ironic dramatic situation. Parmenides, who composes philosophical works in poetic form, is listening to a reading of a written work by his follower Zeno, who is, in turn, facing an attack by Socrates, who wrote nothing.

Another reference to reading discourse in the *Phaedo* exemplified Socrates' frustration with writing. Here Socrates himself may have been reading aloud. One day, Socrates said, he heard someone reading from a papyrus by Anaxagoras (97B). The argument interested him greatly, "and very eagerly taking the papyrus I was reading as quickly as possible, in order that I might know as quickly as possible the best and the worst" (98B). Socrates was so interested in the argument that he grabbed the papyrus from the person reading the discourse aloud. Then his great hopes evaporated, he said, "since continuing the reading" he found that the arguments did not satisfy him (98B). Possibly he would have preferred to have the author present in order to question him regarding the meaning of his ideas. The context did not conclusively indicate whether anyone heard Socrates reading, but since he "continued the reading as quickly as possible" the situation suggested that he continued reading aloud as the previous reader had done.

The *Erotic Essay* attributed to Demosthenes and the *Panathenaicus* of Isocrates provide two further examples of discourse being read aloud. The *Erotic Essay* has an introduction that establishes the dramatic background for the essay as a private reading for two friends by the author. "But indeed since you wish to hear the discourse, I shall exhibit and read it to you"(61.1). The word for "exhibit" here is *deiknymi,* which can also mean "to show forth" or "to explain," and thus "to tell." This usage, in addition to the presence of the two hearers, makes the "reading aloud" quite certain. A similar instance occurs when Isocrates describes the composition of his *Panathenaicus* in detail (12.231–34). While working on it, he was "reading and going through [the discourse] in detail" (12.231). The verb here for "going through in detail,"*diexeimi,* also translates as "recounting in full," which may indicate that Isocrates is reading aloud to himself. A indisputable example of reading aloud to friends follows this passage, when Isocrates brings his admirers together to hear the discourse (12.233). The philosophical literature of Hellenic Greece, in sum, provides abundant evidence that discourse is read aloud as a means of "publishing" the author's work to others. Isocrates' *Antidosis* (15.1), Plato's *Phaedrus* (268C), Philostratus' *Lives of the Sophists* (510–11), and Plutarch's *Moralia* (836D, 840D–E, 845C) all contain examples. By comparison no known examples provide unquestionable evidence that Greeks ever read philosophical discourse silently.

Reading aloud is therefore more widespread than silent reading of philosophical discourse. On the basis of available evidence, one can argue convincingly that such silent reading is entirely lacking in ancient Greece. The simplest practical explanation for this absence is the high cost of papyrus and the expense of having copies written upon it. Making multiple copies of discourses—for each member of a group, for example—would be prohibitively expensive. We must temper these obvious considerations, however, with the extant descriptions of composition, which indicate that practical considerations may be only part of the story.

"WRITING" HELLENIC DISCOURSE

Scholars have made much of the fact that the ancients clearly "wrote" discourse because we have the extant evidence. In chapter two, we discussed Burger's argument that Plato could not possibly have meant to attack writing in the *Phaedrus* because Plato *wrote* the dialogue.[35] On similar grounds, Lockyear argued that Plato, immersed in the written literary tradition yet tied sentimentally to the oral tradition, employed oral recitation of evidence as a literary device.[36] Ancient authors were writers, the argument ran, because we had their written histories and speeches extant. The unstated assumption was that the ancients were writers in the modern sense of the term. The difficulty lay in the use of the word "writing" itself. Modern usage implied written composition, or the recording of words in writing as they were composed. The evidence showed, however, that the ancient practice of composition did not include writing *in that sense* and did not even begin to do so until the time of Isocrates.

A remark by the author of the *Erotic Essay* attributed to Demosthenes illustrates: "all these things have been written from the first as one would store them up in a papyrus-roll" (61.2). The concept of "storing up" (*katatithēmi*) the composition in writing as though inscribing a record of inventories compares to the earliest uses of writing for the recording of properties. The ironic appearance of this archaic view of writing as a list of words for storage—when a few authors are beginning to speak of "writing" discourse—points up the paradoxical nature of the Greek conception of writing. The Greeks value the written word according to the living intelligence of the maker who originated that word in speech. As in this example, the ancients usually draw a distinction between the composition, termed *logos,* and the writing itself. The composition, which we would call "literature," exists in the mind of the maker, and the writing is only a means of storing up that composition against the passage of time.

Thucydides suggests this attitude when he indicates how he records speeches for his history.

> As to the speeches that were made by different men, either when they were about to begin the war or when they were already engaged therein, it has been difficult to recall with strict accuracy the words actually spoken, both for me as regards that which I myself heard, and for those who from various sources have brought me reports. Therefore the speeches are given in the language in which, as it seemed to me, the several speakers would express, on the subjects under consideration, the sentiments most befitting the occasion, though at the same time I have adhered as clearly as possible to the general sense of what was actually said.[37]

In the Greek, he does not use words specifically referring to "writing" in association with the speeches. The events of the war, however, he "writes" after much more strenuous research into the facts of each case than he attempts with regard to the speeches (1.22.). Clearly, in light of Yates' two types of memory, Thucydides is carefully explaining here that he bases many of the speeches that he records upon memory of things (or arguments made) rather than memory of words. From this perspective, the historian seems much more concerned with accuracy; at first glance one might wonder how many other scribes recorded discourses on the basis of what the writer *thinks* the originator of the work *might* have said. Thucydides researches the speeches, however, talking to all those who bring him reports, and he bases his exact wording on the general line of arguments as he and his sources remember them. Most important to our discussion, however, is his distinction between the spoken words and those used to record speeches in writing. Memory is the connection that Thucydides establishes with the speaker through a hearer, drawing upon his personal experiences or upon the testimony of witnesses for his report. Thucydides includes this section of his work, indeed, to demonstrate that he has been as accurate as possible, but at the same time he warns the reader not to expect a verbatim account.

Two descriptions of the composition of discourses indicated that such a distinction was common, and illustrated the importance of memory to preserve discourse *after* an author composed it in his mind and *before* he wrote it down. One appeared in the *Theaetetus* of Plato, a late dialogue (c. 368), and described a situation similar to the Platonic dialogues that employed recitation as a dramatic frame.[38] The character Eucleides reported a conversation between Socrates and Theaetetus that he had not actually heard, but which Socrates later repeated to him (142D). Eucleides told his companion, Terpsion, that he did not have the discourse memorized, or "from the mouth" (142D). After hearing the discourse from Socrates, however, he went home and wrote down notes, or *hypomnēmata* (143A). The actual composition of the notes was unclear; they might have been simply a list of main points.[39] As he remembered other parts of the discourse, he continued writing them down. On later visits to Athens, he questioned Socrates about various points of the discourse he could not remember and continually corrected the notes upon arriving home (143A). "Thus," he told Terpsion, "nearly all of a certain dialogue [*ho logos*] has been written by me" (143A). Here he used a word that referred directly to the process of inscribing marks on a piece of papyrus, *gegraptai*. Plato permitted this use of

104

writing in his attack upon writing, for it reminded an individual of something he already knew—in this case, the dialogue.[40] After Terpsion and Eucliedes retired to the latter's home some distance away, Eucleides' slave read the dialogue. The master had literally ordered the slave to "take the papyrus and speak" (143C).[41]

Throughout the composing process, Eucleides refers back to a living witness, as though composing a history of sorts, and then carries the information home in his memory. The source, in this case Socrates, determines the composition's credibility. Eucleides, in short, describes writing as a method for preserving something that already exists in the mind of the living participant in the original discourse. We must wonder, in light of Plato's attack on writing in the *Phaedrus,* if this portrait depicts Plato's method of preserving the ideas of Socrates, at least for the early dialogues. Scholars will, no doubt, argue that too many inconsistencies of date, place, and character exist for Plato's works to have been "histories" of Socratic dialogues. One could also allege, as in the case of our examples of recitation from memory, that the sheer volume of words makes it highly improbable that Plato could remember so much of so many conversations with Socrates. The response, clearly a powerful one in light of the relationship between oral composition and writing for preservation, is that the importance of memory in the process of writing could explain such lapses of detail. In addition, the concern of such writing primarily with memory of argument, not words, makes the volume of material seem less overwhelming. Therefore it is reasonable to reconsider the extent to which Plato and other Greek philosophers "wrote" their works at all in our sense of the term. We must reexamine the possibility that the works represent the preserved arguments of Socrates as Plato remembered them, heard them from others, and spoke them aloud to his slave.

In the another example of "written" composition, Isocrates described the composition of the *Panathenaicus* as something he originated in conversation as his response to remarks by another: "I did not stop until I dictated to my servant the discourse, which a brief time earlier I delivered with pleasure, but a little time later gave me discomfort" (204–29). After he had spoken, Isocrates rested and whispered the entire discourse to a servant (231). He may have been seated during this time of "rest," as other authors apparently were when "writing" with a scribe.[42] Isocrates later said that the servant was writing the discourse as he dictated it, for he referred to "the things I had written"(232). The word used for the actual dictation, *hypoballō,* meant literally "to throw" or "put under." The word also denoted the making of suggestions, and thus, dictation.[43] The result of the dictation must have been a complete version of the discourse, apparently recited from Isocrates' memory, as he said that he "read through and examined it in detail" (231). Such *ana-gigknoskōn* (reading or "knowing again") probably meant reading aloud. Upon reading through the discourse as recorded, Isocrates was dissatisfied and uncertain whether to burn the work (232). As a result of his indecision, he invited several friends to hear the discourse read aloud (233).

Several interesting inferences emerge in this story of writing and reading aloud. One is the suggestion that Isocrates "distributes" (some would say "publishes") the discourse. He speaks in the same passage of the decision he has to make: "whether it [the discourse] is to be destroyed completely or distributed to those who desire to receive it" (233). He confuses the reference by the use of words that could mean "communicate" as well as "distribute" (*diadosis*), and "understand" as well as "receive" (*lambanō*).[44] The passage could also mean the communication of the discourse to those who wish to understand or comprehend it, instead of the distribution of a written version. The passage, in addition, does not refer to the "things I had written," but to the word *logos* in the sentence preceding. Thus the passage does not clearly substantiate the apparent "publication." Providing written copies for all Isocrates' friends would have been slow and expensive. We may reasonably conclude, therefore, that even the "publication" of an admitted "writer" involved reading aloud in a performance rather than the distribution of written copies.

The second inference is that the "writing" of discourse occurs only, or at *least* primarily, after the maker composes it in his mind. Isocrates, without mentioning notes, implies that he simply sits down with the servant and recites the entire discourse to him from memory. Then he *later* considers erasing or burning the discourse, the first literal reference to writing (232). The composition originates in the mind of the maker. Later the author might alter or destroy the written recording of the composition. The mind of the maker still determines the importance of the written word; Isocrates is present to vouch for his arguments before his friends. The writing is a means of preserving the discourse, a means that the author can forgo by burning the papyrus. The composition does *not* require writing to come into being. It requires writing to survive and uses writing to accomplish its "publication" through reading aloud. Thus, Isocrates, noting the multitude of things to "say" that rush into his mind while composing, laments that as he composes in his mind he is moving away from the tone of speech he planned to maintain when he began to "write" (95). We hear the author developing an awareness of exact wording that goes beyond his concern for leaving his intended line of argument. Clearly he recognizes that writing can preserve words in precise order. Isocrates is the one author of the period who admits writing works primarily for reading aloud in such situations. As he considers revisions of that precise wording, he develops an awareness of written style. We will consider Isocrates' unique position in the change to a more literate culture in chapter eight.

In any case, the oral canon of memory clearly remains vital to the act of writing. Furthermore, writing in Hellenic Greece is not necessarily "publication" for silent reading as we know it. No evidence exists of reading discourse silently to support such a conception of the dissemination of Greek discourse; a composition is apparently published through the act of having it read aloud in public. Since Eucleides and Isocrates both wrote down their discourses to preserve them and to present or "publish" them through reading aloud, both illustrate the importance of memory to our final paradigm of oral composition, written preservation, and publication by reading aloud from the written work.

SUMMARY

The evidence regarding the relationship between writing and intellectual discourse, in short, points to a period of transition between a primarily oral culture and a more consciously literate one. Havelock's "dynamic tension" is evident in the three stages of the relationship between writing and the philosophical literature of the period. First, we see the poetic form of much Presocratic literature and the growing awareness of abstraction in early writings. Second, we see the tension between orality and literacy in the descriptions of recitation recorded in writing and in the ties to the oral tradition of memory and recitation they represent. We must conclude that citizens in the Athenian state retained powerful memories, unless we accuse Plato of using improbable dramatic situations to frame eight of his dialogues. Yates' outline of the importance of the memory of argument adds further support to this conclusion. Third, when Greeks use written discourse for reading, or, literally, "knowing again," it is always for reading *aloud,* indicating that the spoken word retains considerable power over the new writing. Finally, even the "writers" of Hellenic discourse apparently research and compose their creations in memory with little or no aid from writing, in the best style of the oral tradition. They then speak them to scribes who preserve them in writing. Such writing extends the Archaic written tradition that *grammata* were for keeping records of important objects or words.

This picture of the relationship between writing and philosophical discourse reveals a time of transition, a period when powerful memories emerging from the "old education" (chapter four) engage in struggle with the written alphabet. Clearly in ancient Greece the "making" of the poets melds with the new technology of writing to yield the "making" of intellectual discourse preserved in writing. Throughout the Hellenic period, however, "making" is still the word for composition, and that word was spoken.

7

Writing as Sophistry:
From Preservation to Persuasion

Hellenic Greeks publicly acknowledged the spoken word as a powerful force. As Vernant wrote: "The system of the *polis* implied, first of all, the extraordinary preeminence of speech over all other instruments of power. Speech became the political tool par excellence, the key to all authority in the state, the means of commanding and dominating others."[1] For the average citizen, the centrality of rhetoric led to the importance of the logographers and Sophists who helped them face audiences in the Assembly and the courts— for a fee. Recent research efforts have sought to "rehabilitate" the Sophists and their approaches to rhetoric. Scholars, however, have not yet adequately explored either the Sophists' relationship to the new technology of writing or the Hellenic attitude toward that relationship.

Plutarch reports in the *Moralia* that Antiphon set up what we might call the first psychiatrist's office near the marketplace in Corinth, in the days prior to his career in rhetoric (833C–D). He declares "that he has the power to treat those being in pain through words." He writes an advertisement upon the door, but the clinical method is to ask questions, discover the source of the distress, and comfort the suffering. The tale exemplifies Plato's conception of the function of writing in the public life of Greece as described in the *Phaedrus* (247A–248E). The spoken word is the direct tool of the living intelligence; the written word is a form of advertising.

Greeks often publicly acknowledged the spoken word as a powerful force. Plato noted in the *Republic*, for example, that citizens aroused by demagogues paid no attention even to the laws, written or unwritten (563D). For the average citizen, the centrality of rhetoric in politics and law led to the importance of logography and the Sophists. As Jaeger wrote: "In the democratic state, where the whole people assembled for political purposes and where any citizen might speak, a talent for oratory became indispensable to every politician: it was the rudder in the statesman's hand. In classical Greek the politician is simply called *rhētor*, an orator."[2] Eloquence, then, was the point from which any attempt to educate a man for political leadership was bound to start. Jaeger was one of the first to recognize the importance of the Sophists in the development of modern conceptions of higher education.

Recent research efforts have sought further to "rehabilitate" the Sophists and their practical approaches to rhetoric.[3] These scholars' efforts have elaborated Jaeger's contention that the Sophists based their educational practice upon two well-defined philosophical positions on the nature of the mind.[4] Scholars have yet to explore adequately, however, the relationship of writing to the vital role the Sophists played in shaping the origins of education.

Jaeger pointed to two fundamental methods of education that grew out of the differing sophistical conceptions of the mind. "One was to import to it an encyclopaedic variety of *facts*, the material of knowledge, and the other to give it *formal* training of various types."[5] The Sophists employed both written and oral methods to educate the young. The essential point for this study is that *both* written and oral methods faced attack when they disregarded the new conception of knowledge as abstract thought in the mind of an individual. The relationship between writing and the Sophists demonstrated the continuing importance of the spoken word as the antecedent of written words and as the method of training students in abstract thought.

WRITING AS PRESERVATION

Cicero and Plutarch record that speeches are not written as a matter of course before the time of the orator Antiphon, with the exception of brief selections from Pericles in Thucydides.[6] Plato confirms in the *Phaedrus* that many influential men refuse to write their speeches for fear of being called Sophists (257C–D). As the written word becomes more commonplace, Plato consistently criticizes writing, logographers, and the Sophists on the grounds that they present the appearance of knowledge where it does not exist in reality. Greeks first employ writing to preserve functional lists of property and socially valuable ideas. Ethical questions cloud the acceptance of this practical function of writing as the logographers and Sophists adapt the written word to their own purposes.

The exact sequence of events in the dramatic change from illiterate to literate society is a matter of contention. Vermeule reports that writing in the Mycenaean heritage of Homer and Hesiod is a skill held by a few in the palace while the remainder of the people are "locked inside a set of traditional social forms where myths and personal leadership are influential." The collapse of the palace system during the Dark Ages prior to the fifth and fourth centuries B.C., she continues, breeds "strong epic poetry which persuaded toward literacy later and preserved the memories if not the practices of the traditions." The heritage of the Greeks includes a conception of education that does not involve literacy and a perception of society that does not feel "any need for a codified body of cult, law, or past history."[7] Furthermore, little history is preserved by the fragile new alphabet, which progresses from hieroglyphic writing dating roughly 2000–1650 B.C., through a less pictorial script called Linear A from 1750–1450 B.C., to a modified form of the script called Linear B that probably fades out about 1200 B.C.[8] Early history, Plato writes in the *Critias*, is little more than a memorized list of the names of ancestors (109D–110A).

The first writings provided lists of military groups, rowers of ships, jars of oil, cattle, armor, and swords.[9] These lists may have begun as drawings of the objects they recorded, or perhaps as drawn copies of clay tokens used to record possessions. They became vital to Hellenic society. Xenophon recorded Ischomachus in the *Economics* telling Socrates that he showed the housekeeper all the important household items and the places where they were kept, and made a comprehensive list of the items for security (9.10). Plato referred in the *Laws* to records of land ownership as a normal governmental use for writing (714C–D). Other lists important to the Athenian government were the registers of citizens and the rolls of men eligible for military service.[10] Speeches of Demosthenes, Isaeus, and Lysias mentioned written records kept by grain commissioners, inventories of inheritances, and lists of sums deposited with bankers.[11] Plato's attack on writing in the *Phaedrus* does not question such lists. In fact, the only value Socrates admits for the written word is "to remind him who knows about the things which have been written" (275C–D).

There is also direct evidence for the preservation of socially valuable words. The first example is the record of Homer made about 650 B.C.[12] Various ancient sources suggest that Solon, Pisistratus, or Hipparchus redacted Homer. Greeks regarded the works of Homer alone as sufficiently valuable to recite at the great festivals of the day. "Your fathers held the poet [Homer] in such regard that they established a law so that every five-yearly Panathenaea his epic works alone, of all the poets, would be chanted by the rhapsodes."[13] The first written laws in Athens are those of Solon. "And laws established equally for evil men and good,/ Strict justice suited to each case,/ I drafted."[14] The city mounted the laws upon revolving frames that brought them the name "axles" because they could be turned. The Greeks regard accessibility to all of written law as an equalizer between the wealthy and the weak, as Euripides notes in *The Suppliants* (433–34). Consequently Greeks expect citizens to know the law.[15] Lycurgus and Aeschines demonstrate the social value of the laws through their descriptions of the care taken to preserve them accurately.

The first writings of the Sophists appeared in the Archaic tradition as elaborated by Dionysius of Halicarnassus, who said that the early Ionian logographers attempted "to bring to the general knowledge of the public the written records that they found preserved in temples or in secular buildings in the form in which they found them, neither adding nor taking away anything."[16] Their style was "clear, simple, unaffected . . . and not revealing any elaborate art in composition." In the *Brutus,* Cicero described the earliest tradition of sophistic writing in the Archaic tradition of listing and recording, an informal inventory of popular wisdom (46–50). The *technai,* or training manuals of the Sophists, apparently originated with such lists of things. Plutarch, in his *Life of Themistocles,* mentioned that the Sophist Mnesiphilus trained Themistocles according to a *sophia* (wisdom) that Solon, the lawgiver, passed down (2.4). This *sophia,* Plutarch said, was not true wisdom but political cleverness and practical intelligence, a kind of commonsense collection of advice for political living. The phrase describing this succession implied that the Greeks passed this *sophia* down from hand-to-hand, almost like a religious dogma or a family craft.[17] The successors of Mnesiphilus, Plutarch continued, changed the focus of the *sophia* from politics to language, and *then* their contemporaries labeled them Sophists. Plato supported this view of the *sophia* in the *Republic,* claiming that the Sophists merely observed the citizens, collected their opinions, and then called that wisdom (7.493A).

The relationship between rhetoric and writing began to change early in the Hellenic period. Antiphon wrote speeches even before Gorgias arrived in Athens in 427 B.C. to revolutionize the rhetorical practice of the day.[18] As Navarre wrote, "Before Gorgias, prose writing in Greece had been nothing but a literal transcription of everyday language."[19] The Sophists applied writing's ability to preserve maxims to the collection of stylistic devices, with the result that a revolution had begun. By the time of the *Phaedrus,* Plato defined rhetoric in terms of speaking *and* writing (261A–B).

LOGOGRAPHY: PRESERVATION FOR PRESENTATION

Logographers in Hellenic society were more than individuals who simply listed or recorded.[20] They had become creators of words in writing to be spoken by others. The act of writing down an individual's words in itself implied a comparison between those words and the laws of the city, the oracles of the gods, the proclamations of the Assembly, and the poems of Homer, all words the city officially preserved in writing. Furthermore, the difference in Hellenic usage between speechmaking and speech-writing raised the question of unethical misrepresentation.

The public speaker, Plato writes in the *Euthydemus,* is both a doer and a maker (284C). Later in the same dialogue, Plato clarifies his meaning (289C–D). There are speechmakers or composers (*logopoios*) who are unable to use their own words. Others are able to use what the makers compose, but cannot themselves compose a speech. Thus, he concludes, there are two distinct arts in speech, one of making and one of doing. Throughout this discussion he makes no specific mention of writing; when it does appear elsewhere in Plato in the name for speech-writer (*logographos*) he considers it a derogatory term.[21] Here we find respect for the maker of words or discourse juxtaposed with the suspicion of the writer of words. Plato does not praise the speechmaker in the *Euthydemus,* but clearly he has even less regard for the speech-writer.

The Greeks displayed this contrast in attitudes toward *logopoios* and *logographos* in the literal meanings of "word-maker" and "word-writer," respectively. *Logopoios* was originally a word for story-teller. Herodotus called the well-known Aesop a *logopoios,* or story-maker (2.134). Later the word became a general term for speech-makers as well, and it was used when a general term with neutral connotations was in order.[22] Both *logopoios* and *logographos* referred to prose writers in general, but when applied to speeches the word *logographos* carried a negative connotation. For example, many attacks in the courts or the Assembly involved the word "speech-writer," or *logographos.* Speakers did not use the word *logopoios* in similar circumstances. The language employed to describe the composition of speeches displayed the characteristics of an underlying suspicion or distrust of writing. When Plato discussed the general functions of men who "made" or composed speeches in the *Euthydemus,* he called them speechmakers (305B–C). When Plato wished to belittle others in the *Phaedrus,* he called them speech-writers (257C).[23]

The root cause of the difference between these two attitudes is that the speech-writer sells or gives written words to others to employ as if they represent the thoughts of the speaker. This must be the questionable activity for which the word *logographos* takes on such strong negative connotations. The writing of words to preserve them is not the issue here; the concept of "storing up" ideas is not in question. Note how blithely the author of the *Erotic Essay* attributed to Demosthenes says, "all these things have been written from the first as one would store them up in a papyrus roll" (61.2). The practice of giving written ideas to another for presentation as his own is clearly another matter.

Plato's *Phaedrus* illustrated this principle, as the two participants walked about Athens studying a written copy of a work on love by Lysias (228A–E). Socrates refused to hear Phaedrus' recitation of the speech as soon as he realized that Phaedrus had a written copy of the discourse. Having Lysias "present," Socrates said, he had no intention of permitting Phaedrus to practice his memory on him. Phaedrus then proceeded to read the speech aloud to Socrates. It is ironic that Socrates refused to hear the recitation of a work, and preferred to hear a reading from the writing that he later attacked in the same dialogue (275D). The key point, however, was that this reading was clearly an informed one, for Phaedrus had listened to Lysias himself reading or reciting the speech. Socrates preferred writing because it recorded the words of the author, and

114

the author himself provided the interpretation of the lines that Phaedrus was memorizing. The ethical question did not arise, because the written words aided the recollection of that interpretation; thus Socrates spoke of having Lysias "present." Had Lysias presented a written speech to a citizen to memorize for use in court, Socrates would have attacked the practice. He expressly attacked writing in the same dialogue because it always said the same thing, and could not defend itself without the aid of the knowledge *in the mind of its author.*[24] In the *Protagoras,* indeed, Socrates characterized many contemporary speakers as "just like papyrus rolls, being able neither to answer your questions nor to ask questions themselves" (329A, 347A–348A).[25]

Early orators were reluctant to write their speeches because the act implicitly compared their words to those chosen formally by the city for preservation. Thucydides only recorded the words of Pericles after they had been accepted as socially valuable.[26] Being called a Sophist implied a prideful attitude apparently associated with the use of writing.[27] Isocrates reported that many orators destroyed speeches they had written, an action consistent with the view of writing as prideful (15.61). The epithetic *logographos* also implied that unethical behavior was involved in writing a speech. The foundation for both attitudes was the value placed upon the knowledge in the mind of a person. Words society officially accepted as wise or important were worthy of being written down. When one person composed words, wrote them down for transmission, and gave them to another to speak as his own, the words became unethical. The measure of truth was in the mind of a person, and in the words spoken by that person to represent that knowledge. Putting words in the mouth of another was, to the Greeks, obfuscating the truth.

SOPHISTRY: PRESERVATION FOR PERSUASION

The origin of the Hellenic Sophists apparently paralleled the changes in the tradition of logography. The Greeks first associated the word *sophistēs* with craftsmanship and skill, and they employed it to describe a person who practiced a craft with knowledge and mastery. Philostratus wrote in the *Lives of the Sophists* that the word originally referred to wisdom, then degenerated into an epithet for those who presented only the appearance of wisdom (1.483). Eventually it became one of the unpleasant epithets used in the courts and the Assembly.[28] This dramatic shift in meaning was concurrent with the use of writing by the Sophists for purposes beyond that of recording and preserving maxims.

The key to the change, Plutarch wrote, was that the successors of Mnesiphilus (the teacher of Themistocles) changed the focus of the written *sophia* from politics to language, and *then* they were labeled Sophists.[29] This change of focus from maxims was corroborated by Xenophon in the *Cynegeticus*, who refused to give sophistic precepts the name *gnomai* that he applied to principles of virtuous conduct (13.3). The new focus of the *sophia* was apparently upon stylistic techniques, not the preservation of wisdom. Plato presents an enlightening protrayal in his *Euthydemus*, with sparkling wordplay and definitional legerdemain (302A). The passage is a sequence of word games, culminating in a discussion between Dionysodorus and Socrates about the gods. Dionysodorus gets Socrates to admit that some things are "his." He then forces Socrates to admit that he "has" ancestral gods that his family shrines honor. Dionysodorus leads Socrates further to the admission that earlier in the discussion he had agreed that the gods were animals. Consequently, he compels Socrates to agree that the gods are animals that men are able to buy and sell, and with which they may do as they please!

Note the interaction of oral and written traditions in this interchange. The awareness of categories and definitions necessary to continue the discussion is evidence of writing's influence. The misuse of that awareness, however, leads to absurd conclusions that do not match the knowledge of truth in the minds of men. Plato clearly requires both awareness of written abstraction and the pursuit of knowledge in careful discussion of what the individual mind knows, as discussed in chapter two.

The Sophists used writing to record and preserve such stylistic "maxims." If, as Plutarch noted above (n. 29), the collected *sophia* became collected stylistic devices, these originated the *technai*, or manuals, of the Sophists. Such lists of sophistic techniques must have seemed an affront to the dignity of citizens who were accustomed to seeing only the laws of the city, the oracles of the gods, and the decrees of the people preserved in writing. The same would have been true of the more involved *technai* that continued in this tradition, as the collections of precepts or devices grew to include entire speeches.[30] Plato's *Sophist* led his hearers and us to believe that the Sophists had written treatises on all the arts, including everything the skilled craftsman needed to know (232D). Xenophon supported that statement in the *Cynegeticus,* reporting that the Sophists had written on many "useless topics" (13.1–2). Beyond the implicit comparison of such writings to the socially valuable words of the past, however, there was the ethical question of presenting the appearance of wisdom in one who did not have it. The Sophists taught these preserved words, speeches, and techniques to the students by memorization, and the crowning touch was that they charged money to teach them.

Aristotle tells us in the *Sophistical Refutations* that many sophistic instructors make their students memorize rhetorical speeches of works that consist of questions and answers (34.183B). Isocrates compares sophistic teaching to the early use of writing and charges that Sophists taught the knowledge of discourse "just as though they were teaching letters" (13.10, 12–13).[31] The rules the Sophists teach are like the letters of the alphabet, Isocrates continues, in that they remain constant and cannot adapt to the changing requirements of actual speaking or discourse. Just as the logographers are guilty of putting techniques into the mouths of speakers, the Sophists are guilty of putting techniques into the minds of speakers who memorize them like letters of the alphabet. Logographers use writing to preserve the words of one man for another to present as his own, and the Sophists use writing to preserve the techniques of one man for another to use as if they were his own invention. Either of the two would be seen as unethical in a society whose past emphasizes the importance of knowledge in the mind of the individual.

Compounding this ethical problem was the fact that the Sophists accepted money for their services, thus suggesting that for the right fee they could make men appear better than they were. Only the gods and the individual himself had the power to make a man better, Socrates argued in Plato's *Protagoras,* for men were not able to pass virtuous conduct from one to another (320A–B). The acceptance of money for this service approaching hubris clearly aggravated the distaste with which many viewed the Sophists.[32] Philostratus wrote in the *Lives of the Sophists,* for example, that Protagoras was the first to charge money for teaching culture and virtue (10.494–95). If this virtue consisted of the rather glib stylistic devices illustrated in the *Euthydemus,* a contemporary would easily understand the outrage of Socrates at those who sold such "virtue" for money.[33]

This perception also underlines the irony of Socrates, defender of the gods in the *Euthydemus* (304C–307C), who must defend himself in the *Apology* against the charge of treating the gods disrespectfully (17A–C). Socrates emphasizes this irony further by the rather overworked commonplace he employs in the opening of the *Apology*, as he tells the audience that he is not a public speaker in a passage brimming with stylistic figures.[34] Socrates in the *Apology* is the epitome of the ideal orator in the Archaic style, a man telling the truth as he sees it without regard to the consequences. He stands as an electrifying Platonic contrast to those who employ words or stylistic devices "made" by others in order to appear to be what they are not. Socrates is thus a model of oratorical virtue in the plainspoken oral tradition, even as his argument demonstrates an awareness of abstraction clearly drawn from writing. The counterpart is the violation of tradition by the Sophists who sell the written appearance of wisdom to those who have not uncovered the knowledge in their own minds.

WRITING AS SOPHISTRY

Eric Havelock argued in his *Preface to Plato* that Plato allied himself with the abstract visual consciousness promoted by the use of writing.

> *It was his [Plato's] self-imposed task, building to be sure on the work of predecessors, to establish two main postulates: that of the personality which thinks and knows, and that of a body of knowledge which is thought about and known. To do this he had to destroy the immemorial habit of self-identification with the oral tradition.*[35]

Plato, in other words, was a spokesman for a new scientific and abstract view of knowledge that grew out of the written tradition. The oral tradition was, for him, an enemy of the pursuit of knowledge.

We can clarify the place of the Sophists in this theoretical position, using our examination of the Platonic attack on writing in the *Phaedrus* as a context. Plato considers writing as a sign for speech, and speech as a sign for thought. Writing is thus the third place from truth as uncovered by dialectic combat in the mind of a man

118

who knows.[36] He attacks rhetoric and the rhapsodes for similar reasons, rhetoric because it often creates the appearance of knowledge where it does not exist, and the rhapsodes because they rely upon the truth of divine inspiration, not upon knowledge. In short, he finds writing, rhetoric, and the rhapsodes deficient upon the same epistemological grounds, for they do not have the glimpses of truth in the mind of a man who knows. The Sophists receive the same criticism because of their use of writing.

Plato, in the *Sophist,* compares the Sophists to painters, men who are able to create the appearance of all things through the use of a single art or craft (235B–C). Aristotle states the essence of this criticism most succinctly in the *Sophistical Refutations:* "For sophistry is a thing appearing to be wisdom but not being [wisdom]" (11.171B). Plato writes in the *Theaetetus* that Sophists spread tidbits of arguments, little phrases, but refuse to sit and argue or explain their positions (179E–180B). Note the parallel with Plato's criticism of writing in the *Phaedrus* as unable to rise from the page to defend itself, constantly reliant upon the voice of its author to support it (275D–E). The oral technique of the Sophists is like their writing, Plato asserts in the *Protagoras;* both present a man afraid to discuss his position in dialectic combat, the test of true knowledge (347E–348A). Plato repeats the comparison to painters in the *Phaedrus,* saying writing is like painting because it looks like a living being, but is unable to respond to questions (275D, 276A). He associates the Sophists with writing because both are unable to defend themselves with the word of truth, the mind of one who knows. The man who knows a thing, in other words, is able to explain his knowledge and defend his position. The measure of reality is not the appearance of the man or his words, but the undiluted strength of the living intelligence. The truth is to be fired in the furnace of intellectual combat, and the Sophists, insecure about their tricks, avoid head-to-head combat in uncontrolled situations.

The *sophia* of the Sophists, the collections of precepts and the memorized phrases, were at the heart of the criticism. As Aristotle said in the *Sophistical Refutations,* the technique of learning by rote and memorizing speeches may have resulted in rapid teaching, but the instruction was not ultimately of value to the student (34.184A). Aristotle further compared the instruction of the Sophists to teaching a student about prevention of pain in the feet. The Sophist, he said, offered the student an array of shoes from which to choose, but did nothing to instruct the student in the art of shoemaking. The Sophist sold the appearance of wisdom and virtue quickly, but did not help the student develop his own intelligence and knowledge.

Note the parallel with the two types of memory discussed in the previous chapter, memory of things versus memory of words. Aristotle criticizes the Sophists for employing the memory of words (verbatim repetition) without requiring the students to understand the arguments that underlie the words. This perspective on the written word and the Sophists provides new insight into the back-handed compliment Socrates gives Isocrates in the conclusion of the *Phaedrus*. Scholars are spending considerable effort investigating the implied attack upon Isocrates in the *Phaedrus*, an attack Plato clearly relates to Isocrates' use of writing.[37] Isocrates is self-admittedly not a speaker.[38] The apparent source of his success is in the communication of his works through small-group readings such as that which he describes in his *Panathenaicus*. A reading of the first version of the *Panathenaicus* precedes a discussion of the work with colleagues (12.204–29). Isocrates actually defends his written words in discussion, so that the hearers are able to test his ideas in direct questioning. He is thus the first to speak of writing and speaking on an equal basis (8.145). His use of writing is also a close match for the use approved by Socrates in the close of the *Phaedrus*, where he describes those he would call philosophers.

> *Therefore we have already played sufficiently with things concerning words. When you return to Lysias tell him that on coming down to the waters and the temple of Nymphs we heard words which commanded us to speak first to Lysias and anyone else who composes speeches, and second to Homer and anyone else who has composed poetry unadorned or in song, and third to Solon and whoever inscribed in political words forms being called laws. If one composed these works having knowledge of the truth, and being able to support them in vigorous discussion, and declaring in oneself the power to show that the things having been written are trivial, one must not call oneself by name from things one possesses such as these writings, but from the former things that one has taken seriously. (278B–D)*

Those named by these "former things," he continues, are to be called philosophers, or lovers of true wisdom.

120

Thus when Socrates says that Isocrates has a suggestion of philosophy in his mind, the compliment may not be as ironic as it seems to us (279A–B). Isocrates defends his works in the fire of intellectual combat with his friends. Socrates implicitly instructs Isocrates, telling him that the value of his studies is in his mind, not in the words upon the page, however impressive. The attack upon Isocrates, when we see it in this light, appears much less ferocious than those upon other targets of Socratic irony, such as Ion or Euthyphro. Surely any one of Socrates' students would be pleased to hear him say that he has even a suggestion of philosophy in his mind. In any case, when Socrates applies the criticism of writing to Isocrates, he gives Isocrates the benefit of the doubt, a generosity he does not offer to the others known as Sophists.

SUMMARY

The attitude of Hellenic Greeks toward writing paralleled their feelings toward logographers and Sophists as the use of the new technology developed beyond the Archaic model of preservation. These uses of writing brought logographers and Sophists under criticism similar to that leveled against writing. Writing clearly changed the rhetorical pedagogy and practice of the day, but came under attack when its powers of abstraction and preservation became cosmetic. When the ancients separated memorized sophistic techniques and words from the intelligence of the "one who knows," only the appearance of knowledge remained.

8

The Retiring Rhetorician: Isocrates the Writer

Scholars have always thought Isocrates a bit staid and self-righteous in comparison to the wit and brilliance of Plato. The drama of the dialogues presented believable characters and intense mental confrontations; Isocrates offered measured statement of lofty ideals. Socrates offered blazing defiance of death in the *Apology;* Isocrates offered more staid and slightly pompous self-deprecation. Next to the vibrancy of Plato's dramatic situations, Isocrates' carefully written style seemed pedantic and a little dull.

Perhaps this was the origin of scholarly interest in Plato's reference to Isocrates in the *Phaedrus* (279A) and in the apparent reference in the *Euthydemus* (304D). Isocrates, said Socrates, had "something of philosophy" about him. Scholars, attracted to the earthy realism of the Platonic Socrates, found it hard to believe that the statement could have been sincere. "It is surely, Howard wrote, "the most comprehensive damnation with the faintest possible praise."[1]

Yet Isocrates occupies a unique position regarding Plato's epistemological attack on writing and the Sophists. Socrates' selection of this twenty-six-year-old author for a warning that he must beware his *grammata* illustrates the significance of Isocrates' role in the changing conceptions of composition and writing.[2] Even the career of this "writer," however, provides evidence of the continuing dynamic interaction between the traditions of orality and literacy. Isocrates moves writing and composition a step farther away from the memory, recitation, and style of the oral tradition. We see the progression in his epistemological approach to writing, in his development of a more abstract concept of audience, in his movement toward a "written" style, and in the emphasis on writing in his pedagogy. Yet in each of these areas he retains important connections to the strengths of the oral tradition.

Isocrates was the first individual who could be termed a "writer" in the modern sense of the term. He trained in rhetoric and philosophy with the best teachers of his day, yet he admitted that he was never a speaker. He prepared his works orally and then wrote them down, with the ultimate goal of having them read aloud. Thus he was the first who irrefutably goes beyond the Archaic use of writing for preservation and the fifth-century use of writing as a precursor to memorization and recitation. He made no attempt to pretend that his works were recordings of dialogues, and he wrote "speeches" that were never intended for a real audience. He wrote for the developing audience that heard works read aloud. Yet he was sensitive to the Platonic charge that writing was a weak substitute for the knowledge in the mind of a live speaker. He defended his written works in person following their readings among groups of his friends. He offered his "knowledge" face-to-face to those who disagreed or did not understand. When revisions based upon their comments were completed, however, Isocrates considered the final product an accurate image of his thought.

Isocrates' conception of the relationship among writing, composition, and audience is significantly different from that of Plato and others. Plato's dialectic assumes an audience of one, and Plato employs writing to preserve the glimpses of truth uncovered. He uses writing in the only fashion his epistemology will allow—as a reminder (or apparent reminder) of things (dialogues) already known, recording the image of the dialectic that is his path to truth. Sophists surpass the Archaic use of writing to preserve techniques and compositions, developing stylistic devices and argumentative tricks for use in persuasion of real audiences. They also begin to write, implicitly, for fictional audiences beyond specific situations, as in the work by Lysias quoted in the *Phaedrus* (230E). Isocrates' lack of voice, on the other hand, forces him to write exclusively for fictional audiences and to develop an awareness of "audience" more abstract than that of his contemporaries.

Isocrates' style of composition displays further evidence of the interaction between oral and written styles in his work. His compositions have measured style and rhythm. He displays, in other words, characteristics of linear thought and careful preparation that writing both makes possible and reinforces. Yet the measure of his famous periods, his careful attention to rhythm, and his passion for euphony all show the use of writing as a method of reviewing and polishing a work in terms of its sound.

Educational practice also illustrates the tension between orality and literacy in the work of Isocrates. For while students begin work in Isocrates' school by studying composition with the use of writing, his school also requires them to get practical experience in speaking. Furthermore, Isocrates establishes abstract goals for the development of noble character in his students through the concept of a "universal education." This ideal includes an awareness of the written literature and philosophy of the day. This theory assures Isocrates an enduring place in the history of education, for he merges the practical interests of the situation-specific oral culture and the abstract ideals that find their origins in written culture. His ideas therefore match the communication and educational environment for centuries following, with rhetorical training in speech performance in tandem with training in writing and composition.

THE FIRST "WRITER" AND HIS EPISTEMOLOGY

Isocrates apparently studied all the skills associated with the "new education" discussed in chapter four. He trained, further, in the techniques of oratory with the best of the Sophists. Plutarch noted in the *Lives of the Ten Orators* (836F) that he studied with Prodicus, Gorgias, Tisias, Theramenes, Protagoras, and others. He also learned from the philosophers of his day. "Doubtless," Plutarch wrote, Isocrates listened to Socrates as "his code of morals and political teachings are decidedly tinged by the Socratic dialogue."[3]

Despite his association with the Sophists and philosophers, however, Isocrates was not well known as a participant in intellectual discussion or speaking. Plato indicated in the *Euthydemus* (305C) that Isocrates was known as a clever composer of speeches but not as a speaker. Plutarch reported in his *Lives of the Ten Orators* (838E–F) that Isocrates' reticence forced him to develop a retort to those who asked him how he could teach speaking if he was not himself a speaker. "He said that the whetstone was not itself able to cut, but made iron able to cut." Plutarch even recorded the story (838E) that Isocrates once made one person leave his lecture room when three arrived to talk to him at the same time. "For now," he said, "the lecture room is a theatre."

The ancients probably exaggerated stories of his shyness, but Isocrates himself admitted that he was no speaker.[4] He therefore decided, he wrote, to take refuge in philosophy, work, and writing on topics related to the Greeks, kings, and states (12.11). Isocrates turned the weakness into a virtue and reported that he did not show off in public as the Sophists did (15.145–48). Despite his lack of public display, however, he became quite wealthy. The apparent source of his success was in the communication of his works through small-group readings such as that described in the *Panathenaicus* (12.204–29). He clearly was not a speaker or oral debater and consequently developed a relationship with writing that was unique in his day. Isocrates was thus one of the first to speak of writing and speaking on an equal basis, without the hostility to writing found in other authors (8.145). This association led Isocrates to develop a new epistemological viewpoint on the writing of discourse.

Isocrates summed up his conception poetically in the *Antidosis* (15.7). Since he was lacking in voice and self-confidence, the only way to defend himself against his detractors was "if a discourse were written just as an image of my thought and of the other things having been done to me." Writing was, in short, a kind of making itself, in that the written word preserved an image of the word in the mind, in the living intelligence of the maker. Isocrates herein took the Archaic conception of the written word as a form of preservation and molded this preservation into an art that captured the shape and form of the thought of man, in the same way a painter caught the image of an object or of a living form. Writing was not, therefore, "the third place from truth," the symbol of the spoken word that is the symbol of thought. Writing, for Isocrates, was a more direct representation of his thought, with only an implicit relationship to the spoken word. Isocrates did not intend his recorded words to be spoken in a concrete courtroom or assembly situation, nor were they to represent concretely and preserve arguments that he might have spoken in a dialogue.

This does not mean that Isocrates completely breaks with the oral tradition. In several instances he speaks of "making," and not "writing," a discourse for the audience, a phrase that clashes with the other identifications of writing and composition mentioned above.[5] The written discourse preserves the image of thought, however, in the image and dramatic frame of what Isocrates would say to a general audience if he had the voice and the courage. Isocrates herein pictures composition and audience in a more abstract way.

Isocrates thus remained within the framework of Plato's general conception of the written word as a symbol of a spoken word that represents the living intelligence of the maker. He remained within the convention of writing as though he were speaking. But Isocrates' consciousness of abstraction and his lack of voice (or courage) led him to a new and more voiceless understanding of the context for a composition. He saw beyond the use of writing to preserve words actually spoken, beyond the use of writing to preserve words to be spoken in a particular realistic situation, even beyond Plato's use of writing to preserve words as if they were spoken in a dramatic conversation in a specific context. He took the first conscious steps toward an awareness of the implied "voice" of an author's written work and toward an awareness—through abstraction—of a general audience for written works. Further, he made the first attempt to answer Plato's assertion that writing could neither present knowledge nor explain itself.

First, Isocrates recognized the distinction, so important to Plato, between the written words and the thought that they were to represent. Isocrates fell into the common habit of mentioning writing in connection with discourses that he wished to belittle. His tone was reminiscent of Plato's attack on speech-writers for misrepresenting the truth as it was to be found in the mind of a speaker. In the *Panathenaicus* (12.271) he contrasted his type of discourse, that composed with art and wisdom, to those having been "written" for the law courts or for epideictic display. In explaining the composition of the same discourse (268), he said that certain of his friends read "the portion of the discourse having been written," a phrase that implicitly separated the unwritten discourse in the composer's mind from the written form of the discourse. The composition itself, then, existed in the mind of the maker until it was recorded. Yet Isocrates takes his understanding of the difference further than Plato.

He answered the charge that writing did not preserve knowledge by testing his compositions before he considered them complete. His usual practice, as described in his writings, was to present himself at readings of his works to discuss the ideas behind them. His presence gave credibility to the written discourse, and, as discussed in the previous chapter, could have originated the "suggestion of wisdom" that Socrates saw in him. Knowledge, Socrates said, was in the mind of the one who knows. Isocrates discussed his works orally with his students and friends, testing the implicit meanings of the written words to determine if they presented an accurate image of his thought to the listeners. He then either corrected the written version or "destroyed it utterly" to avoid misunderstandings (12.233). Thus Isocrates, in his usual practice, answered Plato's charge that writing was unable to defend itself by meeting with readers in a form of dialectic. He then employed the knowledge gained in oral discourse, revising the written composition to reflect more accurately his intentions.

Isocrates' success at thus presenting an image of his thought and life brought greater credibiblity to the written word. He did not prepare the most important of his works for delivery by someone other than the author in court. He did not write them to deceive, as Socrates might have said, because they did not present the intelligence of one man for that of another. Isocrates saw papyrus and pen not only as writing for preservation but as making itself, as a creative act that provided an image of his thought and life. Yet while he suppressed the spoken word, he did not escape its influence entirely. He revised works based upon oral discussion with readers to avoid misrepresentation of that thought and life. Even his abstracted image remained a symbol for the spoken word as Isocrates himself might have delivered it, complete with all the smoothness of style that writing made possible.

So the fictional audience of Isocrates was not a complete break with dialectic, at least in his first presentation of works through oral reading. On the other hand, Isocrates' storied shyness led him to avoid open intellectual combat in person. He responded in writing to challenges, and this forced opponents to answer him in writing. This adaptation of the give and take of debate or dialectic to the use of writing answered another Platonic objection to writing. Writing, Socrates said, cannot answer questions about its intentions; it must always refer back to its author for defense and clarification. Isocrates adopted this reference as a permanent part of scholarly composition. The example set by Isocrates expected the author to defend his ideas in writing. The written word became the medium through which the author defended his earlier written ideas, presenting the first evidence of an abstracted "dialectic" through written treatises. Isocrates molded the later practice of scholarly debate by his example, building the expectation that other authors would address the general reading audience to defend their ideas in writing. As we see in the next chapter, he apparently succeeded in provoking the first written debate of this kind. Furthermore, he moved closer to an understanding of the new type of audience that would follow scholarly debate.

WRITING FOR FICTIONAL AUDIENCES

Isocrates began the movement toward an awareness of the universal, abstract audience through the creation of entirely fictional speaking situations. Jebb noted the example of the *Archidamos*, a fictional address that was purportedly delivered in 366 B.C. to a specific audience.[6] As Johnson wrote, however, Isocrates developed the concept beyond the creation of fictional audiences to the creation of the abstract audience that Ong associated with writing.[7]

> *It was Isocrates, unable to face an audience but richly gifted as an orator—Isocrates, orator without an audience—who first saw that an orator did not need a single, specific audience, compressed into a single place and time. He turned his own limitations into extraordinary assets, and in so doing, he refined the art of propaganda, gave it a powerful, elegant, and permanent form. In the task of shaping the lives of men and the destinies of nations, the orator need not climb to the rostrum—he could stay in his study, at his desk. After Isocrates, the book, the pamphlet, the letter, need not rely on mere demonstration for its modes of argument.[8]*

Isocrates, in other words, went beyond his conception of writing as an image of one's thought to include the presentation of that thought to the general audience. This step toward an abstract understanding of audience, as Ong noted, required a style shaped by writing's demand for clarity and linear order.

Isocrates was the first to exhibit consistently so many characteristics of written composition and thought throughout his works. On the other hand, however, even this most writing-conscious of Greeks did not make a clean break from the oral tradition of memory and performance for an audience. Isocrates recognized (5.25–26) that his lack of delivery skills was a source of difficulty. A work not delivered by the author, he said in *To Phillip*, lacked the reputation of the one speaking, the sound of his voice, and the variations in his delivery. As a result, he continued (5.26–27), when "one reads it without persuasiveness and without intimating a character but just as though counting, it appears, naturally, to be trivial to those hearing." Isocrates, nevertheless, did not deliver his own works; thus his persuasive impact depended upon the ability of his words not only to portray the image of his thought but to involve the imaginations of those hearing in the dramatic frame of the work. The audience, in other words, had to imagine the discourse as if Isocrates himself were speaking.

As a consequence, his work required the particular audience to learn to consider the discourse in a more abstract fashion. As Isocrates told Philip (5.29), the person hearing had to examine the discourse through reasoning and love of wisdom to determine if there was value to the arguments. He had to disregard the more superficial factors valued by popular opinion. The fact that Isocrates did not speak his own compositions, in short, began to give the written word a measure of credibility, in contrast to the appearance of the individual's wisdom that Plato said other forms of writing presented. Isocrates urged hearers to judge the written word on its own merits, not upon those of the author alone, and certainly not upon the speaking or reciting ability of the author.

At the same time, Isocrates did not entirely escape from his image of thought as a discourse that might have been delivered. The discourse of Isocrates presented the fictive dramatic frame of a work that the author might have spoken and did not address an entirely abstracted "written" audience. This explained, in part, the paradox between Isocrates' references to writing, apparently meaning composition as well, and his numerous references to reading, to hearing aloud, and to himself as though he were speaking the discourse.[9] Even this author who did not speak his works, in short, retained ties to the traditional association between writing and the preservation of the spoken word of the living maker.

The first relation of Isocrates' style to the oral culture was the careful attention to sound in the written composition. Writing, in the case of Isocrates, was not second best to the presence of the maker and the hearing of the maker's words from his own lips.

Isocrates indicated himself that he wrote to be read aloud, perhaps even recited (15.1). He made this clear by the numerous references in his works indicating that he thinks of his discourse as though he were speaking the words aloud.[10] Further, there was no clear evidence that Greeks read his work silently, and abundant evidence that they read it aloud. These ties to oral presentation paralleled the idiom of quotation, suggesting speaking or saying, which predominated in other discourses.

The authors of discourse conceived of literature as something to be recited or read aloud, as displayed in the overwhelming preponderance of quotations introduced by the phrase, "he says," or "he said."[11] The multitude of citations in the spoken idiom dominated the minds of the Greeks, at the very least in the sense that most quotations originated from passages of compositions that the authors had memorized. In contrast, there were relatively few instances where an author quoted an authority in terms of writing. When this occurred, there was generally a direct mention of the discourse in question, as in the statement "as Plato wrote in the *Timaeus*."[12] The citations that did mention writing also noted the names of both the author and the work in question. The works quoted in the spoken idiom were probably common knowledge, poems of which most Greeks were aware, for example, or credible maxims like those discussed in chapter five.

The quotations from written works, however, established credibility through a connection with the author's name and reputation and possibly through public recognition of the name of the discourse. The appearance of quotations that alluded to written discourse suggested the growing availability of written copies of these compositions. Further, they indicated a changing conception of literature itself, in line with the changes demanded by Isocrates' practice of writing for reading aloud. These two factors taken together indicated that the Hellenic practice of writing was moving toward a conception of the composition of literature with the written copy as the ultimate goal.

Isocrates led the way toward this more abstract understanding of both composition and audience. Yet he clearly recognized the power of the spoken word when contrasted with his chosen medium of communication. In addition, he addressed that concern by adapting the oral characteristics of language to the written treatise that addressed a general audience.

Isocrates the Writer

THE ORAL STYLE OF WRITTEN COMPOSITION

Isocrates involved himself so deeply with writing that he began to develop a style that reflected the patterns of thought associated with the new medium. His conception of composing for an abstracted audience as if he were speaking, however, led to the retention of paradoxical ties to more oral style. Ancient criticism of his works recognized the relationship between his works and writing, alleging that he had a style too complex for speaking.[13] Dobson outlined the major characteristics of that style: 1) care to avoid hiatus, or vowel sounds unseparated by consonants; 2) dissonance, or clashing consonants; 3) attention to rhythm; 4) periodic phrasing; and 5) the use of parallel structure.[14] Isocrates was also notable for his copying of passages verbatim from one composition to another, a practice clearly made possible by writing.[15] These details were characteristic of the care in composition that Ong attributed to written composition.

> *To make yourself clear without gesture, without facial expression, without intonation, without a real hearer, you have to foresee circumspectly all possible meanings a statement may have for any possible reader in any possible situation, and you have to make your language work so as to come clear all by itself, with no existential context. The need for this exquisite circumspection makes writing the agonizing work it commonly is.*[16]

With writing, Ong continued, you reviewed, revised, erased, and began again, correcting mistakes that would have been "glossed over" in an oral performance.

All of Isocrates' stylistic characteristics showed the influence of the revision and linear thought associated with writing. Paradoxically, review of written compositions made it possible for Isocrates to avoid the clashing vowels or consonants in this linear sequence that would be difficult to pronounce aloud. The progression of concern for such matters was evident in the gradual disappearance of hiatus as writing became more common. The old-style orators Antiphon and Andocides made little effort to avoid hiatus.[17] Noticeable avoidance occurred in Thrasymachus, then in Gorgias and Alcidamus, with moderate avoidance of hiatus in Lysias and Antisthenes. Isocrates, however, avoided hiatus so completely that Dionysius of Halicarnassus wrote in his *On Literary Composition*

131

(23) that he could find no single instance in the whole of the *Areopagiticus*. The revision made possible by writing allowed Isocrates, ironically, to avoid completely unpleasant sounds in his compositions.

The use of writing was further evident in Isocrates' structure and his choice of words. His formal and stately periods showed the use of writing to examine and reconsider phrasing, and his parallel structure was clearly an effort at linear clarity.[18] Even the accumulation of synonyms to avoid cliché demonstrated the power of writing to allow the conscious avoidance of the oral culture's characteristic repetition.

The careful phrasing and rhythms also illustrate the continuing tension between oral and literate conceptions of style. Aristotle, for example, contrasts the "continuous" and "periodic" styles in the *Rhetoric* (1409A–B) by saying that the continuous style rambles on and on until the sense is complete. The periodic style, however, has sentences with a beginning and end and a length that is *eusynopton*, literally "of a size that can be seen all at once." The awareness of the length of phrases clearly comes with reexamination of texts, with editing. Yet the measure of the appropriate length of the period, Aristotle writes, is that it be easy to repeat in one breath (1409B). So a period is easy to see all at once *and* to say in one breath.

By the same token, parallel structure is a characteristic of oral literature's repetition from the *Psalms* to Homeric literature.[19] Yet parallel structure also matches the "line" of cause-and-effect continuity that writing establishes, the something-does-something-to-something-else linkage. Alternatively, it places a list of parallel items in a category reinforcing the written word's attention to definitions and categories. Thus parallel structure transforms repetition to stress cause-and-effect and categorical links while suppressing mere repetition. Or occasionally the Greeks might vary repetition by the use of stylistic devices like the *chiasmus,* which allows repetition but combines it with changes in linear sequence.

These continuing tensions in the characteristics of language were evident in the way Isocrates spoke of writing, displaying connotations that most others reserved for "making" instead of "writing." He employed the word "writing" in contexts that approached our modern usage of the word, in locations, for example, where it connoted composition instead of simply recording.[20] The composition required for the new universal audience, however, still retained elements of oral style. The abstracted persona of the image of the author's thought, in short, retained a "voice" and a "tone" of its own, and addressed the new audience as if it were speaking. These relationships between oral and written cultures extended from Isocrates' practice to his pedagogy, as he attempted to meld the strengths of both traditions.

ORALITY AND THE "UNIVERSAL EDUCATION"

"If you would be a lover of learning," Isocrates wrote in *To Demonicus* (1.18), "you must be one who learns many things." He developed a concept of education that was the origin of the liberal arts tradition, in that it required one to seek this broad range of knowledge. Further, this concept of education cut across the boundaries between the oral and written traditions. In his final admonition in *To Demonicus* (1.51), he said that the young man should both "learn the best sayings of the poets and, if they have anything valuable to say, read [the sayings of] the other wise men [Sophists]." The wise sayings of the culture, he wrote, were a way to order the judgment, just as the discipline of athletic training ordered the movements of the body (12). Yet this broad education included familiarity with the best written literature as well. The goal of education was philosophy, and, as Robbins wrote, "The study of philosophy is with him the study of literature in its best and most extended sense, and philosophers are students of literature."[21]

Just as Isocrates expected students to know the best from both written and oral culture, he expected them to train in both the practical skills we have associated with the oral mentality and the abstract goals for noble character we have associated with writing.[22] Jebb described Isocratic culture in such a way that it sounded like a synthesis of the practical pedagogy of the Sophists and the ideal education of Plato's *Republic*.[23] He envisioned an education that covered the spectrum from practical to ideal: 1) it was to be practical, while avoiding "barren subtleties" (15.268); 2) it was to be rational, employing "the devices of the whole intelligence," not technicalities; 3) it was comprehensive, not limited to a single professional or vocational plan.

Jaeger recognized this as a major achievement of Isocrates in the context of the "new culture" brought about by rhetoric and the

Sophists. "The particular way in which he distributes the emphasis, magnifying the importance of rhetoric and of practical politics, and pushing mere sophistry and theory into the background, shows his fine perception of the Athenian attitude to the new culture."[24] Isocrates, in other words, began to establish links between the abstract, ideal concepts that writing made possible and the everyday necessity of action in the concrete events of a largely oral culture.

Perkins noted that Isocrates (15.276) rooted his definitions of concepts like "true advantage" and "right conduct" in the context of the social community. The student of government learned and practiced the lessons that allowed the wise governance of *both* home *and* city. "Such a concept of political *aretē* (virtue) was quite close to the moral virtue of Plato. But, it stemmed from the individual as a social creature and not from some external, absolute, and universal reality."[25] So the student of Isocrates learned practical skills, but practical skills organized by and founded in abstract principles.

In daily teaching, Isocrates employed techniques that covered the broad spectrum of available methods from both oral and written traditions. He trained with Prodicus the Grammarian, so writing and the use of written models were important elements of his instruction.[26] Writing made the preservation of wise sayings and examples possible, as we noted in discussing the *technē* of the Sophists. Hubbell pointed out that Isocrates merged the earlier Sophists' "encyclopedic tradition," clearly based on written collections of rhetorical devices and speeches, with the rhetorical tradition of oral performance.[27] His students, Jebb wrote, learned these "artificial resources," but then they developed practical experience in applying those resources.[28]

But this learning experience was not just the regurgitation of sayings and techniques learned by memory on the basis of written texts. Isocrates did not teach *tetagmenē technē,* or "the art of things having already been placed in a certain order."[29] Wagner pointed out that this was a significant difference from previous practice, because Isocrates taught the students abstract principles that they then applied to order their compositions. "Content had mattered little before this; to Isocrates it was all-important."[30] The properly trained Isocratean orator, in other words, was familiar with the forms of argument based upon abstract reason that moved his composition from sophistry to rhetoric.[31] As Robert wrote, "To speak in a less involved way, we mean that a man educated to take a full share in public life on the highest level must be practiced in analyzing all forms of argument, including the scientific."[32] Student and teacher carefully reexamined and revised the finished composition, a process made possible by writing. However, the writing and its critique apparently took place in one-on-one discussion with the master, allowing for something akin to the dialectic Plato required for the acquisition of knowledge.[33]

The ultimate goal remained the production of orators, men who could speak well on broad topics in an abstractly organized fashion. Isocrates recognized the natural ability to speak as a prerequisite to the training he offered in the *Antidosis* (15.186) and openly admitted in *To Phillip* (5.24–30) that the spoken word was more powerful than the writing upon which so much of his reputation and pedagogy relied. So Isocrates was the first self-admitted writer, and he relied upon the technology and abstraction associated with writing. Yet the aim of his pedagogy remained the development of men able to speak in a world where the spoken word was still the dominant force.

SUMMARY

Isocrates, the retiring rhetorician, provided another link in the continuing interaction between oral and written modes of communication and thought. His voice and temperament tied him to the techniques and form of written communication, yet he nevertheless retained ties to the oral culture that placed value on the ability of a citizen to speak. Unable to speak himself, he employed the organizational and educational strengths of writing to make a reputation as an educator of speakers. Unable to address live audiences, he created the fictive universal audience and proved through his appeals to Greek unity that writing could effect persuasion with words that were spoken only to a scribe. Concerned with the revision and analysis of discourse that writing made possible, he made the oral style of the written words the focus of that revision. Isocrates' theory and practice offered a perfect illustration of the continuing competition between written and oral culture as the Hellenic world grew more dependent on writing. The retiring rhetorician was too shy to employ the spoken word he felt to be so powerful, and yet he changed the world with treatises written as if they had been spoken.

9

The Unlettered Author: Alcidamas' Written Attack on Isocrates' Writing

The growing use of writing in the ancient world was the source of many odd tales. Diodorus Siculus said the Spartans were so eager for glory that they inscribed their names upon sticks that were fastened to their arms, creating the equivalent of modern "dog tags" (7.27). Another story recorded by Herodotus (5.35) concerned a rebellious Persian who shaved the head of a slave, cut a message in his scalp, and waited for the slave's hair to grow. He then sent the slave through the Great King's security checkpoints on the great road to Miletus, telling him to give his co-conspirators the message, "Cut my hair and examine my head." Another Diodorus Siculus story (15.52.5) alleged that Themistocles inscribed messages on rocks near the harbors where allies of the Great King would anchor, urging them to defect to the side of the Greeks.

Many of the stories about writing, however, demonstrated that the use of writing had unexpected consequences. An army holding Potidea under siege, Herodotus wrote, had developed a way of contacting their spies behind the city walls (8.128). They simply wrote a message on papyrus, wrapped it around an arrow, and then fired it into a particular area of the city at a specified time. The citizens uncovered the conspiracy one day when, despite the newly discovered science of probabilities, the arrow hit a passerby.

Alcidamas was another ancient Greek who fired off a written message in search of glory but instead suffered unforeseen consequences. The disciple and heir-apparent to Gorgias, his position as the leader of the Gorgianic school of rhetoric placed him solidly in the tradition of those who taught extemporaneous speaking. His work displayed the "gorgeous" style of his mentor, and like Gorgias, he proclaimed his ability to speak on any given topic extemporaneously.[1] The striking differences between his work and the measured phrases of Isocrates inevitably led to conflict. Clearly jealous of Isocrates' fame as a writer of discourse, Alcidamas felt he had to react.

Yet Alcidamas could not get Isocrates into a direct confrontation that would allow him to show off his skill at extemporaneous speaking—Isocrates simply did not speak in uncontrolled situations. The latter's *Against the Sophists* apparently moved Alcidamas to attack openly in the only way possible. The irony was that, like Plato, he attacked writing through a written composition.[2] Thus the continuing tension between the oral and written traditions exhibited itself in an attack on writing, *in* writing, by an advocate of the more oral tradition in sophistic rhetoric. The ironies reverberate throughout the comparison of the two rhetoricians.

A comparison of the two through Alcidamas' attack on Isocrates illustrates several dimensions of the continuing and paradoxical interaction between the oral and written traditions. First, Alcidamas argues against writing upon practical grounds, and only on practical grounds. He offers no theory of writing at all, none of the epistemological foundation that we would expect from a philosopher with awareness of written abstraction. Second, the work records in writing a message replete with the stylistic characteristics of an oral rhetoric, but writing stimulates awareness of those devices and preserves them for memorization. Third, Alcidamas attacks writing as lacking the ability to respond extemporaneously to the immediate situation, but written sophistic *technē* preserves the topics upon which Alcidamas relies. Fourth, the very oral nature of the address, the extemporaneous and lively style Alcidamas defends, makes it less effective as a written composition. Fifth, Alcidamas, true to his "oral" mind-set, clearly shows that he is consistently measuring the effectiveness of rhetoric against a specific audience and a specific situation. Isocrates, however, has begun to consider "audience" as an abstract term, and to conceive of a composition as something created "for all time." Finally, Alcidamas, like Plato, resorts to writing in an effort to attack writing. The motivation to make the attack in this medium indicates that writing is an important part of advanced education such as that practiced in Isocrates' school.

AWARENESS OF ABSTRACTION

Despite their common backgrounds, Isocrates was more aware than Alcidamas of the epistemological issues underlying the debate. The two had much in common, as Van Hook noted.

> *They were contemporaries; both had studied rhetoric under the famous Gorgias, and Alcidamas had even succeeded to the master's school; both were Sophists (although each would deny the orthodox title to the other); both claimed to be "philosophers"; both resided in Athens, and there established influential schools; both belonged to the Epideictic School with respect to their tendencies; both were prominent and gifted men, but almost childishly egotistic, impatient of criticism, and contemptuous of their rivals.*[3]

Isocrates, however, was creating an entirely new vision of the act of composition, one that was developing written style, more premeditated organization, and a new abstract conception of audience.

Alcidamas, meanwhile, remains true to a conception of rhetoric as a practical tool for the development of speakers. He makes no attempt to argue against writing on grounds that would give him support for his claim to being a philosopher. The striking difference between the two rhetoricians marks the powerful influence writing has had upon the concept of composition in the roughly sixty years since Antiphon first wrote a speech.

Their different approaches to written discourse illustrate the point. Alcidamas charges that prepared discourse is unable to adapt to the requirements of the live-speaking situation. Isocrates charges that the techniques taught by the Sophists have the same weakness (13.10, 12–13). Isocrates is clearly aware that such use of either writing or sophistic tricks do not offer knowledge; understanding abstract principles does. The student who understands basic principles can adapt to the immediate situation; the Sophist's student must rely upon "ready-made" phrases or tricks like those we find in the *Rhetoric to Alexander* (attributed to Aristotle). Alcidamas' idea of adaptation is to display the appropriate memorized technique. Isocrates sees writing as a means of teaching students to pursue the connections between ideas at a higher level than their concrete "practical value."

"WRITING" IN ORAL STYLE

As the follower of Gorgias, Alcidamas employed the same poetic style and use of antithesis as his mentor. Gorgias was famous for moving all the elements of poetic style into the realm of prose.[4] As Kennedy summarized, "In essence Gorgias simply borrowed a number of the techniques of poetry and developed to an extreme the natural Greek habit of antithesis."[5] Diodorus Siculus (12.53.4) listed antithesis, isocolon, parison, and homoeoteleuton as the stylistic devices called Gorgianic figures. They were, respectively, contrasting phrases, clauses with equal numbers of syllables, parallel structure, and two or more clauses ending with the same or rhyming words.[6]

These devices are clearly in evidence in Alcidamas' *On the Sophists*. The contrastive structure of Greek discourse is evident in the omnipresence of the *men* . . ., *de* structure;—"on the one hand . . ., on the other hand." Alcidamas, however, shows clearly the extreme to which Gorgias took the usage of this structural framework. Contrast marks nearly every paragraph of the discourse in sentences such as, "Whatsoever things are good and fair are ever rare and difficult to acquire, and are the fruits of painful endeavor; but the attainment of the cheap and trivial is easy."[7] The device clearly overuses a normal oral pattern of conversation to the point that it disturbs the linear progression of words across the written page.

Homoeoteleuton, or rhyming clauses, and isocolon, or clauses with equal numbers of syllables, have more direct ties to the oral tradition. Alcidamas borrows rhyme and a suggestion of metric structure from poetry in an effort to impress the audience with Gorgias' well-known love of sound.[8] Parison, or parallel structure, does move a step closer toward more literate modes of composition, but in Gorgias or Alcidamas the parallel structure is not part of a planned linear progression of thought. Neither does it reemphasize the abstract categories or cause-and-effect reasoning that consciousness of writing would encourage.[9] It is thus episodic, a sequence of phrases or ideas lacking abstract connection through subordination to a category, in the way Ong describes additive oral thought.[10] Perhaps this very attention to sound without substance in the figures is the reason that Aristotle so vehemently condemns the overuse of these Gorgianic figures in the *Rhetoric* (3.3). The key point is that these parallels do not build a link between concrete and abstract, between the observable world and abstract theories about it. This was the central concern of Aristotle's epistemology, and it is little wonder that parallels without purpose infuriate him.

The memorization of these devices was a basic part of the instructional practice of Gorgias, whose works did not include an art of rhetoric.[11] The students learned by rote in the system of Gorgias, as described by Aristotle in the *Sophistical Refutations*. "For some of them gave their pupils to learn by heart speeches which were either rhetorical or consisted of questions and answers, in which both sides thought that the rival arguments were for the most part included. Hence the teaching which they gave to their pupils was rapid but unsystematic."[12] As Milne noted of Alcidamas, "The instruction he gave in oratory was probably merely practical and mechanical."[13]

Yet this use of poetic devices and maxims, which taught through the oral tradition of memory, still relied upon writing. The ancients preserved in written form the discourses that the students learned, as well as the devices and antithetical maxims that they practiced. As Kennedy noted, "One sign of Gorgias's influence is that the account of style in the fourth-century *Rhetoric to Alexander* is concerned with what we think of as Gorgianic figures."[14] Similar manuals certainly provided the basis for memorization of the poetic style reminiscent of the oral formulae of the *aoidoi,* just as we have described their use in schools in chapter four.

So the ability of writing to preserve the lists of figures and antithetical topics makes the extemporaenous style of speaking possible. Alcidamas admits as much at the end of his discourse, when he notes that he does not condemn writing altogether, but that "I believe the art of extemporaneous speech to be in command" (30). Yet we find extemporaneous speech itself is reliant upon written collections of topics and maxims.

THE WRITTEN FOUNDATION OF EXTEMPORANEOUS SPEECH

This leads us to the third paradoxical connection between Alcidamas and writing. His central theme is that extemporaneous speaking is more effective because written speeches cannot adapt to answer new arguments as they arise. Those who prepare discourses for the courts, he alleges, respond clumsily, "For, if any argument not previously thought of occurs to them, it is a difficult matter to fit it in and make appropriate use of it; for the finished nature of their precise diction does not permit improvised interpolations."[15] Yet the same point made about stylistic devices can be made about the antithetical topics that provide the ammunition for extemporaneous responses to unexpected attacks: the topics were preserved in written *technē*, which aided in their memorization. Thus memory and writing were both vital to the extemporaneous speaker trained in oral argumentation.

Furthermore, Isocrates has drawn Alcidamas into a debate in writing about the nature of written composition. As I note in the previous chapter, the growing expectation that authors are to defend their works in writing has weakened the force of this argument. Those who appeal to the developing abstract audience of readers need not necessarily answer unexpected attacks on the spur of the moment. Alcidamas makes the point on practical grounds, in parallel to Plato's epistemological argument on this line, but the timelessness of writing (which Alcidamas admits he hopes to use) soon renders it moot. He argues against writing's inability to respond immediately, in short, at the same time he takes part in a written debate with time to respond deliberately to Isocrates' attack on sophistry.

THE WRITTEN FAILURE OF SPOKEN DISCOURSE

The fourth point of contradiction in Alcidamas' *On the Sophists* grew out of the previous two, for the very extemporaneous style and argumentation that served him well in oral speaking made his words less effective in written form. As Van Hook wrote:

> *Alcidamas's discourse has no orderly or systematic development of divisions. A logical sequence of arguments is lacking in this composition, which is loosely strung together, although there is a formal prooemium and a striking epilogue. The greatest blemish is due to*

141

the frequent repetitions which, in a measure, mar the effectiveness of the presentation.[16]

The organizational plan was that of the extemporaneous speaker, who was sure to mention all the main arguments he had considered in prepration. Yet the overall plan of the work lacked the sense of unity brought by more abstract planning of the overall progression of ideas.

The effect of the resulting jumble on the reader is confusion. The repetition characteristic of the oral tradition works well in oral speaking situations, but in written form the words become inane. The rough and tumble order of ideas and words belies the author's argument (19–22) that precise order of words is not important.

> *Now the main topics in a speech are few, and they are important, but words and phrases are numerous and unimportant, and differ little from one another. Then, too, each topic is brought forward once only, but words, often the same ones, are used again and again. Thus it is that to memorize topics is easy, but to learn by heart an entire speech, word by word, is difficult and onerous.*[17]

The very rambling nature of Alcidamas' discourse demonstrates that his argument does not hold true for *written* discourse. The order of words and topics *is* important in successful written discourse, and his lack of order combines with choppy transitions to confuse the reader.

He does have a case regarding the practical strength of memory and provides more support for the conception of the memorization of argument, which was discussed in chapter six. For if the extemporaneous speaker forgets an argument or a phrase he had intended to use, it is no matter of great difficulty: the speaker simply picks up the expression later on in the speech (20). The individual who memorizes a speech verbatim, however, suffers confusion once the train of thought is broken. Occasionally, he falls silent, embarrassed and unable to continue (21). For the new audience of readers to which Isocrates addresses his works, however, the point is irrelevant. The reader needs only to pay attention to his text to be word perfect in his reading of the piece, and he does not rely upon memory at all. This leads us to the conclusion that Alcidamas' conception of speaking remains so anchored in the lawcourts and the Assembly that he has little understanding of the change Isocrates brings to the nature of writing.

CONCRETE VERSUS UNIVERSAL AUDIENCE

In fact, Alcidamas constantly has in mind a particular audience in the courts or the Assembly. He does not think or argue at all in terms of *written* style and specifically attacks the composers of written discourse for having less power as speakers than laymen (15). This is a clear and rather tasteless reference to Isocrates' admitted lack of voice. Alcidamas refers specifically to the behavior expected of a speaker before an audience. He demonstrates no glimmer of understanding of the new form of composition that Isocrates espouses, no understanding that Isocrates is writing for a general audience.

Isocrates spoke of preserving an image of his thought for all time, "a discourse . . . written just as an image of my thought and of the other things having been done by me; for I hoped through this to make known the best about myself, and at the same time to leave a monument more beautiful than bronze statues" (15.7). He fashioned the written word as a composition to be read aloud as it *might have been spoken,* something written for those who chose to listen to a reading (15.12). Isocrates felt, Milne noted, that extemporaneous speeches did answer the the arguments of the moment—the *kairoi tōn pragmatōn,* but that this was their "only virtue" in comparison to written composition: "The speeches of Isocrates . . . are written for all time; their artistic finish gives them a permanent value. Hence they do not need to comply with the *kairoi in addition: tois de grammasin oudenos touton prosedeēsen* [none of these things are necessary for writings]."[18] Isocrates admitted the usefulness of extemporaneous speaking "for the moment," but added that it had "no value for subsequent time."[19] Alcidamas, in the very act of "writing" his composition, admitted writing's value for this purpose. He weakened his entire case by the admission that he wanted to be remembered through writing and yet displayed little awareness of the stylistic and structural demands of the medium.

ATTACKING WRITING IN WRITING

Even Alcidamas desired to be remembered and admitted in closing that he had chosen to attack writing *in* writing, at least in part

143

because he wished to leave a memorial to himself. He argued from concrete, practical grounds that he did not condemn writing entirely and that he wished to demonstrate that he could easily become a writer while his detractor could only become a speaker with great difficulty.

Yet his effort to be remembered was largely a failure. His lively style and fiery statement may have been amusing and entertaining before a live audience accustomed to the rash charges and accusations common in the Athenian courts or Assembly. As written discourse, however, it was less successful than the plain speaking of the "old orators" Antiphon and Andocides. The measure of the weakness of *On the Sophists* as being written for an audience "for all time" is that, when Caecilius of Calacte established the Canon of Ten Orators, Alcidamus was not among them.[20]

SUMMARY

Alcidamus thus revealed himself as an advocate of the "old school" of oral rhetoric who was out of his depth in written composition. He spoke against Isocrates and his precise diction with the fire and bluntness of the law courts. He thought in terms of concrete situations with which he was familiar and based his argument primarily upon a conception of that which had practical value in those concrete situations. His arguments and words tumbled out as they occurred to him, and he placed more emphasis on simply stating them all than on ordering the structure of his discourse. He stood as an example of a speaker with close ties to the oral tradition in memory and performance, and in his concrete, practical approach to speaking.

Yet even he relies upon writing by the beginning of the fourth century. He preserves and discusses his arguments and stylistic devices in written *technē* that aid his pedagogy, and he must admit the efficacy of using written speech at the same time he attacks it. He remains, however, an unlettered author employing writing in the Archaic tradition of preservation to catch his words as they spill forth. Thus the world remembers the written memorial of Isocrates, as his works address readers "for all time," while it remembers Alcidamas, if at all, as the successor to Gorgias.

10

The Voiceless Muse: Writing and Silent Reading in Greek Literature

The modern world owes much to ancient Greek literature. As Werner Jaeger notes, modern literature derives its basic forms and the concept of a work as an organic whole from the Greeks.[1] We can trace the influence of this literary tradition to the importance of poetry and drama for the Greeks themselves, an importance it is difficult to overestimate. The story of Solon the lawgiver that Stobaeus records in his *Anthologion* (29.88) is an apt ilustration. "Execestides the nephew of Solon the Athenian sang a certain song of Sappho's over the wine, and pleased by the song Solon asked the boy to teach it to him. Being asked by someone why he had been so eager to do this, he replied on the spot, 'So that learning this I may die.'"[2] The tale may be a myth, but it reflects the depth of feeling the Greeks had for their literature. Clearly poetry and the holding of poetry in the memory give Solon a sense of completeness and fulfillment.

Another tale indicative of the importance of literature to the Greeks was the assertion by Plutarch in his *Life of Lysander* (15.2–3) that the Spartans might have razed the city of Athens and sold all its people sold into slavery but for the beauty of Euripides' *Electra*. After the final Athenian defeat in the Peloponnesian War, Plutarch wrote, one of the Spartan allies proposed that the city be razed and its people sold. Later the leaders of the Spartans and their allies held a banquet, however, and a Phocian sang a chorus from *Electra*. The piece was so beautiful that the group decided that it would be a miserable deed to destroy a city that produced such poets.

The ultimate importance of the development of writing to the Western literary tradition would be equally difficult to overstate. The great works of poetry and drama would simply not exist for us today if writing had not come into its own. Yet the relationship between writing and the "oral" literatures of poetry and drama revealed the paradoxical tensions we have found in other areas. As noted in chapter three, poetry became "literature" as it became something subject to verbatim recall based upon writing, and the rhapsode would not have existed as a living library of Greek culture without the writing that allowed verbatim memorization of poetry. Yet poetry and poets apparently never developed strong ties to writing in definition or practice. Drama depended primarily upon memory and oral performance skills but eventually relied on the use of writing for accurate preservation of poets' words.[3] So even in forms of literary expression with direct and continuing ties to the traditions of memory and oral performance, tensions existed between those traditions and the new technology of writing.

Poetry never moves beyond the first stage of the use of writing as we outlined it in chapter six. Poetry apparently relies upon writing to preserve it for history, but there is little or no evidence that Hellenic poets ever move beyond the stage of oral composition, oral preservation by memory, and the consequent oral performance. Poets, in short, never become "writers" in modern parlance. Yet their work, as Bruno Snell attests, shows the influence of written awareness of abstraction.

The evidence regarding the relationship between writing and drama is similarly paradoxical. The composition of drama remains in the realm of the oral tradition, for we find no references to writing as a tool for the creation of dramatic works. The preservation of drama is largely oral in everyday practice, at least in the sense that poets have great influence over the teaching of the play to the actors. Taken in context, evidence for written copies of plays in the audience may be more evidence for the importance of memory than for growth in the use of writing. Formal recording of plays in writing is apparently a very late development, and even then drama relies upon written copies only for preservation in the Archaic tradition. Awareness of abstraction does affect the structure of dramatic thought, however, and the poets' awareness of the self. Yet para-

146

doxically the drama that remains today the most oral of literary forms raises the most interesting question regarding ancient literacy. Through concrete depictions of silent reading in the midst of oral performances, Hellenic drama provides the strongest evidence to prove that Hellenic writing never breaks free of the oral tradition. For silent reading of brief messages clearly is possible for the Greeks, and yet they always read or recite literature aloud. The Greeks continue, by ancient tradition and contemporary choice, to think of literature as an oral form.

POETRY AS "MAKING"

The written and oral traditions of poetry in Hellenic Greece contrasted metaphorically in two stories that later antiquity preserved. A story of Simonides in Phaedrus' collection of tales (4.23.19–24) metaphorically represented the vitality of the oral tradition in the sound and recitation of poetry. Simonides, being poor, began to tour the cities of Asia and sang songs for money in honor of the winners of athletic contests.[4] When shipwrecked at Clazomene, Simonides met a complete stranger who knew much of his poetry and who consequently recognized the poet's "voice" when he spoke.

A story of Philoxenus' "O," as several sources recorded it, represented the written tradition.[5] Dionysius, the tyrant of Syracuse, fancied himself a poet. Like most amateurs, he was very sensitive to criticism of his work. Philoxenus, a prominent poet of the day, was famous for being a little outspoken. After a public performance by Dionysius, the tyrant asked Philoxenus what he thought of the poetry. He told the tyrant exactly what he thought of the performance, and in a rage Dionysius had Philoxenus thrown into the stone quarries. After considerable effort by his friends, Dionysius released Philoxenus from his imprisonment, and the poet returned to the banquet hall. Again Dionysius recited his poetry, and the room quieted as the tyrant waited for the poet's reaction. Philoxenus, presumably after a dramatic pause, grandly gestured for the guard to come and take him to the quarries again.

Somehow the poet managed to escape from Sicily. After a short time Dionysius repented, and when he found out where Philoxenus was staying he wrote to apologize and to beg Philoxenus to come visit him again. Philoxenus replied by inscribing a series of concentric circles on papyrus, representing the abbreviated form of the

147

Greek word for "no," *ou,* in ingenious and emphatic fashion. His answer may well have created the first "concrete" poem. These two stories illustrate both the power of the oral tradition and the growing awareness of writing, even through both originated in sources much later than the Hellenic period.

Contemporary evidence, in fact, reveals little direct connection between poetry and writing, particularly as it relates to composition. Definitions of poetry do not refer to writing, and the terminology referring to the composition of poetry excludes words derived from "writing." Yet poetry, in Aristotle's estimation, retains an awareness of the abstractions that writing fosters.

Aristotle defines poetry, the general term for "making," in the *Poetics* (1447A–B). He includes within the category all types of Hellenic literature, from epic poetry, tragedy, and dithyramb to scientific treatises in meter.[6] Throughout the sequence in which he defines poetry, Aristotle employs the word for "making," *poieō,* which is the origin of all our words for poetry. "Making" refers to composition in general, and there is no specific mention of writing. Rhythm, language, and tune are the tools of the artist, with dance, for example, involving rhythm alone.[7] The Greeks have no truly generic name for poetry, Aristotle writes, beyond the word for "maker," which they apply to all artists and craftsmen. Aristotle therefore declares the art that we call poetry, through which a poet fashions words and meter alone into works of art, to have no name (1447B). People form the name for epic poetry and the other genres of the day, he says, by simply adding the generic word poet or "maker" to the name of the meter. Thus the epic poet is an *epopoios* and an elegiac poet is an *elegeiopoios.*

Perhaps this is because, as Aristotle says in the *Poetics* (1448B), man's natural instinct for imitation, harmony (or tune), and rhythm gives birth to the art of poetry. Unquestionably writing has little place in the consideration of poetry's origins. Further, we find references that suggest a distinction between discussion, writing, and the creation of poetry. Aristotle writes in the *Rhetoric* (1370B) that "those being in love always take pleasure in discussing, writing, or composing [making] something about the beloved." The passage suggests that each is a distinct activity. Demosthenes makes a reference in the *Funeral Speech* to poetry, metric or sung, and the historians, implying the same distinction (60.9).

POETS ARE NOT WRITERS

Contemporary authors support this distance between writing and poetic composition, invariably referring to the composition of poetry as "making" and not "writing." This is the case in most passages modern scholars translate into English as "writing."[8] Sources later in antiquity do speak of individuals' "writing" rather than "making" poetry.[9] A review of the major ancient works for this study, however, finds no Hellenic sources that use such language. Similarly, there is no indication that anyone ever "reads" poetry, either aloud or silently. There are, however, numerous references to poetry's being spoken or sung.[10] Evidence from later antiquity reinforces these references.[11] Pausanias even records that a statue of the poet Anacreon on the Acropolis of Athens represents him in the act of singing his works (1.25.1).

Furthermore, the ancient Greeks never called poets "writers." No name for poet developed that included "writing," as in the word *logographos* or "speech-writer," for example. References to the composition of poetry demonstrated this lack of literal connection with writing. Isocrates (2.7), for example, differentiated between poetry "made" in meter and things written by way of conversation, even though he placed great importance on the sound of his written compositions. The only exception was the connection of writing to the preservation of Homer, discussed in chapters three and seven, a use of writing that was clearly in the Archaic tradition of writing for preservation of important words. The evidence available through Hellenic authors, in short, did not draw an important connection between the composition of poetry and the practice of writing. The Greeks did not define poetry as something written; they defined it in terms of the music, words, and rhythm of spoken language. The poet was literally a maker, not a writer, a creator in the same sense as a painter or other artist.

POETRY AND ABSTRACTION

Even poetry, however, had begun to develop connections to the consciousness of abstraction fostered by writing. A key passage in the *Poetics* (1451A) of Aristotle argued that poetry was more "philosophical" in nature than history, because it provided more than a recording of events. The events recorded by poetry were those that were either probable or necessary, given the circumstances of the characters in a play or poem. Even if one put Herodotus in meter, Aristotle said, the work would remain a record of actual events. Poetry, on the other hand, necessarily presented a reasonable conclusion based upon a kind of abstract reasoning. The poet worked out probabilities and necessary conclusions, just as a philosopher sought the same in terms of abstract terminology. Poetry remained withdrawn from writing in terms of composition, and yet the awareness of abstraction influenced the understanding of poetry's themes and action.

More powerful evidence comes from Bruno Snell's *The Discovery of the Mind in Greek Philosophy and Literature.* Snell traces the growing awareness of abstraction through the poetry of the Greeks, beginning with the Homeric lack of a word for "mind," and extending through the development of an awareness of abstractions in poetry.

> *We must first of all understand that the rise of thinking among the Greeks was nothing less than a revolution. They did not, by means of a mental equipment already at their disposal, merely map out new subjects for discussion, such as the sciences and philosophy. They discovered the human mind. This drama, man's gradual understanding of himself, is revealed to us in the career of Greek poetry and philosophy. The stages of the journey which saw a rational view of the nature of man establish itself are to be traced in the creations of epic and lyric poetry, and in the plays.*[12]

So while poetry apparently remains in the realm of oral composition, memory, and oral performance, it reflects the growing awareness of abstraction that was the inheritance of writing. We find similar contradictions in the relationship between writing and drama.

WRITING'S CHANGING RELATIONSHIP WITH DRAMA

The origins of theatre in Greece dated to the religious festivals of Hesiod's day, such as that described in his *Shield of Heracles* (275–85). These early celebrations consisted largely of music and song in the oral tradition. The names for comedy and tragedy even paralleled the structure of the names for poetry that Aristotle described, with modifiers added to the word *odos* or "song." The popular history was that Thespis invented drama for the entertainment of the villagers when the chorus sang in procession through the town. The prize for the victor was a goat and a basket of figs, thus the name for tragedy was *tragodos,* or "goat song."[13] The etymology of comedy reached back to similar surroundings, with the root word for song, *odē,* added to either *kōmē* (or village) or *kōmos* (or revels). Pindar actually used the word *kōmos* to refer to the song sung as part of a village procession during a general revel.[14] According to Plutarch's *On Music* (1140D–E), this earliest form of theatre consisted of religious music handed down, presumably in oral fashion, in honor of the gods. The *Problems* (19.31.920A) in the Aristotelian corpus suggested that songs were the primary components of early tragedy.

The religious origins of the theatrical performances gave them a special place in the life of Greek civilization. The laws of Hellenic Athens, according to the *Athenian Constitution* attributed to Aristotle (56.3), provided for regular presentation of the dramatic choruses. The Eponymous Archon chose the wealthiest men in the city as *Choregoi* to finance tragedies and comedies for the festivals of the city. The strength of ancient respect for the religious tradition of the theatre was legendary. The leaders of Sparta, for example, refused to stop the chorus in progress at the theatre after they heard of the city's great defeat at Leuctra.[15] The origins of the theatre in religious belief, song, and recitation founded a heritage of reverence for both sacred tradition and the related oral past.

Yet drama offers evidence of the same paradoxical relationship with writing we found in other areas of Greek culture. There was no indication that writing ever became important either in the composition of drama or in the rehearsal of plays. The teaching of performers remained oral, at least in the sense that such teaching consisted primarily of information about oral performance rhythms and movement. The much-discussed written copies of plays were probably in evidence as aids to memory. This left the relationship of drama and writing no further advanced than the second model discussed in chapter six, that of oral composition, writing for preservation, and oral performance based on memorization of the written text. Furthermore, there was evidence that this model did not become important until very late in the era, when cities began to develop "official" texts of the great plays as memories began to fade.

DRAMA AND THE ORAL TRADITION

The references to writing within drama's depiction of daily life showed that Greeks used writing primarily in the tradition of Archaic uses for written records, notes, and diagrams. There were also references to the copying of plays in writing, however, and one intriguing suggestion that the ancient audience either corrected written copies at the second performances of plays or used them as an aid to memorization of dramatic works. An important point, however, was that no ancient author described a composer of plays as "writing" his works. In fact, the expressions "comedy-writer" and "tragedy-writer" dated from the second half of the third century B.C. or later.[16] Playwrights were poets or "makers," and contemporaries called them "comedy-makers" and "tragedy-makers."[17] There was no hard evidence to suggest that they composed with the aid of writing. In all probability they dictated their works after composition; research, however, uncovered no direct evidence of this either.

Translations have confused the issue, for scholars translated many references as "writing" that literally meant "saying" or derived from the word *poeiō,* or "making."[18] Most of the actual references to writing or written materials in the plays themselves spoke of taking mental notes by "writing on the tablets" in a person's mind, decorating statues with symbols, drawing diagrams for placing a tent at the athletic contests, or writing memoranda.[19] One such mention of writing in Aeschylus' *The Suppliants* (946–49) stated that the spoken word of a king was more trustworthy than something written in the folds of papyrus. This "dramatic" support for Plato's attack upon writing (chapter two) was characteristic of the mistrust of writing that we have noted in many contexts.

WRITING DRAMA FOR PRESERVATION

There are few mentions of written copies of plays and no descriptions of their production. The sole reference to the actual copying of plays in drama is a list of the inhabitants of Hades in *The Frogs* (151) of Aristophanes. Heracles describes various crooks, liars, and thieves as the sort of people who inhabit Hades, and adds in conclusion "anyone who made himself a copy of a speech by Morsimus." Morsimus is apparently a well-known bad playwright of the day.[20] Aristophanes' chorus makes a statement in *The Wasps* (1056), which smugly encourages the audience to place a copy of the play into their clothes chests to keep their clothing smelling sweet. The chorus does not, however, specifically mention the act of writing.

The most intriguing reference to the writing of plays, however, was a line in *The Frogs* (1113–14) regarding the competition between Aeschylus and Euripides mentioned above. The line touched on the fact that the play had been performed before.[21] In literal translation it read, "For they have fought themselves, and having the papyrus each one learns the right way." There have been several interpretations of the passage. Rogers stated in his edition that since the play had been presented before, the meaning was simply that the audience had copies of the play in hand.[22] He noted that others explained that the audience was "well-read," and thus the reference to "holding the book." Aristophanes was clearly playing with his battle metaphor, using a word that meant that the audience had "gone into battle" before, and then stating that they learned "the right way." The word he used for "the right way," *ta dexia,* also referred to the right hand that carried a sword, or to the right side of an army that necessarily had strong sword arms.[23] The soldiers' shields did not defend the right side of the body, and thus generals chose only the best fighters for the "right wing" in the line of battle. Another plausible meaning was that the audience had written copies in hand in order to correct them, or to "learn the correct way" from the actors.

There is a further interpretation that appears more likely if we remember Phaedrus' use of the papyrus roll in memorization (228A–E). The passage could also mean that the audience has a written copy and listens to the recitation of the play in order to memorize it correctly themselves. Just as Phaedrus listens to Lysias repeat his own work aloud, the audience listens in search of the "approved version," the oral performance of the play as taught by the author to the actors. There is reason to believe that the dramatic poets teach the choruses their works themselves, or through a chorus-master.[24] Clearly poets are angry if they feel that an actor misrepresents their verses, as Plato attests in the *Charmides* (162D). The public performance of the play, then, provides a basis for the memorization of favorite passages by the public. One of the few references to written copies of plays thus offers possible support for the strength of the oral tradition in Hellenic Greece as represented by the use of memory and recitation.

Another possibility, dating from the late reference in the *Theaetetus* of Plato (142D–143C), was that the audience made written notes as a step toward the eventual compilation of a complete copy of the play. Eucleides talked to the participants in the *Theaetetus,* then made notes, and repeated the process several times. Audiences may have carried written texts of a play in various stages of completion into the theatre as a way of correcting rough copies of a play. Perhaps they also checked for changes the author might have made since they received their copy.

CHORUSES REHEARSE WITHOUT WRITING

We find further suggestions in this direction in descriptions of the function of the playwrights and the chorus masters who supervise the training of the choruses. The language that describes the function of the playwright in Hellenic literature relates the work of the poet to "teaching" or "making" the chorus that recites the plays in choral competitions. There are no references to "writing" plays as such. Xenophon outlines the resposibilities of the two major officials relating to drama in the *Heiro* (9.4). The first is the *choregus,* who is responsible for gathering the chorus. The major responsibility of the *choregus* is apparently to pay the bill for the chorus' costumes and expenses.[25] The second official is "to teach [the chorus] and to deliver punishment to those who make anything badly."[26] This official is the "chorus-maker" or *choropoios* who gives each individual his place in the choir and apparently supervises the production of the chorus.[27] Note again the parallel to Aristotle's description of the naming of poetic forms. Aristophanes emphasizes the teaching function of the chorus-maker in *The Peace* (737), using another word for this individual in the production of comedy, the "comedy-teacher" or *komodidaskalos.* Plato also uses the word for teacher in a general sense in the word "chorus-teacher" or *chorodisdaskalos* found in *Alcibiades* (125E).

The chorus-teacher supervised the singing and movement of the chorus, Plato said in the same work (125D–E). The ancients associated the early poets Pindar and Simonides with such teaching, possibly with reference to the dithyrambic choruses, raising the question whether the poets themselves taught choruses the words

154

to comedy and tragedy as well.[28] Aristophanes indicated that this was the case in *The Peace* (734–38; 765–75) when he sang his own praises as "comedy-maker" and "comedy-teacher." In *The Wasps* (1029), he spoke of the time when he first began "to teach." No words for "comedy-writer" were in evidence. In addition, Plato clearly saw the function of the poets as teaching rhythm, tune, and words to the choruses in the *Laws* (656C) when speaking of the laws to regulate his ideal choruses. Obviously the poet had motivation to get angry with the actors if they misrepresented through a bad oral performance what he himself had taught them.[29]

The image of the author as teacher of the chorus members clarifies the statement in the *The Frogs* (1113–14) concerning the competition between Aeschylus and Euripides. Certainly if an individual invests the considerable time and money to procure a written copy of a play, the most credible source by which to check that copy would be either the author himself or someone who learns the play from the author. The audience member with the papyrus in hand, then, might very well be checking the written copy and/or memorizing the proper pronunciation of the play with the written copy in hand.[30] There is a rather startling implication lying beyond these considerations of the evidence: the poets apparently teach their works to the chorus without the aid of writing.

There is, simply, no evidence of writing being used in the instruction of choruses. Furthermore, it is reasonable to assume that such oral instruction is a vital element of drama before the appearance of writing. The strength of ancient references to Simonides' memory, for example, makes it likely that he, as one of the early chorus-teachers, could function without the aid of writing.[31] An inscription in the *Palatine Anthology* (6.213) states that Simonides won fifty-six victories for teaching choruses. The fact that there are no extant choric works by Simonides, and only a small selection of his other compositions, indicates that this prolific early poet places little of his work in writing.[32] The probable conclusion is that Simonides, and other early Greek poets as well, train choruses without the aid of writing. Dramatic references to writing increase around the end of the fifth century b.c., suggesting that the written version of a play could appear then as an aid to the instruction of the chorus. Yet the date for the formal creation of written texts of dramatic works comes much later, suggesting a lengthy period of transition from oral to written forms in drama.

The possible explanations for the appearance of written copies of a play in the theatre demonstrate the continuing interaction between the dramatic work and the writing that eventually preserves it. The "play-teacher" is responsible for the artistic use of voice and movement by the chorus, and yet writing preserves the works for posterity. Written copies in the theatre declare that audiences are aware of writing's ability to preserve the poetically structured verse of the playwright verbatim. Further, it seems probable that authors begin to make copies of plays for their own use, although lack of evidence leaves this uncertain. Yet there is no evidence that the Greeks write plays down in an official form until the fourth century.

OFFICIAL WRITING OF DRAMA

Evidence for writing plays in the Archaic tradition of formal preservation by society places the event as late as the time of Lycurgus in the mid fourth century B.C. Plutarch records in the *Moralia* that Lycurgus of Athens is responsible for a law, probably in the late Hellenic period, that establishes official written copies of the tragedies of Aeschylus, Sophocles, and Euripides "to protect them." The reference is found in a list of laws Lycurgus pushes through the Assembly: "And one law, that bronze statues be erected of the poets Aeschylus, Sophocles, and Euripides, and their tragedies be written out and preserved at public expense, and that the Clerk of the City read them publicly to those who are going to be actors; and that they not depart from them in acting" (841E). The law does not permit actors to deviate from these copies in performance. The Clerk of the City was to read these texts to the actors, since "they [should] not depart from them in acting" (841E).

The future participle for "actors," *hypokrinoumenois,* suggests purpose, or the intention to be actors. The phrase, then, could be translated reasonably as "the Clerk of the City [to] read [the written tragedies] publicly to those who are going to be actors." Yet the structure of the sentence is such that the "them" that represents the thing from which the actors must not deviate actually refers back, not to the written copy of plays, but to the word "tragedies" itself. The phrasing suggests a subtle distinction between the play and the written copy as though the two are distinct entities. One definition of the word for reading supports this dichotomy. The verb that describes the reading process is *paranagignoskō,* a word meaning both reading one document in comparison to another and simply reading publicly.[33] The passage mentions no other written copy, however, to which the reading could be in comparison.

There remains the interpretation, on the other hand, that the comparison implied by the verb refers not to another written copy but to the version in the memories of the actors or the "teachers" of the actors. In other words, the official written copy "corrects" the version of the play in the minds of the actors verbatim. This suggests that the oral memory of these great works is beginning to falter with the passage of time. Perhaps, as well, a plethora of written copies with variegated histories is diminishing the work of these great poets. This reading demonstrates clearly the intention to use writing in the Archaic tradition of preserving words important to society. The poets themselves are no longer present to teach the most accurate version of the plays; writing holds the best possible version verbatim. Yet even the late formal connection between writing and drama in the fourth century does not imply a connection between writing and composition.

DRAMA AND ABSTRACTION

Yet writing had an impact on drama. While the use of writing in the theatre was predominantly in the Archaic form of *hypomnemata* or official preservation by the city, the dramatic poets grew in awareness of abstraction just as the other poets did. Charles Segal noted in his discussion of writing in Greek tragedy that the playwrights began to display a new awareness of self that he associated with the abstraction fostered by letters. He found the "seeing" and "telling" of the climactic moment of *Oedipus* characteristic of the "self-consciousness" brought into being through writing.

> *This textual self-consciousness, I suggest, owes much to the transitional moment of the form between oral and literate. This concern with the hidden, private, inner space, here and elsewhere in Greek tragedy, points to a poet-writer whose frame of reference is* both *the physical, public space of the oral performance in the theater* and *the graphic space of the text.*[34]

And yet, he continued, tragedy had no word for the self, the *psyche* that Snell noted as evidence of man's discovery of the mind in his book *The Discovery of the Mind*.[35] "The way in which tragedy approaches the relationship between god and man differs from that of the Homeric epic in only one respect. But this one difference is all the more crucial: for the first time in history man begins to look at himself as the maker of his own decisions."[36] Thus, the tragedies provided explicit evidence of the awareness of self, even without a word for the concept, evidence of the ongoing interactive process between writing and the oral tradition in drama.

Segal found further evidence of this interaction in the adaptation of traditional myths to the questioning of an increasingly literate mind. The themes of the tragedies provided examples of this awareness of abstraction, for tragedy had clearly gone beyond the mere repetition of accepted versions of the ancient myths.

> *Tragedy resembles the poetic narrative of an oral culture in that its concern is the present relevance of the myths it uses. These tales are remade to fit a homeostatic present with little concern for historical depth. Yet the quality of that mythical narrative is determined by the spirit of criticism fostered by writing. The myths told by tragedy are no longer the myths of an oral society, clear exemplars of a received truth or accepted communal values.*[37]

Thus the form remained poetic in structure, and the presentation was clearly through memory and oral performance. Yet the words "made" by poets explicitly for recitation showed the results of an interaction with writing's verbatim preservation *and* awareness of abstraction.

In summary, Hellenic drama exhibits signs of the same "tension" between writing and oral culture we found in other contexts. There is no evidence that the ancients composed plays with the aid of writing, but they preserve them in writing after their composition. The version of the play the poet teaches to the performers involves the appropriate "making" of vocal and physical art beyond the mere reproduction of the words. Members of the audience may even be attempting to memorize this "authorized" version of the poet's work, complete with appropriate intonation. Plays retain their poetic structure, yet the elements of visual display, narration, and theme begin to show the awareness of self and the critical evaluation of myth that writing brings to Greece. So writing appears in drama in the late fifth century, and gradually increases its influence over the poets into the fourth century. Yet, ironically, the fictional descriptions of writing in dramatic literature provide the most powerful evidence that writing never completely triumphs over the oral tradition in the Hellenic era.

THE DRAMATIC PORTRAYAL OF SILENT READING

The most patently oral forms of literature in ancient Greece, then, show clear signs of the influence of writing despite their strong and continuing ties to the oral tradition. Yet drama provides the most powerful evidence of the continuing dominance of the oral tradition in Hellenic Greece. For drama provides incontrovertible evidence that silent reading of short messages is possible and leads us to question the lack of evidence for silent reading of written literature. If the Greeks read short passages silently, why do they not do so with longer passages of literature? They read and recite longer passages of literature in great numbers. We must conclude that either tradition or choice binds the Greeks to conceive of literature as an oral form.

Dramatic portrayal provides clear evidence that there was silent reading and writing of brief messages and oracles in the late fifth century. The literature reveals only two instances that unquestionably demonstrate silent reading or writing. The contexts for both of these instances of silent reading and writing make it clear that neither author or reader are saying the words aloud. We can be sure of this because dialogue makes it clear that other characters cannot hear the words the author or reader are writing or reading.

The oldest of the two instances (about 424 B.C.), in *The Knights* of Aristophanes (116–45), is a description of the character Demosthenes reading a written oracle while his friend Nicias eagerly asks him what it says. Demosthenes roars in reaction to the oracle, while his companion mistakes his exclamations for the words of the oracle (116–24). The passage makes it clear that Demosthenes can derive the meaning from the oracle without saying the written words aloud, for he tells his companion the meaning without reading aloud verbatim (127–45).

The second example of silent writing and reading (about 405 B.C.) occurred in the *Iphigenia in Aulis* of Euripides (34–38). The old servant of Agamemnon saw him writing a letter to his wife. The servant made it clear that he had watched Agamemnon write and destroy tablets, crying all the while. The assembled Greeks have forced Agamemnon to summon his daughter to be sacrificed to the

159

gods, using the explanation that she was to marry the warrior Achilles (100). He found the request impossible to make, however, and wrote an additional passage in the letter telling his wife Clytemnestra not to send Iphigenia (108–23). Agamemnon even read the addition aloud to the servant (117–23), both as a stage device to inform the audience, and as insurance for the credibility of the document through a reliable witness. However, Menelaus foiled Agamemnon's effort to save his daughter by intercepting the servant carrying the message. Menelaus read the message silently (307–27). The script made it clear that Menelaus understood the meaning of the writing without reading it aloud (236). These two passages provided conclusive evidence that Greeks could read silently, at least brief messages and oracles. Yet drama abounds with numerous examples, both fictional and historical, of lengthy works being read aloud or recited to an audience.

READING ALOUD IN DRAMA

Within the surviving plays themselves there are several fictional examples of reading aloud. *The Birds* of Aristophanes (959–90) depicts an oracle-seller reading oracles about 414 B.C. The play makes it clear that there is a written copy of an oracle by Bakis, and that the oracle-seller pretends to read from it. The person hearing the oracle read confuses the reference comically; he apparently pulls out an oracle of his own warning that any oracle-makers should be beaten (981–90). There are references throughout to "taking the papyrus" or seeing "for yourself," which suggests that one or both of the characters may be pretending to read the words because they cannot (959–90). The character Peisthetaerus asks several times if such-and-such a thing is actually in the writing, and the oracle-monger replies, "take the book." They repeat the gag several times, suggesting that Peisthetaerus cannot read; the humor of the situation would, indeed, be intensified if it is clear to the audience that the oracle-monger cannot read either.[38] As a result, the story provides little conclusive evidence regarding the practice of reading aloud; the context does not clarify precisely that they are reading or if indeed reading is taking place.

In the *Ecclesiazusae* (1012–20) Aristophanes provides another instance of reading aloud (about 392 B.C.) when an old hag reads a law to a young man that requires him to make love to her before he can lawfully court a young maiden. The reference does not employ the word *anagignoskō* for reading but literally translates "tell me whatever it says." The same mode of statement appears later, when the hag complains that "the writing says" that she is first to wed the youth (1050). The fact that the old woman is reading to the young man from a written document, on the other hand, does not appear to be in doubt from the situation surrounding the event. *The Clouds* of Aristophanes (16–40) offers another humorous use of reading aloud (423 B.C.) as the character Strepsiades examines a register that lists the debts from his son's horse racing. He clearly has a written document, as he awakens in the middle of the night and calls his slave to bring the ledger.

The remaining example of reading aloud in Greek drama appears in Euripides' *Iphigenia in Tauris* (about 412 B.C.). Iphigenia, as the priestess at a temple that sacrifices strangers, offers to help two shipwrecked men escape if they promise to carry a letter to her relatives in Argos (585–94). One of the men is her brother Orestes, who is searching for her (793–830). Neither recognizes the other, and only when Iphigenia reads the letter aloud does he realize that she is his sister.[39] The reading of the letter is a dramatic device for the two characters' recognition of each other, but the reason given for the reading replicates a common occurrence. They are to carry the letter with them, and Iphigenia wants the two men to vouch for the letter, in this case by delivering the message if the tablet is lost at sea (760).

RECITATION IN DRAMA

Recitation also occurs within Greek drama. The poet in *The Birds* (414 B.C.), for example, composes his responses to the character Peisthetaerus in poetic form, apparently on the spot (904–953). There is no mention of a written work from which the poet might be reading. The context makes it clear that the poet composes on the spot, for as Peisthetaerus notes, he speaks the poems to honor a city that has a name only moments old (922). Greek drama gives evidence, then, of oral composition in addition to reading aloud.

Another lengthy sequence dated to 405 B.C. in *The Frogs* (752–1308) makes it clear that recitation is a vital part of life in Greek drama. Much of the play consists of a reciting competition between Aeschylus and Euripides in the underworld; the winner receives the seat of honor next to Hades, the lord of the dead, and a chance to return to life. The lengthy section plays the two rather vain playwrights against each other for successful comic effect, with the recitation providing the basic dramatic frame for the structure of the action. This particular instance of reciting does not seem to be unusual; the procedure appears to be well known. There is also a lengthy section in which Aeschylus and Euripides criticize each other's works as they recite them, interrupting to make negative comments as they see fit (1117–1364).

The evidence in drama, in summary, shows the predominance over silent reading of reading aloud, lengthy recitations of plays within plays in a form of rhapsodic competition, and oral composition of poetry on stage without visible support from written materials. The intriguing question, however, remains: if the Greeks read brief forms of writing silently, why not literature? Why is this most common sign of literacy as we know it not in evidence, with the exception of short messages or phrases? The logical answer, in the light of all the evidence, is that it simply never occurs to the Greeks to read silently. By tradition or choice, they remain true to the conception of literature as a primarily oral form. Despite all the changes writing fosters in modes of thought, organization, and preservation, for the Greeks literature is something that exists in the mind of a person, and the performance of the spoken word continues to be the best medium for experiencing that knowledge.

Some may argue that dramatic convention would preclude the presentation of silent reading of literature in drama due to its length. While actors read many types of written documents aloud on the Greek stage, we should note that, like the two examples of silent reading, these involve only short passages. Certainly the conventions of the stage limit such reading, whether aloud or silent, to brief segments. The cumbersome technology may be a factor as well. It would be more difficult to handle a lengthy roll of papyrus rather than a small piece with a short message or oracle, especially when in full choral costume. Yet the two examples of silent reading stand alone in all of the extant literature of the period, not just in dramatic literature. And even those portrayals retain ties to the oral tradition.

It is significant, as Segal notes, that the portrayal of the uses of the written word demonstrate that it is ambiguous and often untrustworthy.[40] Just as with evidence in the courts, the writing of personal messages requires the testimony of a reliable witness to verify its meaning, and to protect against its loss. It is also significant that writing does not appear in the works of Aeschylus and Sophocles, who lived out their lives in the fifth century B.C. Writing begins to appear in plays around twenty-five years after Antiphon writes the first speeches down, but the references, as Segal notes, point up the ambiguity of writing and the unreliability of its message. In this context, the most logical explanation for the lack of silent reading in ancient Greece is that the majority of Isocrates' contemporaries still regard writing as a less than adequate means of expression.

The attitude of the Greeks toward writing, in other words, retained the heritage of its history as a method of preserving important words and lists in the Archaic tradition. Ironically, it was clear that writing continued to reinforce awareness of abstraction, that it continued to replace memory as a way of preserving important words—even words in poetic form. Yet in their very depiction of writing the Greeks displayed a reluctance to trust this new technology, even as they admitted their growing reliance upon it. They never completely forgot the power of the spoken word, even in silent reading of the written word.

SUMMARY

The general picture of writing Hellenic drama and poetry presents is that of a period of transition for the written word. Poetry remains close to the the oral tradition of the past while demonstrating the influence of writing's awareness of abstraction. The world of drama accepts writing as a part of dramatic daily life beginning around 424 B.C. and depicts it on the stage as a normal activity. Much of the writing the stage portrays, however, is in the model of the Archaic uses of the written word for record-keeping and preservation. Two examples of reading silently in the context of a play are extant, but they represent the only instances of silent reading in major works of Greek literature. Clearly reading silently is possible, but the writings in both instances are brief messages, not literature. The remainder of the evidence regarding writing and reading in dramatic literature provides no evidence of the written composition of drama, and some evidence suggests that that specialized "drama-teachers" teach plays orally to the actors and choruses. As is the case in regard to poetry, there are no words for "drama–writer" in Greek, in contrast to the "speech–writers" in the field of rhetoric. The contradictory attitude Greek drama displays toward writing, in short, matches the depiction of silent reading within it. Dramatic contexts verify that silent reading of literature is possible. The Greeks, however, never read silently simply because they think of the written word as a sign for the spoken word and a means of preserving it. So drama gradually changes form under the influence of writing, and yet drama provides the most powerful evidence that writing never completely triumphs in its competition with the oral tradition. The music of the spoken word is the closest approximation of the making in the poet's mind, and writing is always the child of the voiceless muse.

11

The Unspoken Oral Premise: Aristotle and the Origin of Scientific Thought

There are dangers in following a line of inquiry too intently, as Plato warns in the *Theaetetus* (174A). Socrates tells the humorous story of Thales, who focuses his mind so completely on the study of the stars that he falls into a hole in the ground. "While he was studying the stars and looking upwards, he fell into a pit, and a neat, witty Thracian servant girl jeered at him, they say, because he was so eager to know the things in the sky that he could not see what was there before him at his very feet."[1] We must beware the possibility of seeing evidence of the influence of oral culture where it may not exist. One recalls the story in Aelian's *On the Nature of Animals* about an elephant's writing with a stylus, the author claiming that he has seen it with his own eyes. The owner of the elephant, he says, had merely helped steady the pen.

One seems in danger of making a similar error when looking at the career of Aristotle for signs of the tension between orality and literacy. Few individuals have such a record of influence on human thought. As Lloyd writes, "To attempt to cover the history of Aristotle's influence on subsequent thought in full would be not far short of undertaking to write the history of European philosophy and science, at least down to the sixteenth century."[2] And few people are so clearly associated with the written tradition. Aristotle has a deep impact on succeeding thinkers and scientists precisely because he is the first to identify a method of inquiry that relies heavily on the awareness of linear cause and effect reasoning.

In fact, it was the application of this method across a broad range of fields that made the influence of Aristotle so powerful. "The very comprehensiveness of Aristotle's philosophy was a major factor that contributed to his enormous influence in antiquity: the doctrine of causes laid down both what types of questions to ask and the terms in which to answer them."[3] Thus the pursuit of indications that Aristotle, too, remained at least partially under the influence of oral culture appeared originally to be an invitation to a *makros logos,* or "long story." Aristotle described the term in the *Metaphysics* (1091.A.5), first used by Simonides, as the "long story" a slave told "whenever nothing he says makes sense."

Certainly there is no great wealth of evidence regarding Aristotle's attitude toward writing, other than the number of his written works. In chapter two, we discuss the brief indications that he shares Plato's understanding that the word was a symbol for the thing. In chapter seven, we note his attack on sophistic instruction, on similar grounds to that of Plato. Yet there is no lengthy discussion of writing such as we have regarding Plato, Isocrates, or even Alcidamas. On the other hand, there are a few interesting points that should be made before we complete our consideration of Hellenic orality and literacy.

Certainly Aristotle's works demonstrate the influence and understanding of the cause and effect reasoning and abstract thought that writing fosters. His approach to scientific research demonstrates the influence of abstract thought, and his approach to rhetoric emphasizes reason over the more concrete and emotional techniques from the oral tradition. He contributes the concept of overall abstract unity as a vital component of successful drama. Nevertheless, his work shows the results of the interaction between orality and literacy in Hellenic Greece. Indeed, the work of Aristotle represents a synthesis of oral and written modes of thought. We see this synthesis in the implicitly oral form of his writings, in the appeal to common oral wisdom in his concept of the *enthymeme,* and in the synthesis of both abstract and concrete in his research method.

ORAL FORMS IN WRITING

A significant change took place in the form of Aristotle's writings, a change that some have taken as a consequence of his break with Plato.[4] His early writings were in a dialogue form that showed the

influence of the oral tradition in their composition. The form reflected Plato's care to leave his written works in the form of human
speech that reminded us of the words of everyday people.[5] These
early works, which unfortunately have not survived, impressed the
ancients with their smooth style. "When Cicero, Quintilian and
other ancient literary critics speak of the 'golden stream' of Aristotle's oratory, or of the "grace" or 'sweetness' of his eloquence,
they no doubt had the dialogues primarily in mind: such terms are
certainly inappropriate to the treatises."[6]

Such praise was inappropriate for the later writings because they
were in a form suggestive of lecture notes. Scholars studying the
Rhetoric and *Poetics,* among others, have suffered from the difficulty
of interpreting Aristotle's writing style. "The original Greek is
extremely terse, sometimes to the point of obscurity, and many
passages require 'expansion' before they can be made meaningful."[7]
This raised the interesting possibility that Aristotle wrote his entire
extant corpus in the sole form for which Plato admitted value.
Lecture notes were reminders of what he already knew, and the
earlier dialogues perhaps a record of the argument in a dramatic
dialogue. It was not clear whether the change represented a break
with Plato, or whether Aristotle had merely accepted and adapted
Plato's epistemological position on writing.

Scholars continue the debate over the issue, some believing the
works to be lecture notes for oral presentation, others holding that
they are more detailed notes Aristotle offers to students familiar
with the often cyptic terms.[8] Sir David Ross argues for the second
position.

> *The extant works were not prepared for publication, but they are for
> the most part too full and elaborate to be mere notes for lecture purposes.
> They rather suggest memoranda meant to be shown to students who
> had missed the lectures, and to preserve a more accurate record than
> memory or the notes of the students could provide.*[9]

Whatever the actual case may be, it is intriguing that Aristotle writes
both the early dialogues and the later treatises in forms that suggest
the practical application of Plato's theory of writing.

We conclude that Aristotle wrote his major works in a form that
is not "written" style. His works do not have the polished style
and syntax of Isocratean compositions; he does not write them down
"for all time." They are, instead, works that function as records of

Aristotle's words, with the emphasis on both abstract ideas and concrete examples rather than on style or syntax. Plato's epistemological position, one could argue, is more implicit in Aristotle's works than in Plato's, despite their apparent differences. Yet the polish of Platonic style is not the same as Isocrates' polished written style. Plato preserves in writing compositions with extremely polished *oral* style. Aristotle preserves more abstractly, focusing on the argument and example that to him are the substance of the work. His businesslike approach to writing in the extant works places him between Isocrates and Plato. Unlike Plato, he is not attempting to present a completely preserved oral discourse as it might have been spoken in its entirety, with a fictive audience in a dramatic context. Unlike Isocrates, he retains the explicit concrete audience, for his works are clearly *hypomnēmata* intended for use in a speaking situation. In other words, Aristotle answers Plato's epistemological attack on writing, on the one hand, by employing writing explicitly as a reminder of that which he knows more fully in his mind. On the other hand, he does not rely solely, as Isocrates necessarily would, upon the written word for the preservation of "an image of his thought" in full-blown written style. Aristotle's lecture notes rely upon the author's knowledge to make them clear. So the form of Aristotle's work places him between the oral forms of writing that begin the Hellenic period, and the more explicitly written forms that end it. In that sense, the form of his works is a synthesis of oral and written traditions.

THE *RHETORIC* AND THE ORAL TRADITION

A second matter of interest in the work of Aristotle is the difference between the *syllogism* and the *enthymeme*. The adaptation of the syllogism in Aristotle's rhetorical thought illustrates his awareness of the unspoken common wisdom, part of the oral tradition that he clearly supported as noted in chapter five.

Aristotle was in many ways the father of modern logic. Scholars in this field have known him best for the theory of the syllogism, which had the form of two premises and a conclusion and which established a relationship between two categories.[10] He did not, in fact, invent the syllogism, but "it was Aristotle who conducted the first systematic analysis of the forms of argument as such."[11] The establishment of a necessary relationship between categories based on a causal relationship became the first step toward "scientific knowledge" as we know it today. "The premises must, moreover, contain the causes of the conclusions, for it is only when we know the cause that we have *epistēmē* [scientific knowledge]."[12] Thus in linear reasoning and awareness of abstraction, Aristotle reached the pinnacle of the written tradition in Greece. His "'scientific' knowledge is of things that cannot be otherwise than they are" and "demonstrates connections that are 'universal.'"[13] He details the relationship between the premises and the conclusion in the *Posterior Analytics* (73B.26–88A.10).

The written tradition explicitly influences Aristotle in this work. First, he directs his attention to linear connections, to the subject-verb–object connections implicit in the left-to-right order of written words. He develops from this a focus on cause and effect: something does something to something else. Merging this with the awareness of categories that writing reinforces, he develops the definition of a proposition as a sentence that makes a positive or negative connection between two categories.[14] In fact, as Lloyd notes, the original meaning of the word *kategoria* itself is "predicate." These are simple conceptions with distinctions implicit in daily conversation, but "for the most part, they had not been stated clearly and explicitly before Aristotle."[15]

Furthermore, Aristotle proposes a list of categories for propositions, attempting to label the possible abstract connections between things.[16] Yet even in this most literate and abstract of endeavors, he retains a connection to the concrete world important to oral culture; for the connections he proposes originate in the real world around him.

> *The first question that might be raised is whether the classification is one of things or of terms, an ontological, or a logical, classification. To this the answer must be that the categories are primarily intended as a classification of reality, of the things signified by the terms, rather than of the signifying terms themselves.*[17]

This connection to the concrete world that the word represents provides an introduction to the ultimate synthesis between oral and written modes of thought in Aristotle. For while he recognizes and consciously seeks abstract connections between things, Aristotle never accepts mere connections between abstract things.

Despite his unquestionable tie to the linear reasoning and abstract awareness of the written tradition, two other characteristics of Aristotle's work demonstrate a synthesis with the strengths of oral culture. The first is the change that the syllogism undergoes when it becomes a part of rhetorical argumentation. The second is an essential part of Aristotelian scientific investigation. In each case we find that Aristotle concerns himself with the careful identification of connections between abstractions and the concrete experiences presented by the real world to the minds of men.

When Aristotle enters the world of public argument over matters that humans connect with less certainty, he demonstrates an awareness of the oral opinion to which the speaker must appeal. He introduces the use of the enthymeme in the *Rhetoric* (2.20–24) during a discussion of the *gnomologias* or maxims about everyday events or probabilities that Greeks commonly accept as wise. This common wisdom is similar to the "unwritten law" of the Greeks discussed in chapter five and to the wise sayings or maxims that are the origin of *technē*, as noted in chapter seven. He specifically describes the difference at the beginning of the *Posterior Analytics,* arguing that all teaching and learning applies reason to knowledge that already exists.

> *Similarly too with logical arguments, whether syllogistic or inductive; both effect instruction by means of facts already recognized, the former making assumptions as though granted by an intelligent audience, and the latter proving the universal from the self-evident nature of the particular. The means by which rhetorical arguments carry conviction are just the same; for they use either examples, which are a kind of induction, or enthymemes, which are a kind of syllogism.(1.1)*[18]

Thus while Aristotle goes further in the *Rhetoric* toward making the art logical than any previous author, he remains aware of the fact that uncertain matters require appeals to an audience often unable to follow a complete and detailed chain of argument (1.2.12). Both rhetoric and logic employ the same techniques of argumentation, he says, but rhetoric relies upon the common wisdom of the day.

For rhetoric, he says, applies to controversial issues that permit differing conclusions, and "in the presence of such hearers as are unable to take a general view of many stages, or to follow a lengthy

170

chain of argument."[19] The rhetorical tools of example and enthymeme concern human actions that could often be other than they are, depending upon the point of view. Thus the connections between the things under debate are rarely in the realm of "necessary" cause and effect relationships between categories. In fact, the enthymeme is a type of syllogism that rests on probable rather than necessary premises.[20] But this form of the syllogism has one premise suppressed or unstated. "For if any one of these is well known, there is no need to mention it, for the hearer can add it himself."[21]

Two points are of interest to our line of inquiry. First, the suppression of one premise of the enthymeme assumes knowledge on the part of the audience, a reference back to the communal wisdom of the oral culture. If the audience accepts a premise as common knowledge, in other words, the speaker need not state the connection between premises. Furthermore, the speaker need not make a necessary connection, since enthymemes apply to probabilities and signs, matters about which the conclusions are not necessary. Enthymemes are, in that sense, more oral than literate in that the linear arguments between categories do not necessarily have to be connected by universal truth when applied to a class of things.[22] They must only draw connections that a particular audience accepts as probable or necessary in a particular limited context. They apply to a class of persons, as noted in *Rhetoric* 1.2, but only as regards the probable outcome of a course of action. Thus, secondly, the connections are not between abstract categories exclusively. That is, the goal of this rhetoric is not to reach an abstract ideal truth and then reveal it to the audience by demonstrating the universal inevitablity of its logical proof in abstract terms. Aristotle outlines the pursuit of connections among argument, evidence, and the real world surrounding humankind. In fact, this connection among abstract truth, the human mind, and the particulars of concrete evidence reveals the synthesis of oral and literate modes of thought in the scientific method of Aristotle.

THE ORAL TRADITION AND THE SCIENTIFIC METHOD

Aristotle retains a connection to the practical, everyday world around him in his new "scientific" approach to the world. The "forms" of Plato and the focus on universal truths reached solely through abstract argument have little interest for Aristotle. "Indeed," he says in the *Metaphysics,* "to say that the ideals exist and that other things are part of them is to say nothing and to speak poetic metaphors" (1079B). For Aristotle, the meaningful connections are those between the events of the world around us and the first principles, or universally true propositions, that relate causally to them. As Lloyd notes, "Aristotle clearly recognised that theories must wait on evidence and he reversed Plato's view that abstract argument is more trustworthy than observation."[23] That does not mean that Aristotle accepts the vacillations of changing human impressions. He specifically states in the *Metaphysics* (87B) that humans cannot acquire knowledge by sense-perception alone. Yet the universal truths must apply consistently to the real world around us. Thus his method for pursuing scientific knowledge involves the rigorous application of abstract logic to the concrete details of the world around us.

Aristotle does not take us all the way to a truly scientific approach in the modern experimental sense and gives short shrift to discussion of the inductive method of research.[24] In fact, he demonstrates an interesting contradiction in his scientific method. His method takes two forms.[25] The first is the application of the kind of rigorous syllogistic argument already discussed, and the second is an appeal to data. Yet the constant appeal to data is in itself paradoxical, for the data take two forms. One is the product of concrete observation, the detailed examination of events that would match the oral culture's predilection for practical and concrete everyday knowledge. The second form of data, however, refers to common opinion, or whatever is thought in general about a particular item of research.[26] "The key methodological doctrine that stimulated and guided Aristotle's own researches and those of the Lyceum after him was that in dealing with a problem one must first examine both the particular data and the common opinions before attempting to resolve the issues."[27]

Thus the scientific method begins with close examination of the evidence available and with a "survey of the literature," both of which seem remarkably contemporary. But while Aristotle initiates the rigorous application of logic to the understanding of phenomena around us, he retains ties to the common wisdom and concrete particulars that are a staple of the oral culture.

SUMMARY

So in fact the Aristotle who is so clearly tied to the written tradition offers evidence that he is not the ultimate example of the scholar in the written tradition. On the contrary, his work represents a synthesis of the best of both traditions. A student of Plato, he demonstrates awareness of the epistemological pitfalls of the use of writing, and in the form of his works he employs writing in a fashion consistent with Plato's epistemology. Aware of abstract logic as a measure of scientific knowledge, Aristotle nevertheless understands the importance of common wisdom to everyday argumentation about uncertain matters. Pursuing scientific wisdom by rational argument to a degree unheard of before his day, he nevertheless carefully considers the opinions of previous researchers and never forgets the importance of concrete observation. He may therefore stand as the final product of the interaction between orality and literacy in Hellenic Greece. He is a man aware of the strengths and weaknesses of both traditions and able to employ the strengths of both in the pursuit of truth.

For Aristotle, truth does not rely solely upon the rigorous discussion of abstractions that writing fosters. Neither does it exist only in the preservation and application of context-specific wise sayings or sophistic literary devices. For Aristotle, truth is a pursuit in rigorous logical fashion of the ever-changing connections between the abstractions we think we know and the evidence our senses provide from the world around us. Aristotle synthesizes the world of the oral culture's maxims and practical knowledge with the logical rigor of writing's consciousness of abstraction. In so doing, he lays the undergirding for the contemporary model of scientific method with surveys of literature, establishment of hypotheses, control of context to focus on cause-and-effect connections between concrete events, replication of results, and rhetorical argument about resulting courses of action. The Sophists argue for a definition of truth resting on practical value, on the daily usefulness of techniques to get a job done. Their perspective matches the context-specific point of view we associate with an oral culture. Plato argues for an ideal truth that men pursue through the creation of connections between abstractions without reference to the distractions of the everyday world. His perspective is the apogee of writing's consciousness of abstraction in Hellenic Greece. Aristotle synthesizes the two positions and identifies the relationship *between* abstractions and the real world as the key to truth. So Aristotle's synthesis of the strengths of orality and literacy provides the foundation for the humanistic approach to research that is a cornerstone of Western culture. He seeks to apply abstract reasoning to concrete problems for the betterment of humankind.

12

Conclusion:
The Synthesis of Oral
and Written Traditions

Aristotle recorded the story of a young scholar intimidated by uncertain expectations in *Parts of Animals* (645A). A budding philospher was eager to meet the famous Heracleitus but was struck by timidity as he approached the presence of the great man, for he was uncertain what the great man's response would be. He found the philosopher warming himself in the kitchen. Heracleitus looked up and invited the novice to enter unafraid, "for even here there are gods."

Like the timid philospher, I have been intimidated by the lengthy tradition of classical scholarship and the colossal standing of the Greeks astride the history of Western culture. Furthermore, in beginning this research I found no "smoking gun," no short and incontrovertible evidence that precisely defined the relationship between orality and literacy in Hellenic Greece. As a result, I have been, perhaps, overly cautious and careful in stating conclusions as sections of this work were finished. The overall pattern of the evidence, however, has given me confidence that the positions I have argued are reasonable.

The most significant conclusion I draw is that the symbiosis of writing and oral culture may have been a vital part of the origins of Western culture itself. That is, the vital element for the creation of philosophy and science was not the dominance of written abstraction or oral culture but the relationship between the two. First, the "tense" relationship between the two continues unabated

175

throughout the period. The evidence simply does not support a conception of "victory" by one medium over the other. Second, the tension between the two modes of thought and communication is beneficial to the culture. They interact so as to match the strengths of oral memory and the strengths of written preservation, the strengths of oral communication skill with the strengths of writing's consciousness of abstraction. Finally, this interaction is directly related to the development of the humanistic tradition of research, testing, and verification, which has formed the core of Western civilization.

First, I argue that the pattern of the evidence we have discussed supports my contention that writing's common appearance around 450 B.C. marks only the beginning of its interaction with oral culture. Writing gradually becomes more evident as time goes on, appearing more frequently in all areas of society from the law courts to the schools. This pattern supports a conception of gradual increase in the influence of writing throughout the Hellenic period, not an immediate, or even an eventual, triumph over the older oral culture.

We see supporting evidence in other areas as well. The tradition of admittedly written discourse does not really begin until the time of Isocrates. His concern with parallel structure and other forms associated with written thought is unmatched in the work of others, and he is clearly an exceptional case due to his lack of performing ability. In the realm of philosophy, we see reliance upon both written and oral traditions in the works of Plato, the development of Isocrates' attempt to legitimize writing epistemologically, and finally Aristotle's synthesis of the strengths of both modes of thought. Yet Aristotle does not embrace writing as enthusiastically as Isocrates and clearly does not think of his written works as the ultimate source of information about his knowledge.

In sum, the evidence indicates that writing did not really dominate the oral tradition until well after the Hellenic era. There was no general acceptance of "written" composition in the style of Isocrates. There was, apparently, no "literacy" as we know the term. Training in letters was limited for all but the most highly educated few, and the awareness of abstraction, consequently, was limited as well. Clearly the influence of written modes of thought grew as people took advantage of writing's practical ability to record and preserve. Ultimately the Greeks preserved the advanced works of the day, which displayed writing's awareness of abstraction, in that medium.

These works then were accessible to future generations, and throughout the period we find the growing sophistication of thought as scholars build upon the writings of the previous generation. Yet writing's consciousness of abstraction and its ability to preserve verbatim are constantly balanced by the memory, performance, and attention to situation-specific concrete detail inherent in the oral culture. Furthermore, the interaction of the two was beneficial.

Indeed, the general pattern of the evidence supported the second contention of this book, that writing and the oral tradition shared strengths during the period. Oral memory was still highly developed, and people such as Plato, Socrates, and Isocrates were clearly trained in this skill. These memories complemented writing's ability to preserve data permanently and accurately. Thus powerful memories augmented writing's absolute preservation, allowing individuals to consider complicated problems, to remember lengthy sequences of argument during discussions, and to hold them in memory for later preservation in writing.

Oral performance was complemented by the detailed verbatim reproduction such writing made possible and by the improvements in composition revision allowed. Rhapsodes and others had access to accurate versions of important works, and they were able, through writing's preservation, to reproduce them precisely. Revision made it possible for writers such as Isocrates to begin avoidance of unpleasant sounds in their compositions and for speakers to become more aware of the structure of their discourse.

Writing's new reinforcement of abstraction was complemented by the concrete imagery of the oral tradition that made writing sensible to the reader. No matter how far-flung Plato's abstractions became, he always settled on a concrete image to make a conception accessible, whether ideal table or shadowy cave. Aristotle employed the strengths of both abstraction and concrete imagery in his research method, examining the data, considering the wisdom of those who had considered the matter before (much of which wisdom was available in detail through writing), and then moving back from the concrete sense perception of the world to the abstractions that made knowledge attainable. For him, it was not the written abstraction that constituted knowledge, nor was it the sense perception that could not always be trusted. For Aristotle, knowledge consisted, ultimately, in the constant exploration of the relationship *between* abstract and concrete. If the things we think we see in the world are true, he said, they will be reflected in universal principles that can be discovered by rational argument. If the universal principles that we believe to be true are, indeed, then they will be apparent in careful observation of the real world.

Thus abstract thought and logical argument from the written world merge with common knowledge and concrete evidence from the oral world in the pursuit of an ever-growing wisdom. The strength of this relationship between the two modes of thought forms the foundation of Western culture, and leads, ultimately, to contemporary scientific methods. This perspective on science certainly reinforces the importance of a liberal education for scientists, to train them in the logic, rhetoric, and epistemology that form the foundation of modern research. Furthermore, viewed in the historical context of the gradual transition from oral to written cultures, this conception of their mutual reinforcement leads to another conclusion regarding the influence of media on culture.

The interaction of writing and the oral tradition during the time period chosen for this study shows clearly that they functioned in support of each other. Furthermore, the overall view of the gradual increase in the interaction, as writing grows in popularity, supports the revision of Innis' postulated relationship between media and culture as proposed in chapter one. Stated simply, culture flourishes when media interact so as to complement each other. The time frame of this gradual increase in interaction between writing and oral tradition is the Golden Age of Greek civilization, and this period lays the foundation for all of Western culture. There is thus little question that culture flourished during the period. In each area of culture, writing and the oral tradition together stimulate and support cultural developments across the society, from the legal system to the educational system, from the social performance of literature to the creation of new conceptions of literature. Thus the general pattern of the evidence across each of the areas demonstrates that the interaction of orality and literacy contributed to the blossoming of creativity in Greek culture.

Finally, there is the conclusion that this interaction between oral and written modes of thought is a significant part of the foundation for Western culture itself. The general pattern suggests ways in which both writing and oral communication skills are vital to Western culture. Writing and its use allows the individual to escape the narrow, self-centered focus of the oral culture, the unquestioning acceptance of the traditions and wise sayings that Socrates forces individuals like Euthyphro to reexamine. The memory, performance skills, and concrete imagery of the oral tradition make communication about those newly discovered abstractions more efficient. Thus both traditions are an essential part of the new attitude toward change and learning that is central to Western culture.

Literacy fosters the abstract ideals that make democracy possible, for example. Abstract ideas like justice make democracy possible as individuals with closed concrete perspectives on their own lives learn to become aware of other points of view. Thus one can conceive of "equal treatment under the law," and realize that everyone is entitled to a fair trial, no matter how unpleasant the specific individual being tried might be. Abstract ideas of law make it possible for citizens to think beyond their own points of view, to allow other persons to have other ideas, and to accept for the final product of a given case a compromise bringing the most good to the most citizens. To compromise, one must be able to think abstractly, to allow that there are differing perspectives on the world. Democracy can survive only through this compromise, for otherwise it deteriorates into self-serving groups convinced of their own righteousness who attempt to create a tyranny over others.

To negotiate these compromises, democracy needs the reasonable rhetoric that writing makes possible. Writing's preservation of words and reinforcement of cause and effect reasoning can create persuasive speakers and communicators, people who can pursue the changing truth on controversial matters, convincing audiences of the need for either constructive change or conservative opposition to alteration. This rhetoric, in turn, requires speakers with the ability to see beyond their own points of view in order to understand those of their audience. One cannot analyze an audience unless one can imagine him- or herself in the audience's place, and consider which connections to their beliefs would allow them to understand the author's point of view. Writing also avoids some conflicts because it preserves verbatim the important words of those who precede us. Writing offers the wisdom of early Americans as first principles in the Constitution, for example, principles that we constantly reconsider in light of the sense perception of changing times.

Oral performance fosters the communication of thought to others. People skilled in the variety possible through voice and gesture are capable of more subtlety of expression, and, literally, of more detail about what is being said. Intonation can provide phonemic information about the intended meaning of passages, and those skilled in adaptation to audiences of various types can literally offer more cues to that intention. Gesture, as modern kinesic researchers are discovering, is a tremendously complex and subtle tool on its own. Thus performance skills in speaking and listening support effective discussion regarding the differing perceptions of which writing makes people aware. Furthermore, possible variations in intonation or "tone" are the source of ambiguities in written composition, and the the individual who composes in writing must be aware of them to avoid possible misinterpretations. Other charactistics of the oral culture are vital as well. Memory in the time of the Greeks improved the quality of thought by allowing individuals to hold great masses of detail in their minds. Concrete imagery made possible the metaphorical understanding of abstract principles.

The interaction of oral and written modes of thought thereby supports the development of a conception of political or scientific truth that can change and adapt, both to changes in human perception and to changes in the evidence provided by the world around us. The works of Aristotle begin the great adventure of Western technology's pursuit of progress, making it conceptually possible. The relationship between writing and the oral culture reflects the tension between abstract and concrete in his thought and in his adaptation to Plato's epistemological critique of writing. This conception of an abstracted truth, with its appeal to evidence through close observation of the concrete world, makes changes possible in the basic assumptions that order our society. Once we accept the basic framework of reason, evidence, and research, major shifts in our assumptions about the world, our oral maxims, or unwritten laws become possible. Thus Copernicus, Newton, and Einstein were able to change the way the world looked to us by making connections between new abstractions and the observable evidence around us. In a very real sense, this interrelationship between abstract and concrete is the core of Western progress, for it allows changes in the conservative traditions of cultures based on the force of reason rather than the force of arms.

These perceptions of the interaction of oral and written modes of thinking suggest a vital role for both speaking and literacy in the future of Western culture. The evidence we have examined shows that both are essential for the adaptation of culture, both to new abstract ideas and to new evidence about the world from observation. Furthermore, the evidence provides a powerful answer to the pundit at a forum on literacy who defiantly asked: "Why do we need literacy? We've got television!" We clearly need both oral and literate modes of thought interacting in symbiosis for culture as we have known it to continue. Literacy is essential if we are to be able to abstract ourselves from our personal situations and emotions to consider evidence and other points of view rationally. Oral communication skills are essential if we are to be able to talk to each other about our differing points of view.

Finally, the results of this study suggest that serious examination of the impact of video and film on our culture be continued and extended. The Greeks underwent tremendous changes in the ways they thought about themselves and their world and were largely unaware of the influence that writing and the oral tradition had on them. By chance they stumbled into a situation where both media were working in concert for the benefit of mankind. If our revised Innis principle is correct, however, we can infer that it is also possible for media to work together in ways that are *not* complementary.

In short, both writing and oral communication are vital to our culture for the same reasons they reinforced each other in ancient times. In ancient Greece, the interaction of the media to the benefit of culture was a happy accident. Unless we consciously strive to balance the media's strengths, however, the resulting accident may lead us away from the conscious, rational modes of thought that have made Western culture unique. The Western world could literally lose consciousness of its self and its responsibility to a heritage of reason.

Notes
Bibliography
Index

Notes

CHAPTER 1

1. Mimi Sheraton, "De Gustibus: Sit Down Comedy," *New York Times,* June 19, 1982.

2. Harold Innis, *The Bias of Communication* (Toronto: Univ. of Toronto Press, 1951), 3–32.

3. Milman Parry, *L'Epithète traditionnelle dans Homère: Essai sur un problème de style homerique* (Paris: Société D'Editions Les Belles Lettres, 1928), 1. Author's translation.

4. Walter J. Ong, S.J., *Orality and Literacy: The Technologizing of the Word* (London & New York: Methuen, 1982), 30–77.

5. Ong, 1982, 51.

6. Bruno Snell, *The Discovery of the Mind in Greek Philosophy and Literature,* trans. T. G. Rosenmeyer (New York: Dover Publications, 1982), 122–23.

7. Ong, 1982, 55.

8. Albert B. Lord, *The Singer of Tales* (New York: Atheneum, 1976), 141–97; Berkley Peabody, *The Winged Word: A Study in the Technique of Ancient Greek Oral Composition as Seen Principally through Hesiod's "Works and Days"* (Albany: State Univ. of New York Press, 1975); Eric A. Havelock, *Preface to Plato,* vol. 1, *A History of the Greek Mind* (Cambridge, MA: Belknap Press of Harvard Univ. Press, 1963), *The Literate Revolution in Greece and Its Cultural Consequences* (Princeton, NJ: Princeton Univ. Press, 1982), and *The Muse Learns to Write: Reflections on Orality and Literacy from Antiquity to the Present* (New Haven & London: Yale Univ. Press, 1986).

9. Havelock, 1982, 9–10.

10. Innis, 3–32.

CHAPTER 2

1. Eric A Havelock, *The Literate Revolution in Greece and Its Cultural Consequences* (Princeton, NJ: Princeton Univ. Press, 1982), 31–32.

2. Eric A. Havelock, *Preface to Plato,* vol. 1, *A History of the Greek Mind* (Cambridge: Belknap Press of Harvard Univ. Press, 1963).

185

3. J. P. Pritchard, review of *Preface to Plato,* by Eric A. Havelock, *Books Abroad* (now *World Literature Today*) 38 (1964): 70; Walter J. Ong, S.J., Review of *Preface to Plato,* by Eric A. Havelock, *Manuscripta* 8 (1964): 179.

4. Ong, 1964, 181.

5. W. M. A. Grimaldi, S.J., review of *Preface to Plato,* by Eric A. Havelock, *Classical World* 55 (1963): 257; N. Gulley, Review of *Preface to Plato,* by Eric A. Havelock, *Classical Review* 14 (1964): 31.

6. Havelock, 1982, 9.

7. Havelock, 1963, 208.

8. Havelock, 1963, 208. Cf. 137, 189, 292.

9. Havelock, 1963, xi.

10. Procope S. Costas, Review of *Preface to Plato,* by Eric A. Havelock, *Classical Journal* 60 (1964): 78–80.

11. Elizabeth Sydney Engel, "Plato on Rhetoric and Writing," Ph.D. Diss., Yale Univ., 1973. Engel approaches Plato's view of rhetoric and writing through the context of a philosophical ideal, a perspective that foreshadows this analysis of the tension between oral and literate traditions in Plato.

12. Author's translations unless otherwise noted.

13. *Republic* 401D–403C; *Timaeus* 88C; *Phaedo* 61A; *Protagoras* 340A. Cf. L. M. De Rijk, "*Engkyklios Paideia:* A Study of Its Original Meaning," *Vivarium* 3 (1965): 24–93, esp. 88–93; and Henri Irénée Marrou, *A History of Education in Antiquity,* trans. G. Lamb (New York: Sheed & Ward, 1956), 36–45.

14. Erwin Rohde, *Psyche: The Cult of Souls and Belief in Immortality Among the Greeks,* 8th ed., trans. W. B. Hillis (New York: Harper Torchbooks, 1966), 2:470).

15. Plato's conception of mind was not static. Cf. David S. Kaufer, "The Influence of Plato's Developing Psychology on His View of Rhetoric," *Quarterly Journal of Speech* 64 (1978): 63–78.

16. Cf. LaRue Van Hook, "Alcidamas Versus Isocrates: The Spoken Versus the Written Word," *The Classical Weekly* 12 (1919): 89–94.

17. Havelock, 1963, 261.

18. Havelock, 1963, 30.

19. Havelock, 1963, 207.

20. Havelock, 1963, 42.

21. Cf. *Republic* 614A.

22. Cf. Aristotle, *On Memory and Recollection* 450A; *On the Soul* 427B; *Topics* 163B.

23. Havelock, 1963, 266.

24. Havelock, 1963, 209.

25. Ronna Burger, *Plato's Phaedrus: A Defense of a Philosophic Art of Writing* (University: Univ. of Alabama Press, 1980), 2–3.

26. Compare the discussion of listing and the early logographers in chapter seven.

27. W. B. Dinsmoor, Jr., "The Royal Stoa in the Athenian Agora," American School of Classical Studies lecture on the site, July 2, 1981. Cf. Lycurgus, *Against Leocrates* 66–67.

28. R. C. Jebb, *Selections from the Attic Orators* (London: Macmillan, 1880), ix.

29. Havelock, 1963, 9–10.

30. Paul Shorey, Introduction, in Plato, *Republic*, vol. 2, trans. Paul Shorey (Cambridge, MA, & London: Harvard Univ. Press & William Heinemann, 1935), xxxii.

31. Burger, 1980, 8.

32. *Gorgias* 486B, 521C; *Meno* 100B-C; *Phaedo* 118A.

33. Havelock, 1963, 4. Cf. *Republic* 604B.

34. Cf. *Republic* 330C, 477C.

35. *Physics* 199A; *Rhetoric* 1355B, 1357A, 1362A.

36. Havelock, 1963, 242.

37. Paul Shorey, Introduction, in Plato, *Republic*, vol. 1, trans. Paul Shorey (Cambridge, MA, & London: Harvard Univ. Press & William Heinmann, 1930), xxiv.

38. Havelock, 1963, 3–4.

39. Cf. Everett Lee Hunt, "Plato on Rhetoric and Rhetoricians," *Quarterly Journal of Speech* 6 (1920): 33–53; Robert W. Smith et al., *Ancient Greek and Roman Rhetoricians: A Biographical Dictionary*, ed. Donald C. Bryant (Columbia, MO: Artcraft Press, 1968).

40. E. R. Dodds, *The Greeks and the Irrational* (Berkeley & Los Angeles: Univ. of California Press, 1951).

41. Havelock, 1963, 4.

42. C. K. Ogden & I. A. Richards, *The Meaning of Meaning: A Study of the Influence of Language Upon Thought and of the Science of Symbolism*, 8th ed. (New York: Harcourt, Brace, 1946); S. I. Hayakawa, *Language in Thought and Action* (New York: Harcourt, Brace, 1949).

CHAPTER 3

1. Carl Blegen and Marion Rawson, *A Guide to the Palace of Nestor* (Meriden, CT: Univ. of Cincinnati, 1967), 10–11.

2. Bergen Evans, *Dictionary of Quotations* (New York: Delacorte Press, 1968), 772.

3. Sir Arthur Evans, *The Palace of Minos: A Comparative Account of the Successive Stages of the Early Cretan Civilization as Illustrated by the Discoveries at Knossos* (New York: Biblo & Tannen, 1964), 1:222. See also Joan Evans, *Index to the Palace of Minos* (New York: Biblo & Tannen, 1964), 41.

4. Richard Leo Enos, "The Etymology of Rhapsode," *Issues in Interpretation* 3 (1978), n. pag.

5. See Eugene Bahn, "Interpretive Reading in Ancient Greece," *Quarterly Journal of Speech* 18 (1932): 432–40; Donald E. Hargis, "The Rhapsode," *Quarterly Journal of Speech* 56 (1970): 388–97; Richard Leo Enos, "The Hellenic Rhapsode," *Western Journal of Speech Communication* 41 (1978): 134–43; Lee Hudson, "Between Singer and Rhapsode," *Literature in Performance* 1 (1980): 33–44.

6. Raphael Sealey, "From Phemios to Ion," *Revue des Etudes Grecques* 70 (1957): 347. Cf. James A. Notopoulos, "The Homeric Hymns as Oral Poetry," *American Journal of Philology* 83 (1962): 353.

7. Mary Mino, "The Relative Effects of Content and Vocal Delivery on Interviewers' Assessments of Interviewees During a Simulated Employment Interview," Ph.D. Diss., Pennsylvania State Univ., 1986, 30. Cf. Gerald M. Phillips, "Science and the Study of Human Communication: An Inquiry from the Other Side of the Two Cultures," *Human Communication Research* 7 (1981): 361–70. Phillips argues that "scientific" knowledge about human communication may not be possible.

8. Scholiast on Aristophanes' *The Wasps* 1222. Text and translation found in *Lyra Graeca: Being the Remains of All the Greek Lyric Poets from Eumelus to Timotheus Excepting Pindar*, vol. 2, trans. J. M. Edmonds, rev. ed. (Cambridge, MA, & London: Harvard Univ. Press & William Heinemann, 1964), 2:268–71.

9. Homer, *Iliad* 1.234, 18.505, 23.568; *Odyssey* 2.37.

10. Henry George Liddell and Robert Scott, *A Greek-English Lexicon*, rev. Sir Henry Stuart Jones (Oxford: Clarendon Press, 1973), 371. See Harold Othmar Lenz, "Laurus Nobilis," and "Myrtus Communis," in his *Botanik der alten Griechen und Romer deutsch in Auszügen aus deren Schriften nebst Anmerkungen* (Gotha: Verlag von Thienemann, 1859); and Alta Dodds Niebuhr, "Laurus Nobilis" and "Myrtus Communis" in her *Herbs of Greece* (Athens: New England Unit of Herb Society of America, 1970).

11. Scholiast on Plato's *Gorgias* 451E. Text and translation found in *Lyra Graeca*, 3:548–81. Ancient sources provide differing versions of the origin and nature of the skolion, or the song sung over the wine. The name apparently derives from *skolios* (crooked), but the sources do not agree as to why that label was applied. Some report that the path of the wand from person to person was "crooked", and thus the use of the term. Others felt that the word "crooked" referred to the metrical pattern of the skolion.

Another explanation offered was that the number of dining couches in the rooms required a "crooked" pattern for the passage of the wand as it was passed in a circle.

12. Scholiast on Aristophanes' *The Clouds* 1364. Text and translation found in *Lyra Graeca* 3:550–51. Scholiast on Aristophanes' *The Wasps* 1222. Text and translation found in *Lyra Graeca* 3:552–53. See also Plutarch's reference as recorded in *Lyra Graeca* 3:550–53.

13. Scholiast on Plato's *Gorgias* 451E. Text and translation found in *Lyra Graeca* 3:548–51.

14. Hargis, 393.

15. See Martin Litchfield West, "Homeridae," in *The Oxford Classical Dictionary,* ed. N. G. L. Hammond and H. H. Scullard, 2nd ed. (Oxford: Clarendon Press, 1972), 526; also Thomas W. Allen, *Homer: The Origins and the Transmission* (Oxford: Clarendon Press, 1969), 42–50.

16. Enos, "The Hellenic Rhapsode," 1978, 142.

17. Paul Shorey, Introduction, in Plato, *Republic,* vol. 2, trans. Paul Shorey (Cambridge, MA, & London: Harvard Univ. Press & William Heinemann, 1935), lxiii.

CHAPTER 4

1. *Codex Atheniensis* 1201. Greek text and translation available in B. E. Perry, "Two Fables Recovered," *Byzantinische Zeitschrift* 54 (1961): 5–7.

2. Harold Frederick Cherniss, *The Riddle of the Early Academy* (Berkeley & Los Angeles: Univ. of California Press, 1945), 61–62.

3. George Kennedy, "Speech Education in Greece," *Western Journal of Speech Communication* 31 (1967): 7.

4. L. M. De Rijk, "*Engkyklios Paideia*: A Study of Its Original Meaning," *Vivarium* 3 (1965): 24–93. See 88–93.

5. Quintilian, *Institutes of Oratory* 3.1.11. Cf. John Frederic Dobson, "Antiphon," in *The Oxford Classical Dictionary*, ed. N. G. L. Hammond and H. H. Scullard, 2nd ed. (Oxford: Clarendon Press, 1972), 74.

6. Frederick A. G. Beck, *Album of Greek Education: The Greeks at School and Play* (Sydney: Cheiron Press, 1975).

7. Martin Lowther Clarke, *Higher Education in the Ancient World* (Albuquerque: Univ. of New Mexico Press, 1971), 11. Cf. John W. H. Walden, *The Universities of Ancient Greece,* reprint ed. (Freeport, NY: Books for Libraries Press, 1970), 18.

8. Walden, 23–24.

9. Walden, 19.

10. *Anacreontea* 52.

11. Henri Irénée Marrou, *A History of Education in Antiquity,* trans. George Lamb (New York: Sheed & Ward, 1956), 36–45; Aristophanes, *The Clouds* 961.

12. Marrou, 43.

13. Marrou, 42.

14. Cf. Kenneth J. Freeman, *Schools of Hellas,* Classics in Education No. 38 (New York: Teachers' College Press, 1969), 43–44; and Walden, 11.

15. Quintilian, *Institutes of Oratory* 1.10. 17–22.

16. Cicero, *Tusculan Disputations* 1.2.4. Plutarch also mentions the importance of music to the Greeks. See Plutarch, *On Music* 1140C.

17. Freeman, 1969, 52–53.

18. Freeman, 1969, 60–61.

19. Frederick A. G. Beck, *Greek Education: 450–350* B.C. (London: Methuen, 1964), 78–80.

20. Walden, 11.

21. Beck, 1964, 80.

22. Beck, 1964, 80.

23. De Rijk, 85 ff. See also Aristotle, *Politics* 1337B.

24. Marrou, 146.

25. Beck, 1964, 111–26.

26. Marrou, 45. See Xenophon, *Memorabilia* 3.7.6–7.

27. Clarence A. Forbes, *Greek Physical Education,,* reprint ed., (New York & London: The Century Co., 1971), 85.

28. Freeman, 1969, writing at the turn of the century, cites this passage as evidence that books were challenging the spoken word as a means of communication, page 207. Students, in other words, expected the teacher to have a copy of Homer. While the relative status of the grammar teacher is a matter of some dispute, I argue that the lack of a book may have been more a matter of price than choice. Cf. notes 29 and 30.

29. Ambroise-Firmin Didot and [no first name] Egger, *Sur le prix du papier dans l'antiquité* (Paris: Imprimerie de Dubuisson, 1857), 10; reprinted from *Revue Contemporaine et Athénée Français,* Sept. 15, 1856.

30. A. E. R. Boak, ed., *Michigan Papyrii,* vol. 2, *Papyrii from Tebtunis,* University of Michigan Studies, Humanistic Series, vol. 28 (Ann Arbor: Univ. of Michigan, 1933), 98. See also Naphtali Lewis, *Papyrus in Classical Antiquity* (Oxford: Clarendon Press, 1974), 132–33.

31. Marrou, 146.

32. Freeman, 1969, believes books were readily available. Cf. 207.

33. Cf. Dionysius of Halicarnassus, *On Literary Composition* 9.

34. Beck, 1975, plates 261–76B.

35. Clarke, 22.

36. Freeman, 1969, 81.

37. *The Greek Anthology* 11.400–401; 11.278–79; 9.173; 9.385.
Text and translation in *The Greek Anthology,* trans. W. R. Paton, 5 vols. (Cambridge, MA, & London: Harvard Univ. Press & William Heinemann, 1956–60).

38. Freeman, 1969, cites this passage as evidence of the low status of the grammar teacher, 81.

39. Marrou, 146.

40. Stanley Wilcox, "Isocrates' Fellow-Rhetoricians," *American Journal of Philology* 66 (1945): 172, and "The Scope of Early Rhetorical Theory," *Harvard Studies in Classical Philology* 53 (1942): 129.

41. Arnold Wycombe Gomme and Robert J. Hopper, "Population (Greek World)," *Oxford Classical Dictionary,* 861. Estimates vary; Cf. James Bowen, *A History of Western Education* (New York: St. Martin's Press, 1972), 74.

42. Kennedy, 1967, 7.

43. Bureau of the Census, *Historical Statistics of the United States: Colonial Times to 1970* (Washington, D.C.: GPO, 1975), H–664–68.

44. Leslie Maitland Werner, "U.S. Study on Adult Literacy Finds the Results Are Mixed," *New York Times,* Sept. 25, 1986, D27.

45. Walter J. Ong, S.J., *Orality and Literacy: The Technologizing of the Word* (London & New York: Methuen, 1982), 31–78, 94.

46. Plato, *Protagoras* 326C.

47. Walden, 20.

48. John Patrick Lynch, *Aristotle's School: A Study of a Greek Educational Institution* (Berkeley, Los Angeles, & London: Univ. of California Press, 1972), 40.

49. Lynch, 38.

50. Werner Jaeger, *Paideia: The Ideals of Greek Culture,* vol. 1, *"Archaic Greece"* and *"The Mind of Athens,"* trans. Gilbert Highet, 2nd ed. (New York: Oxford Univ. Press, 1945), 290.

51. Jaeger, 1945, 296–97.

52. Jaeger, 1945, 296–97.

53. Lynch, 51–52.

54. Lynch, 47–48.

55. Lynch, 64.

56. Lynch, 65.

57. Jaeger, 1943, 2:5. See also Thucydides 2.40–41.

58. Bruno Snell, *The Discovery of the Mind in Greek Philosophy and Literature,* trans. T. G. Rosenmeyer (New York: Dover Publications, 1982), 122–23, 234 ff.

59. Walden, 11.

60. Freeman, 1969, 44–45.

61. Lynch, 75.

62. Lynch, 76–78.

63. H. Curtis Wright, *The Oral Antecedents of Greek Librarianship* (Provo, Utah: Brigham Young Univ. Press, 1977), 157 ff.

64. Wright, 164–65. Wright relies heavily on Rudolf Pfeiffer, *History of Classical Scholarship from the Beginnings to the End of the Hellenistic Age* (Oxford: Clarendon Press, 1968), 31 ff.

65. Pfeiffer, 206.

CHAPTER 5

1. Eugene Bahn and Margaret L. Bahn, *A History of Oral Interpretation* (Minneapolis, MN: Burgess Publishing Co., 1970), 3.

2. Wallace A. Bacon, *The Art of Interpretation,* 3rd ed. (New York: Holt, Rinehart & Winston, 1979), 4–5.

3. G. L. Hendrickson, "Ancient Reading," *The Classical Journal* 25 (1929–30): 182–90; W. B. Stanford, *The Sound of Greek: Studies in the Greek Theory and Practice of Euphony* (Berkeley & Los Angeles: Univ. of California Press, 1967), 2.

4. William Chase Greene, "The Spoken and the Written Word," *Harvard Studies in Classical Philology* 60 (1951): 23–59, esp. 36. Cf. Greene's "'Gentle Reader': More on the Spoken and the Written Word," in *The Classical Tradition: Literary and Historical Studies in Honor of Harry Caplan,* ed. Luitpold Wallach (Ithaca, NY: Cornell Univ. Press, 1966), 391–405.

5. Eric A. Havelock, *Preface to Plato,* vol. 1, *A History of the Greek Mind* (Cambridge, MA: Belknap Press of Harvard Univ. Press, 1963), 201.

6. Elizabeth Sydney Engel, "Plato on Rhetoric and Writing," Ph.D. diss., Yale Univ., 1973.

7. Plato, *Protagoras* 347E–348A.

8. Plato, *Sophist* 263E; *Phaedrus* 276A.

9. Plato, *Phaedrus* 274C–275E; *Philebus* 39A; *Theaetetus* 191C–195A.

10. Eric A. Havelock, "The Preliteracy of the Greeks," *New Literary History* 8 (1977): 369–99, esp. 370.

11. George Kennedy, *The Art of Persuasion in Greece* (Princeton, NJ: Princeton Univ. Press, 1963), 230.

12. George Miller Calhoun, "Oral and Written Pleading in Athens," *Transactions and Proceedings of the American Philological Association* 50 (1919): 177–93, esp. 178, 181, 191–92.

13. Calhoun, 192.

14. Havelock, 1977, 369.

15. The water clock or *klepshydra* was a vessel similar in function to the modern hourglass and measured time by the flow of water out of the vessel. See Demosthenes 45.8; 47.82.

16. Andocides 1.15; Demosthenes 45.31, 44.46, 44.54, 23.115; Lysias 13.33, 14.47, 17.9, 19.57, 1.28.

17. Calhoun, 183–90.

18. Kennedy, 1963, 230. Jurors often saw the defendants' families shedding tears as well. Cf. Kathleen Freeman, "Legal Code and Procedure," in her *The Murder of Herodes and Other Trials from the Athenian Courts* (New York: W. W. Norton, 1963), 18.

19. Alan L. Boegehold, "Toward a Study of Athenian Voting Procedure," *Hesperia* 32 (1963): 366–75; "Philokleon's Court," *Hesperia* 36 (1967): 111–21; "Ten Distinctive Ballots: The Law Court in Zea," *California Studies in Classical Antiquity* 9 (1976): 7–19. Professor Boegehold is preparing a thorough study of Athenian legal procedure.

20. A lid for an echinus apparently used in fourth century B.C. to seal up documents has been found in the Agora expedition of the American School of Classical Studies at Athens but remains to be published. Agora PZT 470.

21. Cf. [Aristotle], *Rhetoric to Alexander* 1432A, regarding the introduction of evidence orally without risk of perjury.

22. Diodorus Siculus 9.27.27; Plutarch, *Life of Solon* 25.1.

23. Cf. Isocrates 7.41, 14.82. Herodotus 1.29; [Aristotle], *Athenian Constitution* 7.1.

24. W. B. Dinsmoor, Jr., "The Royal Stoa in the Athenian Agora," American School of Classical Studies lecture on the site, July 2, 1981. Cf. Andocides 1.85.

25. Cf. [Aristotle], *Athenian Constitution* 3.4.

26. Aristotle, *Politics* 1269A; Andocides 1.83–84.

27. Dinarchus 1.42–43; Lysias 30.1, 30.3–4, 30.10–14, 30.17, 30.21–22, 30.25.

28. Thucydides 2.37.3; Lysias 6.10.

29. [Aristotle], *Rhetoric to Alexander* 1446A; Aristotle, *Rhetoric* 1368B, 1373B, 1374A, *Nicomachean Ethics* 8.13.5; Demosthenes 23.61, 23.70; Xenophon, *Memorabilia* 4.4.19.

30. Plutarch, *Life of Lycurgus* 13; *Moralia* 221B, 227B.

31. Alfred P. Dorjahn, "Poetry in Athenian Courts," *Classical Philology* 22 (1927): 85–93, esp. 89.

32. John Chadwick, *The Decipherment of Linear B* (Cambridge: Cambridge Univ. Press, 1969), 12–13, 67 ff.; see also Hans Jenson, *Sign, Symbol and Script: An Account of Man's Efforts to Write*, trans. George Unwin, 3d rev. ed. (New York: G. P. Putnam's Sons, 1969), 451–71.

33. John Frederic Dobson, "Lysias," in *The Oxford Classical Dictionary*, ed. N. G. L. Hammond and H. H. Scullard, 2nd ed. (Oxford: Clarendon Press 1972), 631–32. See also Kennedy, 1963, 133–40; [Aristotle], *Athenian Constitution* 42.1; Isocrates 8.88; Isaeus 7.16.

34. [Aristotle], *Athenian Constitution* 55.1–4.

35. Xenophon, *Cyropaedia* 2.1.18. Cf. [Aristotle], *Athenian Constitution* 49.2; Aristophanes, *The Acharnians* 569, *The Birds* 1172, *The Peace* 353; Thucydides 4.4, 7.60; Lysias 16.16.

36. Lysias 16.13, 9.4, 15.7; Thucydides 8.24.2–3.

37. [Aristotle], *Economics* 1347A, 1348A, 1349B, 1350A, 1353A; [Aristotle], *Athenian Constitution* 47.2–3, 48.1–2.

38. [Aristotle], *Athenian Constitution* 43.4; Lysias 28.5.

39. Demosthenes 20.32; Lysias 9.6–7; Isaeus 5.3; Lysias 32.14; Demosthenes 49.43, 52.4.

40. [Aristotle], *Athenian Constitution* 36.2; Xenophon, *Hellenica* 2.3.20; Lysias 25.8.

41. Xenophon, *Hellenica* 2.3.51.

42. Xenophon, *Hellenica* 2.3.51–52.

43. Demosthenes 45.8; Isaeus 4.14; Lysias 32.5–6, 32.14.

44. Cf. Aeschines 1.165.

45. Hippocrates, *Oath.* See *Hippocrates,* trans. and ed. W. H. S. Jones and E. T. Withington, 4 vols. (Cambridge, MA, & London; Harvard Univ. Press & William Heinemann, 1923–31), 1:292; Aeschines 1.165.

46. Isaeus 10.1, *Fragment* 4.4; Isocrates 17.33–34. Cf. Kennedy, 1963, 206–07, regarding Demosthenes' court battle over his inheritance; also Adolf Berger and Barry Nicholas, "Inheritance, Law, of," in *The Oxford Classical Dictionary,* 546–47.

CHAPTER 6

1. See Kevin Robb, "Introduction," Eric A. Havelock, "The Linguistic Task of the Presocratics," and Arthur W. H. Adkins, "Orality and Philosophy," in *Language and Thought in Early Greek Philosophy,* ed. Kevin Robb (LaSalle, IL: Hegeler Institute, 1983).

2. Eric A. Havelock, *Preface to Plato,* vol. 1, *A History of the Greek Mind* (Cambridge: Belknap Press of Harvard Univ. Press, 1963), 207–8.

3. Eric A. Havelock, *The Literate Revolution in Greece and Its Cultural Consequences* (Princeton: Princeton Univ. Press, 1982), 8.

4. Havelock, 1982, 9–10.

5. Charles W. Lockyear, Jr., "The Fiction of Memory and the Use of Written Sources: Convention and Practice in Seneca the Elder and Other Authors," Ph.D. diss., Princeton Univ., 1971, 52–53.

6. Lockyear, 194.

7. John Frederic Dobson, "Antiphon," in *The Oxford Classical Dictionary,* ed. N. G. L. Hammond and H. H. Scullard, 2nd ed. (Oxford: Clarendon Press, 1972), 74. Cf. Plutarch, *Lives of the Ten Orators* 832B–834B, and Photius, *Bibliotheca* cod. 259, 485B9.

8. Philip Wheelwright, *The Presocratics* (New York: Odyssey Press, 1966), 1.

9. Havelock, 1982, 232 & 205.

10. Frances A. Yates, *The Art of Memory* (Chicago: Univ. of Chicago Press, 1966), 29–31.

11. Yates, 8–9.

12. Yates, 9.

13. Walter J. Ong, S.J., *Orality and Literacy: The Technologizing of the Word* (London & New York: Methuen, 1982), 20–21.

14. Edward Hussey, *The Presocratics* (New York: Charles Scribner's Sons, 1972), 78–79.

15. Philostratus, *Lives of the Sophists* 1.2.1–7; Plato, *Hippias Minor* 368B, *Hippias Major* 285B; Xenophon, *Symposium* 4.62.

16. Plato, *Protagoras* 339A.

17. Hermann Diels, *Die Fragmente Der Vorsokratiker,* rev. by Walther Kranz (Dublin & Zurich: Weidmann, 1966), 1:126–38, 227–46, 308–70.

18. Wheelwright, 181. Cf. Diels, 2:130–207; and chapter seven on the early logographers.

19. Wheelwright, 275.

20. Hussey, 61.

21. Hussey, 61. Cf. Diels, 1:449–78.

22. William David Ross, "Dissoi Logoi," in *The Oxford Classical Dictionary,* 356.

23. Hussey, 96.

24. Hussey, 104 & 114.

25. Hussey, 118.

26. Cf. Alfred P. Dorjahn, "Poetry in Athenian Courts," *Classical Philology* 22 (1927): 85–93.

27. Aristotle, *Rhetoric* 1415B; Plutarch, *Lives of the Sophists* 482–83, *Moralia* 836F.

28. Plato, *Protagoras* 315A.

29. Plato, *Protagoras* 315B–C; *Hippias Minor* 363A–B.

30. Hippocrates, *Paranggeliai* 12.1–8, 13.1–10; *Mochlia* 33.7–10.

31. Cf. chapter seven discussion of the defenses rhetoricians developed against charges that they prepared speeches with the aid of writing.

32. Richard George Frederick Robinson, "Plato," in *The Oxford Classical Dictionary,* 839–42.

33. Cf. chapter seven on the use of writing for storehouse records.

34. Cf. Plato, *Protagoras* 347E–348A.

35. Ronna Burger, *Plato's Phaedrus: A Defense of a Philosophic Art of Writing* (University: Univ. of Alabama Press, 1980), 2–3.

36. Lockyear, 52–53. See chapter five for a discussion of the growing use of written evidence in the law courts.

37. Thucydides 1.22. From *Thucydides,* trans. Charles Foster Smith (Cambridge, MA, & London: Harvard Univ. Press & William Heinemann, 1962), 39.

38. Robinson, 842.

39. Xenophon, *Memorabilia* 4.2.13–15.

40. Plato, *Phaedrus* 275C–D.

41. They are "resting" when the reading takes place. This "rest" probably involves sitting or lying down; Aristotle suggests an association between sitting and writing, although he does not mention listening to an oral reading as part of such composition. Aristotle, *Topics* 8.10.160B.

42. See note 41.

43. Isocrates, 5. 149. Cf. Plato, *Gorgias* 491A.

44. Epicurus, *Epistle* 2.

CHAPTER 7

1. Jean-Pierre Vernant, *The Origins of Greek Thought* (Ithaca: Cornell Univ. Press, 1982), 49. Cf. Plato, *Republic* 563D.

2. Werner Jaeger, *Paideia: The Ideals of Greek Culture,* vol. 1, *"Archaic Greece"* and *"The Mind of Athens,"* trans. Gilbert Highet, 2nd ed. (New York: Oxford University Press, 1945), 290–91.

3. See George Kennedy, *The Art of Persuasion in Greece* (Princeton, NJ: Princeton Univ. Press, 1963), 13–15; Richard Leo Enos, "The Persuasive and Social Force of Logography in Ancient Greece," *Central States Speech Journal* 25 (1974): 4–10, esp. 9–10; Keith V. Erickson, *Plato: True and*

Sophistic Rhetoric (Amsterdam: Rodopi, 1979); Bruce E. Gronbeck, "Gorgias on Rhetoric and Poetic: A Rehabilitation," *Southern Speech Communication Journal,* 38 (1972): 27–38.

4. Jaeger, 1:292.

5. Jaeger, 1:292.

6. Cicero, *Brutus* 7.27; Plutarch, *Moralia* 832C–D.

7. Emily Vermeule, *Greece in the Bronze Age* (Chicago & London: Univ. of Chicago Press, 1974), 237–38.

8. John Chadwick, *The Decipherment of Linear B* (Cambridge: Cambridge Univ. Press, 1969), 12–13. Cf. Lilian H. Jeffrey, *The Local Scripts of Archaic Greece* (Oxford: Clarendon Press, 1961); and Vermeule, 138–39.

9. Chadwick, 104–33. Cf. Hans Jensen, *Sign, Symbol and Script: An Account of Man's Effort to Write,* trans. George Unwin, 3rd rev. ed. (New York: G. P. Putnam's Sons, 1969), 31–49; and Boyce Rensberger, "Roots of Writing Traced Back More Than 10,000 Years," *New York Times,* July 9, 1977, 19.

10. See [Aristotle], *Athenian Constitution* 42.1, 49.2; Isocrates 8.88; Xenophon, *Cyropaedia* 2.1.18.

11. Demosthenes 20.32; 49.43; 52.4. Lysias 9.6–7; 32.14. Isaeus 5.3.

12. G. S. Kirk, *The Songs of Homer* (Cambridge: Cambridge Univ. Press, 1962), 306–7. Cf. Lycurgus, *Against Leocrates* 102; [Plato], *Hipparchus* 228B; Diogenes Laertius 1.57; Cicero, *De Oratore* 3.137. Havelock argues for a mid-sixth-century date. Cf. Eric A. Havelock, *The Muse Learns to Write* (New Haven & London: Yale Univ. Press, 1986), 19.

13. Richard Leo Enos, "The Hellenic Rhapsode," *Western Journal of Speech Communication* 42 (1978): 139.

14. [Aristotle], *Athenian Constitution* 12.4. Cf. Diodorus Siculus 9.27.27, and Plutarch, *Life of Solon* 25.1.

15. Aristotle, *Nicomachean Ethics* 3.5.8; [Aristotle], *Athenian Constitution* 12.4. Cf. Lycurgus, *Against Leocrates* 66–67; Aeschines 3.76; and the tradition of unwritten law in Sparta from Plutarch, *Life of Lycurgus* 13, *Moralia* 221B, 227B.

16. Dionysius of Halicarnassus, *On Thucydides* 5, trans. Lionel Pearson, in *Early Ionian Historians* (Oxford: Clarendon Press, 1939), 3–4. Cf. Enos, 1974, 5.

17. Hippocrates, *Oath* 11. Cf. *Hippocrates,* trans. W. H. S. Jones (Cambridge, MA, & London: Harvard Univ. Press & William Heinemann, 1951), 1:xlv–xlvi.

18. Quintilian, *Institutes of Oratory* 3.1.11; and John Frederic Dobson, "Antiphon," in *The Oxford Classical Dictionary,* ed. N. G. L. Hammond and H. H. Scullard, 2nd ed. (Oxford: Clarendon Press, 1972), 74.

19. Octave Navarre, *Essai sur la rhétorique grecque avant Aristote* (Paris: Librairie Hachette, 1900), 86.

20. Enos, 1974, 4.

21. Plato, *Phaedrus* 257C. Cf. Kennedy, 1963, 177.

22. Dinarchus 1.35–36; Isocrates 5.75. Cf. Aeschines 1.94, 3.173; Aristotle, *Rhetoric* 1408A; Demosthenes 19.250, 58.19; Dinarchus 1.3; Hyperides 3.3–4; Plato, *Phaedrus* 257C.

23. Plato, *Phaedrus* 257C. Cf. Kennedy, 1963, 177.

24. Plato, *Phaedrus* 275C–E. Cf. Paul Plass, "The Unity of the Phaedrus," in Erickson, 196–97.

25. Cf. Plato, *Phaedrus* 276A.

26. Cicero, *Brutus* 7.27; Plutarch, *Moralia* 832C–D.

27. Plato, *Phaedrus* 257C–D.

28. Aeschines 1.125, 3.202.

29. Plutarch, *Life of Themistocles* 2.4.

30. Kennedy, 1963, 52–54.

31. Cf. LaRue Van Hook, "Alcidamas Versus Isocrates: The Spoken Versus the Written Word," *The Classical Weekly* 12 (1919): 89–94.

32. Plutarch, *Life of Lycurgus* 9.3.

33. Plato, *Protagoras* 348E–349A.

34. Cf. Plato, *Meno* 92C–96C.

35. Eric A. Havelock, *Preface to Plato*, vol. 1, *A History of the Greek Mind* (Cambridge, MA: Belknap Press of Harvard Univ. Press, 1963), 201. Cf. Bruno Snell, *The Discovery of the Mind in Greek Philosophy and Literature*, trans. T. G. Rosenmeyer (New York: Dover Publications, 1982), 71, where writing is called "the source and foundation of all civilized life."

36. See chapter two. Cf. Elizabeth Sydney Engel, "Plato on Rhetoric and Writing," Ph.D. diss., Yale Univ., 1973.

37. R. L. Howland, "The Attack on Isocrates in the *Phaedrus*," in Erickson, 265–79. Cf. Kennedy, 1963, 79.

38. Isocrates 5.81–82, 12.9–10, *Epistle* 1.9, *Epistle* 8. See Dionysius of Halicarnassus, *Isocrates* 1; Plutarch, *Moralia* 838D–E.

CHAPTER 8

1. R. L. Howland, "The Attack on Isocrates in the *Phaedrus*," in Keith V. Erickson, ed., *Plato: True and Sophistic Rhetoric* (Amsterdam: Rodopi, 1979), 279.

2. R. C. Jebb, *The Attic Orators from Antiphon to Isaeus*, vol. 2 (London: Macmillan, 1893), 3.

3. R. D. C. Robbins, "Isocrates," *Bibliotheca Sacra* 35 (1878): 403.

4. Isocrates 5.81–82, 12.9–10, *Epistle* 1.9, *Epistle* 8. See Dionysius of Halicarnassus, *Isocrates* 1; Plutarch, *Moralia* 838D–E.

5. Isocrates 8.26, 41; 12.35; 15.8.

6. R. C. Jebb, *Selections from the Attic Orators* (London: Macmillan, 1880), 294.

7. Walter J. Ong, S.J., *Interfaces of the Word: Studies in the Evolution of Consciousness and Culture* (Ithaca & London: Cornell Univ. Press, 1977), 53–81.

8. W. R. Johnson, "Isocrates Flowering: The Rhetoric of Augustine," *Philosphy and Rhetoric* 9 (1976): 224.

9. Isocrates 4.14; 5.72; 12.24; 12.96; 12.136–37; 12.201; 15.12; 15.55.

10. Isocrates 1.18; 3.11; 4.4–5; 5.4; 5.23; 5.151; 12.137; 15.12; 15.47–48.

11. Aristotle, *On the Air* 2.4.415B; Plato, *Gorgias* 484B; Aristotle, *Rhetoric* 1.7.33.1365A.

12. Aristotle, *On the Generation of Animals* 2.5.332A, *Eudemian Ethics* 1.8.17.

13. Dionysius of Halicarnassus, *Isocrates* 2, 13.

14. John Frederic Dobson, *The Greek Orators* (London: Methuen, 1919), 131–34.

15. Jebb, 1880, 276.

16. Walter J. Ong, S.J., *Orality and Literacy: The Technologizing of the Word* (London: Methuen, 1982), 104.

17. Walter Haywood Shewring and Kenneth James Dover, "Hiatus in Greek Prose," in *The Oxford Classical Dictionary,* ed. N. G. L. Hammond and H. H. Scullard, 2nd ed. (Oxford: Clarendon Press, 1972), 513.

18. Dobson, 1919, 133–34.

19. George Arthur Buttrick, ed., *The Interpreter's Bible* (New York: Abingdon-Cokesbury Press, 1951–57), 4:11–12; Ong, 1982, 39.

20. Isocrates 1.5; 5.83–84; 12.262.

21. R. D. C. Robbins, "Isocrates," *Bibliotheca Sacra* 35 (1878): 610.

22. Ong, 1982, 49; Bruno Snell, *The Discovery of the Mind in Greek Philosophy and Literature,* trans. T. G. Rosenmeyer (New York: Dover Publications, 1982), 236–37.

23. Jebb, 1893, 2:9.

24. Werner Jaeger, *Paideia: The Ideals of Greek Culture,* vol. 3, *The Conflict of Cultural Ideals in the Age of Plato,* trans. Gilbert Highet (New York: Oxford Univ. Press, 1944), 49–50.

25. Terry M. Perkins, "Isocrates and Plato: Relativism vs. Idealism," *Southern Speech Communication Journal* 50 (1984): 61–62.

26. Goodwin F. Berquist, Jr., "Isocrates of Athens: Foremost Speech Teacher of the Ancient World," *Speech Teacher* (now *Communication Education*) 8 (1959): 252–54.

27. Harry Mortimer Hubbell, *The Influence of Isocrates on Cicero, Dionysius and Aristides* (New Haven & London: Yale Univ. Press & Oxford Univ. Press, 1913), x.

28. Jebb, 1893, 2:37–38.

29. Jebb, 1880, 249–50.

30. Russell H. Wagner, "The Rhetorical Theory of Isocrates," *Quarterly Journal of Speech* 8 (1922): 329.

31. Jebb, 1880, 249–50.

32. Brother S. Robert, "What Should Gorgias Know?" *Western Speech* (now *Western Journal of Speech Communication*) 24 (1960): 163.

33. Dobson, 1919, 143.

CHAPTER 9

1. Stanley Wilcox, "Isocrates' Fellow-Rhetoricians," *The American Journal of Philology* 66 (1945): 179; Alcidamas, *On the Sophists; or, On the Writers of Written Discourse,* 31.

2. Marjorie Josephine Milne, *A Study in Alcidamas and His Relation to Contemporary Sophistic* (Bryn Mawr, PA: Westbrook Publishing, 1924), 32.

3. LaRue Van Hook, "Alcidamas Versus Isocrates: The Spoken Versus the Written Word," *The Classical Weekly* 12 (1919): 89.

4. Octave Navarre, *Essai sur la rhétorique grecque avant Aristote* (Paris: Librairie Hachette, 1900), 93.

5. George Kennedy, *The Art of Persuasion in Greece* (Princeton, NJ: Princeton Univ. Press, 1963), 64.

6. Kennedy, 1963, 64–65.

7. *On the Sophists* 5. Translated by Van Hook, 91.

8. Kennedy, 1963, 62.

9. Van Hook, 90.

10. Walter J. Ong, S.J., *Orality and Literacy: The Technologizing of the Word* (London & New York: Methuen, 1982), 37.

11. Kennedy, 1963, 62.

12. Aristotle, *On Sophistical Refutations* 183B. Translation by E. S. Forster in Aristotle, *On Sophistical Refutations; On Coming-To-Be and Passing-Away; On the Cosmos* (Cambridge, MA, & London: Harvard Univ. Press & William Heinemann, 1955), 154–55.

13. Milne, 23.

14. Kennedy, 1963, 64.

15. *On the Sophists* 25. Translated by Van Hook, 93.

16. Van Hook, 90.

17. *On the Sophists* 19. Translated by Van Hook, 93.

18. Milne, 28.

19. Milne, 29.

20. George Kennedy, *The Art of Rhetoric in the Roman World: 300* B.C.–A.D. *300* (Princeton, NJ: Princeton Univ. Press, 1972), 367, n. 89.

CHAPTER 10

1. Werner Jaeger, *Paideia: The Ideals of Greek Culture,* vol. 1, *"Archaic Greece"and "The Mind of Athens,"* trans. Gilbert Highet, 2nd ed. (New York: Oxford University Press, 1945), xxi. Cf. Aristotle, *Poetics* 1451A.

2. Text and translation in *Elegy and Iambus: Being the Remains of All the Greek Elegiac and Iambic Poets from Calinus to Crates Excepting the Choliambic Writers and the Anacreontea,* ed. J. M. Edmonds (Cambridge, MA, & London: Harvard Univ. Press and William Heinemann, 1968), 1:109.

3. Charles Segal, *Interpreting Greek Tragedy: Myth, Poetry, Text* (Ithaca & London: Cornell Univ. Press, 1986), 77.

4. Text and translation in *Aesopic Fables in Babrius and Phaedrus,* trans. B. E. Perry (Cambridge, MA, & London: Harvard Univ. Press and William Heinemann, 1965), 336–39.

5. *The Suda,* "Philoxenou grammation," or "The letter of Philoxenus"; Diodorus Siculus 15.6; Plutarch, *De Tranquillitate Animi* 12; Apostolius 6.68. Cf. Scholiast on Aristides, text and translation in *Lyra Graeca: Being the Remains of All the Greek Lyric Poets from Eumelus to Timotheus Excepting Pindar,* trans. J. M. Edmonds (Cambridge, MA, & London: Harvard Univ. Press and William Heinemann, 1964), 3:371–73.

6. Aristotle's definition of poetics as his specific concern (1447.7) is the art that employs only words and meter. "Making" in general, however, apparently includes all types of literature. See Gerald F. Else, *Aristotle's Poetics: The Argument* (Cambridge, MA: Harvard Univ. Press in cooperation with The State Univ. of Iowa, 1967), 1–16, esp. 12–13.

7. Cf. Plato, *Republic* 3.10.

8. Aristophanes, *The Acharnians* 410; Aristotle, *Poetics* 1459A–B, 1460A–B; *Eudemian Ethics* 1214A; *On the Classification of Animals* 673A.15–16; *Rhetoric* 1405B; Isocrates 10.65; Plato, *Phaedo* 94E; Xenophon, *Symposium* 4.6.

9. [Longinus], *On the Sublime* 9.13; *Inscriptiones Graecae,* vol. 12, *Inscriptiones insularum maris Aegeai praeter Delum,* fasc. 5, *Inscriptiones Cycladum,* pars 1, *Inscriptiones Cycladum praeter Tenum,* ed. F. Hiller von Gaertringen (Berlin: George Reimer, 1903), 455, p. 315; Plutarch, *Life of Solon* 14.5–6; *The Suda,* "Mimnermos."

10. Aristophanes, *Thesmophoriazusae* 160; Demosthenes 19.252; Herodotus 5.67; Isocrates 12.18, 33; Thucydides 3.104.5.

11. Athenaeus 14.620C; Diogenes Laertius 9.18; *Greek Anthology* 7.664; Plutarch, *Life of Themistocles* 5.

12. Bruno Snell, *The Discovery of the Mind in Greek Philosophy and Literature,* trans. T. G. Rosenmeyer (New York: Dover Publications, 1982), v.

13. *Greek Anthology* 7.410.

14. Pindar, *Olympian Odes* 4.10, *Pythian Odes* 8.20, 70; Bacchylides 8.103. Cf. Pindar, *Nemean Odes* 3.5, and Aristophanes, *Thesmophoriazusae* 104, 988.

15. Xenophon, *Hellenica* 6.4.16; Plutarch, *Life of Agesilaus* 29.2–3.

16. *Inscriptiones Graecae* 12.5.433; Polybius 2.17.6, 3.48.8, 12.13.7; Diodorus Siculus 12.14, 14.43; Apollonius Dyscolus, *De Adverbiis* 188.27; *Greek Anthology* 7.708; Philodemus, *De Musica* 88K.

17. Aristophanes, *Thesmophoriazusae* 30; Plato, *Apology* 18D, *Cratylus* 425D, *Phaedo* 17C, *Republic* 408B, 606C; Aristotle, *Poetics* 1449A.

18. Aristophanes, *The Frogs* 12–15, *Thesmophoriazusae* 85, 450–51; Xenophon, *Economics* 3.9.

19. Aeschylus, *Prometheus Bound* 789, *The Suppliants* 463; Aristophanes, *The Peace* 878–98, *The Wasps* 530–35, 559.

20. Benjamin Bickley Rogers, ed. and trans., *Aristophanes* (Cambridge, MA, & London: Harvard Univ. Press and William Heinemann, 1967), 2:311, note "d."

21. Rogers, 2:400, note "b."

22. Rogers, 2:400, note "b."

23. Xenophon, *Agesilaus* 2.9.

24. Aristophanes, *The Wasps* 1029; Plato *Alcibiades* 125D–E; Xenophon *Heiro* 9.4.

25. Xenophon, *Athenian Republic* 1.13.

26. Xenophon, *Heiro* 9.4.

27. Xenophon, *Agesilaus* 2.9.

28. Eustathius, *Introduction to Pindar* 27; *Greek Anthology* 6.213. Cf. *Lyra Graeca: Being the Remains of All the Greek Lyric Poets from Eumelus to Timotheus Excepting Pindar,* 3 vols., trans. J. M. Edmonds, rev. ed. (Cambridge, MA, & London: Harvard Univ. Press and William Heinemann, 1964), 2:388–89.

29. Plato, *Charmides* 162D.

30. Cf. Plato, *Phaedrus* 228A–E.

31. Cicero, *De Oratore* 2.357; Aristides 2.510.

32. C. M. Bowra, "Simonides," in *The Oxford Classical Dictionary*, ed. H. G. L. Hammond and H. H. Scullard, 2nd ed. (Oxford: Clarendon Press, 1972), 991.

33. Henry George Liddell and Robert Scott, *A Greek-English Lexicon*, rev. Sir Henry Stuart Jones (Oxford: Clarendon Press, 1973), 1319.

34. Segal, 99.

35. Snell, 7–22.

36. Snell, 122.

37. Segal, 107.

38. There were ancient references to people who made money as scribes by pretending to be able to read and write. Cf. Herbert C. Youtie, "*Agrammatos*: An Aspect of Greek Society in Egypt," and "*Bradeos Graphon*: Between Literacy and Illiteracy," in his *Scriptiunculae* (Amsterdam: Adolf M. Hakkert, 1973), 2:611–51.

39. Cf. Segal's extended discussion of this passage as an example of Euripides' awareness of the relative value of writing and speech, 102–5.

40. Segal, 101–2.

CHAPTER II

1. Trans. H. N. Fowler, *Plato: Theaetetus and Sophist* (Cambridge, MA, & London: Harvard Univ. Press & William Heinemann, 1967), 121.

2. G. E. R. Lloyd, *Aristotle: The Growth and Structure of His Thought* (Cambridge: Cambridge Univ. Press, 1968), 306.

3. G. E. R. Lloyd, *Early Greek Science: Thales to Aristotle* (New York & London: W. W. Norton, 1970), 122.

4. Frederick Copleston, S.J., *A History of Philosophy*, vol. 1, *Greece & Rome*, pt. 2, new rev. ed. (Garden City, NY: Doubleday Image Books, 1962), 12.

5. One exception is part of the *Topics*. Cf. E. S. Forster, Introduction, in Aristotle, *On Sophistical Refutations; On Coming-To-Be and Passing-Away; On the Cosmos* (Cambridge, MA, & London: Harvard Univ. Press & William Heinemann, 1955), 4, and Lloyd, 1968, 27.

6. Lloyd, 1968, 10.

7. Alex Preminger, O. B. Hardison, Jr., and Kevin Kerrane, eds., *Classical and Medieval Literary Criticism* (New York: Frederick Ungar, 1974), 99.

8. Preminger et al., 99.

9. Gwilym Ellis Lane Owen, "Aristotle," in *The Oxford Classical Dictionary*, ed. N. G. L. Hammond and H. H. Scullard, 2nd ed. (Oxford: Clarendon Press, 1972), 116.

10. Lloyd, 1968, 116.

11. Lloyd, 1968, 120–21.

12. Lloyd, 1968, 123.

13. Aristotle, *Nicomachean Ethics* 3.3, 6.3; *Metaphysics* 2.1. Cf. Lloyd, 1968, 123.

14. Aristotle, *On the Soul* 3.8.

15. Lloyd, 1968, 112. Cf. Bruno Snell, *The Discovery of the Mind in Greek Philosophy and Literature,* trans. T. G. Rosenmeyer (New York: Dover Publications, 1982), 236.

16. Aristotle, *Categories* 4.

17. Lloyd, 1968, 113.

18. Trans. Hugh Tredennick, in *Aristotle: Posterior Analytics; Topica* (Cambridge, MA, & London: Harvard Univ. Press & William Heinemann, 1960), 25.

19. Aristotle, *Rhetoric* 1.2, trans. John Henry Freese in *The "Art" of Rhetoric* (Cambridge, MA, & London: Harvard Univ. Press & William Heinemann, 1967), 23.

20. Aristotle, *Prior Analytics* 70A; *Rhetoric* 1.1.

21. Aristotle, *Rhetoric* 1.2. Cf. *Prior Analytics* 70A.

22. Aristotle, *Metaphysics* 2.1.993B.

23. Lloyd, 1968, 79.

24. Lloyd, 1970, 101.

25. Lloyd, 1968, 285.

26. Cf. Aristotle, *Eudemian Ethics* 1145B.2.

27. Lloyd, 1968, 102.

Bibliography

PRIMARY SOURCES

References to works by the Attic orators are by canon number as listed in the Loeb Classical Library.

Aelian
  On the Nature of Animals.
Aeschines
Aeschylus
  Prometheus Bound.
  The Suppliants.
Aesopic Fables in Babrius and Phaedrus. Trans. B. E. Perry. Cambridge, MA, & London: Harvard Univ. Press & William Heinemann, 1965.
Alcidamas
  On the Sophists.
Anacreontea
Andocides
Apollonius Dyscolus
  De Adverbiis.
Apostolius
Aristides
Aristophanes
  The Acharnians.
  The Birds.
  The Clouds.
  Ecclesiazusae.
  The Frogs.
  The Knights.
  The Peace.
  Thesmophoriazusae.
  The Wasps.
Aristotle
  Categories.
  Eudemian Ethics.

  Metaphysics.
  Nicomachean Ethics.
  On Memory and Recollection.
  On the Air.
  On the Classification of Animals.
  On the Generation of Animals.
  On the Soul.
  Parts of Animals.
  Physics.
  Poetics.
  Politics.
  Posterior Analytics. Translation found in Hugh Tredennick, ed. *Aristotle: Posterior Analytics; Topica.* Cambridge, MA, & London: Harvard Univ. Press & William Heinemann, 1960.
  Prior Analytics.
  Rhetoric. Translation found in John Henry Freese, ed. *Aristotle: The "Art" of Rhetoric.* Cambridge, MA, & London: Harvard Univ. Press & William Heinemann, 1967.
  Sophistical Refutations.
  Topics.
[Aristotle]
  Athenian Constitution.
  Economics.
  Problems.
  Rhetoric to Alexander.
Athenaeus

Bacchylides

Cicero
  Brutus.
  De Oratore.
  Tuscalan Disputations.

Codex Atheniensis.

Demosthenes
  Erotic Essay.

Dinarchus

Diodorus Siculus

Diogenes Laertius

Dionysius of Halicarnassus
  Demosthenes.
  Isocrates.
  On Literary Composition.
  On Thucydides.

Dissoi Logoi.

Elegy and Iambus: Being the Remains of All the Greek Elegiac and Iambic Poets from Calinus to Crates Excepting the Choliambic Writers and the Anacreontea. Ed. J. M. Edmonds. Cambridge, MA, & London: Harvard Univ. Press and William Heinemann, 1968.

Epicurus
  Epistle.

Euripides
  Electra.
  Iphigenia in Aulis.
  Iphigenia in Tauris.
  The Suppliants.

Eustathius
  Introduction to Pindar.

The Greek Anthology. Trans. W. R. Paton. 5 vols. Cambridge, MA, & London: Harvard Univ. Press & William Heinemann, 1956–60.

Herodotus

Hesiod
  Shield of Heracles.
  Theogony.

Hippocrates

Text and translation in *Hippocrates.* Trans. and ed. W. H. S. Jones and E. T. Withington. 4 vols. Cambridge, MA, & London: Harvard Univ. Press & William Heinemann, 1923–31.
  Mochlia.
  Oath.
  Paranggeliai.
  Regimen.

Homer
  Iliad.
  Odyssey.

Hyperides

Inscriptiones Graecae. Vol. 12, *Inscriptiones insularum maris Aegeai praeter Delum.* Fasc. 5, *Inscriptiones Cycladum praeter Tenum.* Ed. F. Hiller von Gaertringen (Berlin: George Reimer, 1903).

Isaeus

Isocrates
  Epistles.

[Longinus]
  On the Sublime.

Lycurgus
  Against Leocrates.

Lyra Graeca: Being the Remains of All the Greek Lyric Poets from Eumelus to Timotheus Excepting Pindar. Trans. J. M. Edmonds. 3 vols. 2nd ed. Cambridge, MA, & London: Harvard Univ. Press & William Heinemann, 1928–64.

Lysias

Pausanias

Phaedrus
  Fables.

Philodemus
  De Musica.

Philostratus
  Lives of the Sophists.

Bibliography

Photius
  Bibliotheca.
Pindar
  Nemean Odes.
  Olympian Odes.
  Pythian Odes.
Plato
  Alcibiades.
  Apology.
  Charmides.
  Cratylus.
  Critias.
  Euthydemus.
  Euthyphro.
  Gorgias.
  Hippias Major.
  Hippias Minor.
  Ion.
  Laws.
  Lysis.
  Menexenus.
  Meno.
  Parmenides.
  Phaedo.
  Phaedrus.
  Philebus.
  Politicus.
  Protagoras.
  Republic.
  Sophist.
  Symposium.
  Theaetetus. Translation found in
    H. N. Fowler, ed. Plato: Theae-
    tetus and Sophist. Cambridge,
    MA, & London: Harvard Univ.
    Press & William Heinemann,
    1967.
  Theages.
  Timaeus.
[Plato]
  Cleitophon.
  Hipparchus.

Plutarch
  De Tranquillitate Animi.
  Life of Agesilaus.
  Life of Alcibiades.
  Life of Cimon.
  Life of Demosthenes.
  Life of Lycurgus.
  Life of Lysander.
  Life of Nicias.
  Life of Solon.
  Life of Themistocles.
  Lives of the Sophists.
  Lives of the Ten Orators.
  Moralia.
  On Music.
  On the Sign of Socrates.
Polybius
Quintilian
  Institutes of Oratory.
Stobaeus
  Anthologian.
Strabo
  Geography.
The Suda. (Formerly known as Sui-
    das' Lexicon.)
Thucydides
  Text and translation in Thucy-
    dides. Trans. Charles Foster Smith.
    Cambridge, MA, & London:
    Harvard Univ. Press & William
    Heinemann, 1962.
Xenophon
  Agesilaus.
  Anabasis.
  Athenian Republic.
  Cynegeticus.
  Cyropaedia.
  Economics.
  Heiro.
  Hellenica.
  Lacedaemonian Republic.
  Memorabilia.
  Symposium.

Bibliography

SECONDARY SOURCES

Books

Allen, Thomas W. *Homer: The Origins and the Transmission.* Oxford: Clarendon Press, 1969.

Bacon, Wallace A. *The Art of Interpretation.* 3rd ed. New York: Holt, Rinehart & Winston, 1979.

Bahn, Eugene, and Margaret L. Bahn. *A History of Oral Interpretation.* Minneapolis, MN: Burgess Publishing Co., 1970.

Beck, Frederick A. G. *Greek Education: 450–350 B.C.* London: Methuen, 1964.

———. *Album of Greek Education: The Greeks at School and Play.* Sydney: Cheiron Press, 1975.

Blegan, Carl, and Marion Rawson. *A Guide to the Palace of Nestor.* Meriden, CT: Univ. of Cincinnati, 1967.

Boak, A. E. R., ed. *Michigan Papyrii.* Vol. 2, *Papyrii from Tebtunis.* Univ. of Michigan Studies, Humanistic Series, vol. 28. Ann Arbor: Univ. of Michigan, 1933.

Bowen, James. *A History of Western Education.* New York: St. Martin's Press, 1972.

Bureau of the Census. *Historical Statistics of the United States: Colonial Times to 1970.* Washington, D.C.: GPO, 1975.

Burger, Ronna. *Plato's Phaedrus: A Defense of a Philosophic Art of Writing.* University: Univ. of Alabama Press, 1980.

Buttrick, George Arthur, ed. *The Interpreter's Bible.* New York: Abingdon-Cokesbury Press, 1951–57.

Chadwick, John. *The Decipherment of Linear B.* Cambridge: Cambridge Univ. Press, 1969.

Cherniss, Harold Frederick. *The Riddle of the Early Academy.* Berkeley & Los Angeles: Univ. of California Press, 1945.

Clarke, Martin Lowther. *Higher Education in the Ancient World.* Albuquerque: Univ. of New Mexico Press, 1971.

Copleston, Frederick, S.J. *A History of Philosophy.* Vol. 1, *Greece & Rome,* pt. 2. New rev. ed. Garden City, NY: Doubleday Image Books, 1962.

Didot, Ambroise-Firmin, and [no first name] Egger. *Sur le prix du papier dans l'antiquité.* Paris: Imprimerie de Dubuisson, 1857. Reprinted from *Revue Contemporaine et Athénée Français,* Sept. 15, 1856.

Diels, Hermann. *Die Fragmente Der Vorsokratiker.* Rev. by Walther Kranz. Dublin & Zurich: Weidmann, 1966.

Dobson, John Frederic. *The Greek Orators.* London: Methuen, 1919.

Dodds, E. R. *The Greeks and the Irrational.* Berkeley & Los Angeles: Univ. of California Press, 1951.

Bibliography

Else, Gerald F. *Aristotle's Poetics: The Argument*. Cambridge, MA: Harvard Univ. Press in cooperation with The State Univ. of Iowa, 1967.

Erickson, Keith V. *Plato: True and Sophistic Rhetoric*. Amsterdam: Rodopi, 1979.

Evans, Sir Arthur. *The Palace of Minos: A Comparative Account of the Successive Stages of the Early Cretan Civilization as Illustrated by the Discoveries at Knossos*. New York: Biblo & Tannen, 1964.

Evans, Bergan. *Dictionary of Quotations*. New York: Delacorte Press, 1968.

Evans, Joan. *Index to the Palace of Minos*. New York: Biblo & Tannen, 1964.

Forbes, Clarence A. *Greek Physical Education*. Reprint ed. New York & London: The Century Co., 1971.

Freeman, Kathleen. *The Murder of Herodes and Other Trials from the Athenian Courts*. New York: W. W. Norton & Co., 1963.

Freeman, Kenneth J. *Schools of Hellas*. Classics in Education, no. 38. New York: Teachers' College Press, 1969.

Havelock, Eric A. *Preface to Plato*. Vol. 1, *A History of the Greek Mind*. Cambridge, MA: Belknap Press of Harvard Univ. Press, 1963.

———. *The Literate Revolution in Greece and Its Cultural Consequences*. Princeton, NJ: Princeton Univ. Press, 1982.

———. *The Muse Learns to Write: Reflections on Orality and Literacy from Antiquity to the Present*. New Haven & London: Yale Univ. Press, 1986.

Hayakawa, S. I. *Language in Thought and Action*. New York: Harcourt, Brace, 1949.

Hubbell, Harry Mortimer. *The Influence of Isocrates on Cicero, Dionysius and Aristides*. New Haven & London: Yale Univ. Press & Oxford Univ. Press, 1913.

Hussey, Edward. *The Presocratics*. New York: Charles Scribner's Sons, 1972.

Innis, Harold. *The Bias of Communication*. Toronto: Univ. of Toronto Press, 1951.

Jaeger, Werner. *Paideia: The Ideals of Greek Culture*. Vol. 1, *"Archaic Greece" and "The Mind of Athens."* Trans. Gilbert Highet. 2nd ed. New York: Oxford Univ. Press, 1945.

———. *Paideia: The Ideals of Greek Culture*. Vol. 2, *In Search of the Divine Centre*. Trans. Gilbert Highet. New York: Oxford Univ. Press, 1943.

———. *Paideia: The Ideals of Greek Culture*. Vol. 3, *The Conflict of Cultural Ideals in the Age of Plato*. Trans. Gilbert Highet. New York: Oxford Univ. Press, 1944.

Jebb, R. C. *Selections from the Attic Orators*. London: Macmillan, 1880.

———. *The Attic Orators from Antiphon to Isaeus*. 2 vols. London: Macmillan and Co., 1893.

Jeffrey, Lilian H. *The Local Scripts of Archaic Greece*. Oxford: Clarendon Press, 1961.

Jenson, Hans. *Sign, Symbol and Script: An Account of Man's Efforts to Write*. Trans. George Unwin. 3rd rev. ed. New York: G. P. Putnam's Sons, 1969.

209

Bibliography

Kennedy, George. *The Art of Persuasion in Greece.* Princeton, NJ: Princeton Univ. Press, 1963.

―――. *The Art of Rhetoric in the Roman World: 300 B.C.–A.D. 300.* Princeton, NJ: Princeton Univ. Press, 1972.

Kirk, G. S. *The Songs of Homer.* Cambridge: Cambridge Univ. Press, 1962.

Lewis, Naphtali. *Papyrus in Classical Antiquity.* Oxford: Clarendon Press, 1974.

Liddell, Henry George, and Robert Scott. *A Greek-English Lexicon.* Rev. Sir Henry Stuart Jones. Oxford: Clarendon Press, 1973.

Lloyd, G. E. R. *Aristotle: The Growth and Structure of His Thought.* Cambridge: Cambridge Univ. Press, 1968.

―――. *Early Greek Science: Thales to Aristotle.* New York & London: W. W. Norton & Co., 1970.

Lord, Albert B. *The Singer of Tales.* New York: Athenaeum, 1976.

Lynch, John Patrick. *Aristotle's School: A Study of a Greek Educational Institution.* Berkeley, Los Angeles, & London: Univ. of California Press, 1972.

Marrou, Henri Irénée. *A History of Education in Antiquity.* Trans. George Lamb. New York: Sheed & Ward, 1956.

Milne, Marjorie Josephine. *A Study in Alcidamas and His Relation to Contemporary Sophistic.* Bryn Mawr, PA: Westbrook Publishing, 1924.

Navarre, Octave. *Essai sur la rhétorique grecque avant Aristote.* Paris: Librairie Hachette, 1900.

Ogden, C. K., and I. A. Richards. *The Meaning of Meaning: A Study of the Influence of Language Upon Thought and of the Science of Symbolism.* 8th ed. New York: Harcourt, Brace, 1946.

Ong, Walter J., S.J. *Interfaces of the Word: Studies in the Evolution of Consciousness and Culture.* Ithaca & London: Cornell Univ. Press, 1977.

―――. *Orality and Literacy: The Technologizing of the Word.* London & New York: Methuen, 1982.

Parry, Milman. *L'Epithète traditionelle dans Homère: Essai sur un problème de style homérique.* Paris: Société D'Editions Les Belles Lettres, 1928.

Peabody, Berkley. *The Winged Word: A Study in the Technique of Ancient Greek Oral Composition as Seen Principally Through Hesiod's "Works and Days."* Albany: State Univ. of New York Press, 1975.

Pearson, Lionel. *Early Ionian Historians.* Oxford: Clarendon Press, 1939.

Pfeiffer, Rudolf. *History of Classical Scholarship from the Beginnings to the End of the Hellenistic Age.* Oxford: Clarendon Press, 1968.

Preminger, Alex, O. B. Hardison, Jr., and Kevin Kerrane, eds. *Classical and Medieval Literary Criticism.* New York: Frederick Ungar Publishing Co., 1974.

Rogers, Benjamin Bickley, ed. and trans. *Aristophanes.* 3 vols. Cambridge, MA, & London: Harvard Univ. Press and William Heinemann, 1955–61.

Bibliography

Rohde, Erwin. *Psyche: The Cult of Souls and Belief in Immortality Among the Greeks*. 8th ed. Trans. W. B. Hillis. New York: Harper Torchbooks, 1966.

Segal, Charles. *Interpreting Greek Tragedy: Myth, Poetry, Text*. Ithaca & London: Cornell Univ. Press, 1986.

Smith, Robert W., et al. *Ancient Greek and Roman Rhetoricians: A Biographical Dictionary*. Ed. Donald C. Bryant. Columbia, MO: Artcraft Press, 1968.

Snell, Bruno. *The Discovery of the Mind in Greek Philosophy and Literature*. Trans. T. G. Rosenmeyer. New York: Dover Publications, 1982.

Stanford, W. B. *The Sound of Greek: Studies in the Greek Theory and Practice of Euphony*. Berkeley & Los Angeles: Univ. of California Press, 1967.

Vermeule, Emily. *Greece in the Bronze Age*. Chicago & London: Univ. of Chicago Press, 1974.

Vernant, Jean-Pierre. *The Origins of Greek Thought*. Ithaca: Cornell University Press, 1982.

Walden, John W. H. *The Universities of Ancient Greece*. Reprint ed. Freeport, NY: Books for Libraries Press, 1970.

Wheelwright, Philip. *The Presocratics*. New York: Odyssey Press, 1966.

Wright, H. Curtis. *The Oral Antecedents of Greek Librarianship*. Provo, UT: Brigham Young Univ. Press, 1977.

Yates, Frances A. *The Art of Memory*. Chicago: Univ. of Chicago Press, 1966.

Youtie, Herbert C. *Scriptiunculae*. Amsterdam: Adolf M. Hakkert, 1973.

Articles

Adkins, Arthur W. H. "Orality and Philosophy." In *Language and Thought in Early Greek Philosophy*, ed. Kevin Robb. LaSalle, IL: Hegeler Institute, 1983.

Bahn, Eugene. "Interpretive Reading in Ancient Greece." *Quarterly Journal of Speech* 18 (1932): 432–40.

Berger, Adolf, and Barry Nicholas. "Inheritance, Law of." In *The Oxford Classical Dictionary*, ed. N. G. L. Hammond and H. H. Scullard. 2nd ed. Oxford: Clarendon Press, 1972.

Berquist, Goodwin F., Jr. "Isocrates of Athens: Foremost Speech Teacher of the Ancient World." *Speech Teacher* (now *Communication Education*) 8 (1959): 251–55.

Boegehold, Alan L. "Toward a Study of Athenian Voting Procedure." *Hesperia* 32 (1963): 366–75.

———. "Philokleon's Court." *Hesperia* 36 (1967): 111–21.

———. "Ten Distinctive Ballots: The Law Court in Zea." *California Studies in Classical Antiquity* 9 (1976): 7–19.

Bowra, C. M. "Simonides." In *The Oxford Classical Dictionary*, ed. N. G. L. Hammond and H. H. Scullard. Oxford: Clarendon Press, 1972.

211

Bibliography

Calhoun, George Miller. "Oral and Written Pleading in Athens." *Transactions and Proceedings of the American Philological Association* 50 (1919): 177–93.

De Rijk, L. M. "*Engkyklios Paideia:* A Study of Its Original Meaning." *Vivarium* 3 (1965): 24–93.

Dobson, John Frederic. "Antiphon." In *The Oxford Classical Dictionary,* ed. N. G. L. Hammond and H. H. Scullard. 2nd ed. Oxford: Clarendon Press, 1972.

———. "Lysias." In *The Oxford Classical Dictionary,* ed. N. G. L. Hammond and H. H. Scullard. 2nd ed. Oxford: Clarendon Press, 1972.

Dorjahn, Alfred P. "Poetry in Athenian Courts." *Classical Philology* 22 (1927): 85–93.

Enos, Richard Leo. "The Persuasive and Social Force of Logography in Ancient Greece." *Central States Speech Journal* 25 (1974): 4–10.

———. "The Etymology of Rhapsode." *Issues in Interpretation* 3 (1978), n. pag.

———. "The Hellenic Rhapsode." *Western Journal of Speech Communication* 42 (1978): 134–43.

Forster, E. S. Introduction. In Aristotle, *On Sophistical Refutations; On Coming-To-Be and Passing-Away; On the Cosmos.* Cambridge, MA, & London: Harvard Univ. Press and William Heinemann, 1955.

Gomme, Arnold Wycombe, and Robert J. Hopper. "Population (Greek World)." In *The Oxford Classical Dictionary,* ed. N. G. L. Hammond and H. H. Scullard. 2nd ed. Oxford: Clarendon Press, 1972.

Greene, William Chase. "The Spoken and the Written Word." *Harvard Studies in Classical Philology* 60 (1951): 23–59.

———. "'Gentle Reader': More on the Spoken and the Written Word." In *The Classical Tradition: Literary and Historical Studies in Honor of Harry Caplan,* ed. Luitpold Wallach. Ithaca: Cornell Univ. Press, 1966.

Gronbeck, Bruce E. "Gorgias on Rhetoric and Poetic: A Rehabilitation." *Southern Speech Communication Journal* 38 (1972): 27–38.

Hargis, Donald E. "The Rhapsode." *Quarterly Journal of Speech* 56 (1970): 388–97.

Havelock, Eric A. "The Preliteracy of the Greeks." *New Literary History* 8 (1977): 369–99.

———. "The Linguistic Task of the Presocratics." In *Language and Thought in Early Greek Philosphy* ed. Kevin Robb. LaSalle, IL: Hegeler Institute, 1983.

Hendrickson, G. L. "Ancient Reading." *The Classical Journal* 25 (1929–30): 182–90.

Howland, R. L. "The Attack on Isocrates in the *Phaedrus.*" In *Plato: True and Sophistic Rhetoric,* ed. Keith V. Erickson. Amsterdam: Rodopi, 1979.

Hudson, Lee. "Between Singer and Rhapsode." *Literature in Performance* 1 (1980): 33–44.

Bibliography

Hunt, Everett Lee. "Plato on Rhetoric and Rhetoricians." *Quarterly Journal of Speech* 6 (1920): 33–53.

Johnson, W. R. "Isocrates Flowering: The Rhetoric of Augustine." *Philosophy and Rhetoric* 9 (1976): 217–31.

Kaufer, David S. "The Influence of Plato's Developing Psychology on His View of Rhetoric." *Quarterly Journal of Speech* 64 (1978): 63–78.

Kennedy, George. "Speech Education in Greece." *Western Journal of Speech Communication* 31 (1967): 2–9.

Lenz, Harold Othmar. "Laurus Nobilis" and "Myrtus Communis." In his *Botanik der alten Griechen und Romer deutsch in Auszügen aus deren Schriften nebst Anmerkungen*. Gotha: Verlag von Thienemann, 1859.

Niebuhr, Alta Dodds. "Laurus Nobilis" and "Myrtus Communis." In her *Herbs of Greece*. Athens: New England Unit of Herb Society of America, 1970.

Notopoulos, James A. "The Homeric Hymns as Oral Poetry." *American Journal of Philology* 83 (1962): 337–68.

Owen, Gwilym Ellis Lane. "Aristotle." In *The Oxford Classical Dictionary*, ed. N. G. L. Hammond and H. H. Scullard. 2nd ed. Oxford: Clarendon Press, 1972.

Perkins, Terry M. "Isocrates and Plato: Relativism vs. Idealism." *Southern Speech Communication Journal* 50 (1984): 49–66.

Perry, B. E. "Two Fables Recovered." *Byzantinische Zeitschrift* 54 (1961): 5–7.

Phillips, Gerald M. "Science and the Study of Human Communication: An Inquiry from the Other Side of the Two Cultures." *Human Communication Research* 7 (1981): 361–70.

Plass, Paul. "The Unity of the Phaedrus." In *Plato: True and Sophistic Rhetoric*, ed. Keith V. Erickson. Amsterdam: Rodopi, 1979.

Rensberger, Boyce. "Roots of Writing Traced Back More Than 10,000 Years." *New York Times*, July 9, 1977, 19.

Robb, Kevin. Introduction. In *Language and Thought in Early Greek Philosophy*, ed. Kevin Robb. LaSalle, IL: Hegeler Institute, 1983.

Robbins, R. D. C. "Isocrates." *Bibliotheca Sacra* 35 (1878): 401–24, 595–618.

Robert, Brother S. "What Should Gorgias Know?" *Western Speech* (now *Western Journal of Speech Communication*) 24 (1960): 160–63.

Robinson, Richard George Frederick. "Plato." In *The Oxford Classical Dictionary*, ed. N. G. L. Hammond and H. H. Scullard. 2nd ed. Oxford: Clarendon Press, 1972.

Ross, William David. "Dissoi Logoi." In *The Oxford Classical Dictionary*, ed. N. G. L. Hammond and H. H. Scullard. 2nd ed. Oxford: Clarendon Press, 1972.

Sealey, Raphael. "From Phemios to Ion." *Revue des Etudes Grecques* 70 (1957): 312–55.

Sheraton, Mimi. "De Gustibus: Sit Down Comedy." *New York Times,* June 19, 1982.

Shewring, Walter Haywood, and Kenneth James Dover. "Hiatus in Greek Prose." In *The Oxford Classical Dictionary,* ed. N. G. L. Hammond and H. H. Scullard. 2nd ed. Oxford: Clarendon Press, 1972.

Shorey, Paul. Introduction. In Plato, *Republic,* vol. 1. Trans. Paul Shorey. Cambridge, MA & London: Harvard Univ. Press & William Heinemann, 1930.

———. Introduction. In Plato, *Republic,* vol. 2. Trans. Paul Shorey. Cambridge, MA, & London: Harvard Univ. Press & William Heinemann, 1935.

Van Hook, LaRue. "Alcidamas Versus Isocrates: The Spoken Versus the Written Word." *The Classical Weekly* 12 (1919): 89–94.

Wagner, Russell H. "The Rhetorical Theory of Isocrates." *Quarterly Journal of Speech* 8 (1922): 323–37.

Werner, Leslie Maitland. "U.S. Study on Adult Literacy Finds the Results Are Mixed." *New York Times,* Sept. 25, 1986, D27.

West, Martin Litchfield. "Homeridae." In *The Oxford Classical Dictionary,* ed. N. G. L. Hammond and H. H. Scullard. 2nd ed. Oxford: Clarendon Press, 1972.

Wilcox, Stanley. "The Scope of Early Rhetorical Theory." *Harvard Studies in Classical Philology* 53 (1942): 121–55.

———. "Isocrates' Fellow-Rhetoricians." *The American Journal of Philology* 66 (1945): 171–86.

Reviews

Costas, Procope S. Review of *Preface to Plato,* by Eric A. Havelock. *Classical Journal* 60 (1964): 78–80.

Grimaldi, W. M. A., S.J. Review of *Preface to Plato,* by Eric A. Havelock. *Classical World* 55 (1963): 257.

Gulley, N. Review of *Preface to Plato,* by Eric A. Havelock. *Classical Review* 14 (1964): 31.

Ong, Walter J., S.J. Review of *Preface to Plato,* by Eric A. Havelock. *Manuscripta* 8 (1964): 179.

Pritchard, J. P. Review of *Preface to Plato,* by Eric A. Havelock. *Books Abroad* (now *World Literature Today*) 38 (1964): 70.

Dissertations

Engel, Elizabeth Sydney. "Plato on Rhetoric and Writing." Ph.D. diss., Yale Univ., 1973.

Lockyear, Charles W., Jr. "The Fiction of Memory and the Use of Written

Sources: Convention and Practice in Seneca the Elder and Other Authors." Ph.D. diss., Princeton Univ., 1971.

Mino, Mary. "The Relative Effects of Content and Vocal Delivery on Interviewers' Assessments of Interviewees During a Simulated Employment Interview." Ph.D. diss., Pennsylvania State Univ., 1986.

Papers

Dinsmoor, W. B., Jr. "The Royal Stoa in the Athenian Agora." American School of Classical Studies lecture on the site, July 2, 1981.

Index

Abstraction: Alcidamas, lack of awareness of, 141–42; Aristotle, awareness of, 168–72; Aristotle, linkage with concrete data, 171–72; awareness of, 3–6, 12–13, 90–91, 116–17, 123, 125–31, 133–35, 141–42, 143, 168–72; drama, writing's influence on, 157–59; Isocrates, abstract audience of, 123, 125–31, 143; Isocrates, universal education, 133–35; Isocrates, writing's influence on style, 131–33; poetry influenced by, 149–50; syllogism linked to, 169–70. *See also* Alcidamas; Aristotle; Isocrates; Plato; Sophists

Alcidamas: abstraction, lack of awareness of, 138–39, 141–42; extemporaneous speech, argument for, 140–41; Gorgias, debt to, 137–40; oral style of, 138–40; organization, lack of, 141–42; particular audience of, 143; Sophists, defense of, 136–44; writing, failure of his attack on, 143–44. *See also* Isocrates

Aristotle: artist and his work, 27–28; dialogue, early works in, 166–67; do-it-yourself books, 28; enthymeme, 168–71; epistemology, abstract and concrete connected, 21–22, 171–72; history, influence on, 165–66; Isocrates, contrasted with, 167–68; later works, lecture note form of, 167–68; laws, unwritten, praise of, 81; Plato, attack on writing reflected in, 167–68; scientific knowledge, 171–72; scientific knowledge, oral tradition in, 171–72; Sophists, attack on, 30–31; syllogism, 168–71; witnesses, credibility of, 82–83; writing, associated with, 165–66. *See also* Aristotle; Plato

Athens: literacy in, 60; oral and written pleading in, 121–22

Audience: Alcidamas' particular, 143; Isocrates' abstract, 123, 125–31, 143

Calhoun, George Miller: oral and written legal pleading, 73–74

Choruses: plays taught by poets, 154–56; training for, 49–51

Contracts: importance of, 85–86; reliance on witnesses, 86–87

Depositions: credibility tied to witnesses, 82

Dialectic: epistemology, importance to Plato's, 22–27, 29–30; oral tradition, weapon against, 22–23

Discipline: in education, 55

Divine inspiration: rhapsode, reliance upon, 31–32; symbols of, 39–41. *See also* Rhapsodes

Dorjahn, Alfred P.: poetry as legal evidence, 82–83

Drama: abstraction, awareness of, 157–59; choruses taught without writing, 154–56; composers (playwrights) not writers, 152; origins of, 150–51; reading aloud in, 160–61; recitation in, 161–63; silent reading in, 159–60; writing used to preserve, 152–54, 156–57. *See also* Segal, Charles

216

Index

Index

Literate Revolution in Greece (Havelock): dynamic tension, 11–12

Lockyear, Charles W., Jr.: memory displays called literary devices, 91–92

Logographers: function in Hellenic society, 113–15; *logopoios,* contrasted to, 113–14; poets lack similar name, 149; writings, first, 112, 114

Logopoios: logographers, contrasted to, 113–14

Maker: name, importance of, 113–15, 149, 152, 154–56; poetry and the, 147–49; spoken words closest to knowledge, 99–100; work of, 27–28

Memory: displays called literary devices, 91–92; oral performance and, 93–99; Plato, comparison to writing, 19–22; Plato, paradoxical defense of, 18–22; Plato's works, recitation in, 96–99; preliterate society, importance to, 18–19; recitation in philosophy, 95–99; Sophists, training of, 65–66, 112–13, 115–21, 138–40; "storing up" words, 17; "things," 92–93, 103–4, *topoi,* 92; "words," 92–93; writing, as support for, 54–58, 99–100; writing, vital to process of, 104–7

Mētrōon: laws, repository for, 25, 79

Mousikē: amousos, "unmusical" persons considered uneducated, 39–40, 50; meaning, change of, 48

Myrtle: divine inspiration, symbol of, 63–67

Ong, Walter J., S.J.: oral culture, characteristics of, 3–4

Oral composition: Alcidamas, his use of, 138–40; preceding writing, 102–8

Oral performance: Isocrates, in his universal education, 133–35; memory in, 93–99; Plato's works, recitation in, 95–99; *skolion,* 39–40;

society, importance to, 38–41. *See also* Recitation

Oral tradition: Aristotle's link to scientific knowledge, 172; characteristics of, 4–7; dialectic as weapon against, 22–23; education, oral origins of, 50–51; enthymeme's link to, 170–71; laws, unwritten, 80–81; Plato's attack on, 15, 17–18

Papyrus: cost of, 53

Paradox: Alcidamas, attack on writing in writing, 136–44; Aristotle's links to oral tradition, 166–72; drama's ties to writing, 150–59; grammar defined by sound, 63–65; Isocrates' oral writing style, 131–32; Plato, consistency in attacks on rhetoric, poetry, Sophists, and rhapsodes, 29–33; Plato, dialectic identification, 22–27; Plato, epistemological attack on writing, 12–18; Plato, popularity of attack on writing, 27–29; poetry's ties to writing, 36–38, 149–50; rhapsodes' reliance on writing, 36–38

Parry, Milman: challenged assumptions about oral culture, 2

Phaedrus (Plato): epistemology of, 14–15; Isocrates, "attacked" in, 120–24; oral tradition, attack on, 15; reading aloud in, 114–15; writing, attack on, 15–18, 118–21; writing, for memorization, 99–100. *See also* Isocrates; Paradox; Plato

Philosophy: education, different from Sophists, 67–68; education, ties to "old," 66–69; oral preservation of, 93–95; Presocratic fragments in oral form, 93–94; recitation in discourse, 95–99

Philoxenus: first concrete poet, 147–48. *See also* Poetry

Plato: consistency of attacks on rhetoric, poetry, Sophists, and rhapsodes, 29–33; dialectic, importance to epistemology of 22–27, 29–30; epistemology, 14–15; Isocrates, "attack"

Tony M. Lentz, is a member of the faculty of the Department of Speech Communication, The Pennsylvania State University. He is the author of numerous articles appearing in such journals as *American Behavioral Scientist, Southern Speech Communication Journal, Communication Quarterly, Philosophy and Rhetoric, Literature in Performance,* and *Rhetoric Society Quarterly.*